THE CONSTITUTION OF RIGHTS

THE CONSTITUTION OF RIGHTS

Human Dignity and American Values

Edited by Michael J. Meyer
and William A. Parent

Cornell University Press Ithaca and London

First published 1992 by Cornell University Press.

International Standard Book Number 0-8014-2650-2 (cloth)
International Standard Book Number 0-8014-9950-x (paper)
Library of Congress Catalog Card Number 91-55535

Printed in the United States of America

Librarians: Library of Congress cataloging information appears on the last page of the book.

⊗ The paper in this book meets the minimum requirements of the American National Standard for Information Sciences—Permanence of Paper for Printed Library Materials, ANSI Z39.48-1984.

To William J. Brennan, Jr.

Contents

Acknowledgments

The editors thank Santa Clara University's Center for Applied Ethics for its generous support, and our editor at Cornell, John Ackerman, for his encouragement throughout.

M. J. M. and W. A. P.

THE CONSTITUTION OF RIGHTS

Introduction

MICHAEL J. MEYER

The year 1991 marks the bicentennial of the ratification of the Bill of Rights. The ten original amendments to the United States Constitution, when taken together with the sixteen others ratified since 1791, are surely to be regarded as one of the nation's most esteemed political accomplishments. This collection of essays is devoted to investigating the normative foundations of the amended Constitution and the relationship between rights, especially moral and constitutional rights, and human dignity. It is striking that in recent interviews with Bill Moyers for his PBS series "In Search of the Constitution," both Associate Justice William J. Brennan, Jr., and Professor Ronald Dworkin emphasized that the fundamental value affirmed by the Constitution, and especially the Bill of Rights, was the value of human dignity.[1]

Clearly, this idea of human dignity bespeaks a certain vision of a citizen, a vision of one's status in political society, of one's rights, duties, capacities, and inclinations. We hope that the essays in this collection will result in a richer understanding of both the moral commitments that justify our democratic institutions and the place of the idea of human dignity within the broader moral, political, and legal scheme. Ours is the oldest functioning written constitution and one that has withstood a civil

1. "In Search of the Constitution": "Mr. Justice Brennan" and "Ronald Dworkin: The Changing Story," both produced by Public Affairs Television, Inc., New York, 1987.

war, though ultimately only with revolutionary change. It is fitting that Americans should continue to reflect on fundamental questions concerning their own constitutional rights and the ways in which these rights affirm the dignity of human beings. Maintaining a constitutional democracy requires serious and sustained reflection on its basic institutions. Indeed, in a constitutional democracy the very practice of questioning these foundations is not undemocratic, but rather the essence of a commitment to true citizenship.

Furthermore, the idea of human dignity is increasingly employed in the widespread discussion of human rights, which over the years has been greatly influenced by the establishment and the continuing authority of the Bill of Rights.[2] The United Nations' Universal Declaration of Human Rights begins with the assertion that "the inherent dignity" and "the equal and inalienable rights" of all persons is "the foundation of freedom and justice and peace."[3] The constitutions of both West Germany and Canada make explicit commitment to the dignity of man.[4] A probing investigation into the foundations of the constitutional rights of American citizens is the only way to ensure that the powerful influence of the Bill of Rights and allied amendments will remain vital for Americans and a positive influence for others into the next century. This bicentennial seems an especially opportune time for such an investigation.

A federal bill of rights was from the very start a controversial idea.[5] After its rejection by the Constitutional Convention in Philadelphia— because state bills of rights were said to provide sufficient protection—

2. Carl J. Friedrich, *The Impact of the American Constitution Abroad* (Boston: Boston University Press, 1967); Louis Henkin and Al Rosenthal, eds., *Constitutionalism and Rights: The Influence of United States Constitutional Rights Abroad* (New York: Columbia University Press, 1989).

3. G.A. Res. 217A, U.N. Doc. A/810 at 71 (1948); see also arts. 1, 22, 23, and U.N. Charter, preamble (1945). For a good general account of employment of the ideal of human dignity by the United Nations and other international organizations, see Haim H. Cohn, "On the Meaning of Human Dignity," *Israel Yearbook on Human Rights* 13 (1983): 226–51.

4. See the Basic Law of the Federal Republic of Germany: "Article 1 (1) The dignity of man shall be inviolable. To respect and protect it shall be the duty of all state authority. (2) The German people therefore acknowledge inviolable and inalienable human rights as the basis of every community, of peace and justice in the world" (translation published by the Press and Information Office of the Federal Government, Bonn; Public Document, 1987, by Grenzland-Druckerei Rock & Co., D-3340 Wolfenbuttel); see the preamble to the Canadian Bill of Rights, S.C. 1960, c. 44. For other instances of national constitutional recognition of human dignity, see Cohn, "On the Meaning of Human Dignity," 3, pp. 232–33.

5. For this sketch I rely in part on Leonard Levy, *Constitutional Opinions: Aspects of the Bill of Rights* (New York: Oxford University Press, 1986), pp. 105–34.

it quickly became an issue again during ratification.[6] Supporters of a federal bill of rights in nine states, buttressed by influential founders at the time overseas, notably Thomas Jefferson and John Adams, insisted that a written document was a necessity. James Madison, at first unenthusiastic about a federal bill of rights, persistently proposed a variety of amendments in the first session of the House of Representatives which were later altered in the Senate and in a conference committee. When the requisite ratification by three-fourths of the states finally culminated with Virginia in December of 1791, ten of those amendments became part of the fundamental law of the United States. Whereas the lack of a bill of rights had been an emotional issue, exploited in the end unsuccessfully by Anti-Federalists bent on upending the new constitution, its adoption had a great healing effect.[7]

Clearly, the Bill of Rights and constitutional rights in subsequent amendments are regarded as basic rights. They are basic in the sense that they preexist (historically, logically, morally, or politically) and on some fundamental level preempt the powers of government. As such, they are of crucial importance for the various interests they protect. They are also significant for the example they provide of this nation's willingness to amend the Constitution so as to provide substantive protection for what it believes to be its most fundamental values. The Bill of Rights and later amendments (especially the "Civil War amendments"), together with their ongoing interpretation by the courts and the public, remain at the core of the political culture of the United States and its unfolding moral imagination.

The term *dignity* appears frequently in political rhetoric and increasingly in legal argument. Although the concept of human dignity has been used by the U.S. Supreme Court in connection with the First, Fourth, Fifth, Sixth, Eighth, Ninth, and Fourteenth amendments, its precise meaning has rarely been clarified.[8] The value of human dignity is often presupposed in moral and legal argument, but the precise function of the concept is almost never explained. In comparison with the attention it

---

6. Hamilton's well-known reasons for rejecting any call for a federal bill of rights are in The Federalist No. 84 at 555–61 (Modern Library n.d.).

7. Levy, *Constitutional Opinions*, pp. 116, 124.

8. See Jordan Paust, "Human Dignity as a Constitutional Right: A Jurisprudentially Based Inquiry into Criteria and Content," *Howard Law Journal* 27 (1984): 150–58. Paust has noted that the phrase *human dignity* was first used by the Supreme Court in 1946, and that in a majority of cases *dignity* is used without explanation or citation to other cases. Although the frequency of use has increased, the justices who employ the notion of human dignity also cover a wide range of political and legal thought.

has paid to such notions as justice, equality, and rights, contemporary scholarship has devoted surprisingly little analysis to the concept of human dignity. Even a partial analysis of the concept of the dignity of human beings is beyond the scope of this introduction, but it is useful to explore some of its Enlightenment origins.[9] This background is significant not only because the Bill of Rights itself is grounded in Enlightenment thought but also because of the appearance at that time of a uniquely modern notion of human dignity.

In political thought at the time of the Enlightenment revolutions two quite distinct concepts of dignity were in use, not only in politics proper but also in philosophical thought. This divide can, at the outset, be understood quite simply. On the one hand, some political thinkers used the idea of dignity to refer to a rank within a recognized and established social hierarchy—for example, the dignity of a king, of a noble, or of a bishop. For these thinkers a person's dignity was simply a function, or a sign, of an individual's elevated social rank. In contradistinction other thinkers understood the notion of dignity to have a much wider application—for example, the dignity of man or the dignity of humanity.

The famous debate over the French Revolution between Edmund Burke and Thomas Paine sets this difference in clear relief. When in the *Reflections on the Revolution in France* Burke writes about "men of dignity," he refers exclusively to the nobility as a hereditary order.[10] He simply assumes that the nobility and the king have dignity, yet when he turns to the dignity of the common man, his position changes crucially. For Burke, and for others who thought of dignity in a similar way, the very idea that the common person could have dignity is a kind of contradiction. Indeed, dignity is just what the common person lacks—social rank. Of course the common person has a place in society, but it is not a position of any rank or esteem—the lowest rank in society is not a "ranking position" (in the same sense a private in the army can be said to "have no rank"). Burke, at least in the *Reflections*, talks of the dignity of commoners only ironically or even bitterly: "I should have thought that the hangman of Paris . . . is allowed his rank and arms in the Heralds College of the rights of men . . . full of his sense of his new dignity."[11] The dignity of the hangman of Paris is, for Burke, comparable only to

---

9. In the next two paragraphs I follow the argument I develop in "Kant's Concept of Dignity and Modern Political Thought," *History of European Ideas* 8 (1987): 319–32.

10. Edmund Burke, *Reflections on the Revolution in France* (New York: Anchor, 1973), p. 60.

11. Ibid., p. 83.

the "awful dignity of a handful of country clowns who have seats in that Assembly."[12]

Thomas Paine, one of the leading figures of both Enlightenment revolutions, directly challenges the traditional employment of the idea of dignity and writes, in self-conscious opposition to Burke, of "the serene dignity of the members of the present National Assembly."[13] The major change from Burke's conception of dignity is Paine's call for the recognition of the "natural dignity of man," which is a status that all people, not just the ranking members of society, enjoy. He promotes this "natural dignity," noting, "The Patriots of France have discovered in good time, that rank and dignity in society must take a new ground. The old one has fallen through. It must now take the substantial ground of character instead of the chimerical ground of titles."[14]

There is strong evidence that Burke's use of the word *dignity* was standard for the time. Samuel Johnson's *Dictionary of the English Language*, published roughly four decades before the Enlightenment revolutions and a widely recognized authority on usage at the time, defines *dignity* as "rank of elevation" and *dignitary* as a "clergyman advanced to some dignity, to some rank above that of a parish priest."[15] Nathan Bailey, the first lexicographer to compile a full dictionary of English (1772), defines *dignity* as "rank of elevation" and then adds with self-assurance: "Dignity is properly represented by a lady richly clothed, and adorned ... beautified with ornaments of gold and precious stones. The meaning is quite obvious."[16] Keeping in mind that *lady* was itself an indication of social rank, we can see that Paine and others (most notably Immanuel Kant in his moral philosophy) were extending the traditional "Burkean" conception of dignity in a way that dramatically alters its meaning and indeed requires significant elaboration.

The American Enlightenment offers further evidence of this ambiguous and evolving employment of the idea of dignity. In The *Federalist* papers and in Madison's notes on the Constitutional Convention, *dignity* is usually used not to refer to the idea of human dignity proffered by Paine and others, but typically in the more traditional sense, exalting the dignity

---

12. Ibid., p. 55.
13. Thomas Paine, *The Rights of Man* (New York: Anchor, 1973), pp. 329–30.
14. Ibid., p. 320.
15. Samuel Johnson, *A Dictionary of the English Language* [1746–55] (Philadelphia, 1819), I sig. 3x2, 3v.
16. Nathan Bailey, *Dictionarium Britannicum* (London, 1736), sig. 3ulv. See also *Black's Law Dictionary*, 5th ed. (St. Paul, Minn.: West, 1979), p. 411, and the references there to vol. 1 and 2 of Blackstone's *Commentaries on the Laws of England*.

of some eminent person or the dignity of the state.[17] Of course, given the American antipathy to and the constitutional ban on titles of nobility, even the dignity of such eminent persons was presumably not intended to be exactly the same as the traditional dignity of social rank. The constitutional ban on titles of nobility (Article 1, section 9, clause 8; section 10, clause 1) was both a hedge against corruption and a gesture toward a recognition of a dignity for human beings not based on social hierarchy—seemingly a move toward Paine and away from Burke.

Some shift away from an understanding of the dignity of persons simply as a function of traditional social status was clearly afoot in the Enlightenment revolution in America. Indeed, Alexander Hamilton, at the very outset of his defense of the Constitution, recommended it as the "safest course for your liberty, your dignity and your happiness."[18] Jefferson clearly rejected the traditional hierarchically based conception of basic human worth in favor of some changing conception of human dignity. In writing to Jean Nicolas Démeunier, the author of an encyclopedia article on the United States, Jefferson insisted that in Europe "the dignity of man is lost in arbitrary distinctions [of "birth or badge"], . . . the human species is classed into several stages of degradation" and "the many are crushed under the weight of the few."[19] Hamilton, of course, was concerned less with the equal dignity of all human beings than with that of all white men of at least some wealth and prestige. Nonetheless, since Publius does write to "the People of the State of New York," and not just to an established aristocracy, some notion of hierarchy is overtly, if in part symbolically, rejected. Jefferson, at least, clearly believed human dignity to be independent of the "arbitrary distinctions" of the hierarchy of the ancien régime. Yet in the society of Enlightenment America this nascent change did not explicitly include an elimination of those often unacknowledged but degrading hierarchies based on race, gender, religion, and property.

This brief sketch is not meant to suggest that any of the Framers explicitly cared as much for the protection of human dignity as they did for the protection of liberty, property, or peace. At best they were, along with many others, leading an intellectual and social revolution that they did not always fully grasp (and perhaps, in some cases, would not later

17. See The Federalist Nos. 6, 15, 17, 19, 30, 45, 46, 58, 67, 69, 70, 71, 78, 81.
18. The Federalist No. 84 at 6 (Modern Library n.d.).
19. "Answers and Observations for Démeunier's Article on the United States in the *Encyclopédie Methodique*, 1786," *Thomas Jefferson: Writings* (New York: Library of America, 1984), p. 587.

have endorsed) even while they laid the political and legal groundwork for it. That they were at the forefront of such conceptual and philosophical changes means that any of their direct remarks on the subject of human dignity carry significant ambiguity. Nonetheless, the story of the formation of the Constitution and the Bill of Rights is, along with the rejection of traditional hierarchy, unambiguously one of the preservation of liberty. But what reason is there to preserve individual liberty? One answer, of course, is that individuals, and not the state, have the highest dignity.[20] That is, individuals have a unique worth and standing vis-à-vis the state, and, in addition, all individuals should enjoy equal public standing, at least insofar as they occupy the role of citizen.

Such a point is recognized by the first constitutional case decided by the Supreme Court. In Chisholm v. Georgia (1793) Justice James Wilson, also one of the Framers in Philadelphia, notes: "A State, useful and valuable as the contrivance is, is the inferior contrivance of man, and from his *native* dignity derives all its *acquired* importance."[21] The general Enlightenment vision of human dignity—especially prominent in, but clearly not limited to, Kant's moral philosophy—is tied inextricably to the human capacity and inclination for self-government. To make this assertion is not to advance the questionable notion that the Framers were Kantians. It is, rather, to say that the tenor of much Enlightenment moral, political, and legal thought clearly leads in the direction of the *equal* recognition of individual human dignity, and it does so because of a belief in the citizenry's capacity for self-government and a commitment to their equal right to the same. Of course, just exactly what such equal recognition entails remains at the heart of many ongoing debates over the existence and the scope of various moral and legal rights.

The very notion of equality is at the root of much of the earlier Enlightenment rejection of hierarchy in the name of human dignity. It did not formally enter the U.S. Constitution, however, until the ratification of the Fourteenth Amendment in 1868.[22] This amendment was passed in part to secure the constitutionality of the Civil Rights Act of 1866.

20. Leonard Levy has noted: "Ours is an extraordinary system of government. We do not believe that the state is obligated to keep citizens from lapsing into political and religious errors. We believe, rather, that citizens have the right and duty of preventing the government from falling into error." *Constitutional Opinions*, p. vii.

21. 2 U.S. (2 Dall.) 419, 455 (emphasis in the original).

22. Of course, other documents of the American Enlightenment, especially the Declaration of Independence, are famously explicit about equality. The Fourth and Fifth amendments also adumbrate a commitment to equality. For a more detailed argument on this, see the essay by Martha Minow in this volume.

Along with the other Civil War amendments, it dramatically enhanced the standing of individuals before the states.[23] In abolishing the slave codes and then trying to ensure the demise of the black codes, the Civil War amendments were a step of unsurpassed importance along the path toward protection for human dignity. The explicit guarantee of the "equal protection of the laws" was a step in a movement from the first constitutional acknowledgment of some significant equality in social status toward a more robust, indeed more egalitarian, commitment to equality before the law. This elimination of various forms of degrading hierarchy is a theme clearly echoed by Justice John Marshall Harlan's famous dissent in Plessy v. Ferguson that "in view of the Constitution, in the eye of the law, there is in this country no superior, dominant, ruling class of citizens. There is no caste here. Our Constitution is color-blind, and neither knows nor tolerates classes among citizens. In respect of civil rights . . . [t]he humblest is peer of the most powerful."[24] The continuing weakening of degrading hierarchies in favor of equality is part of the growing recognition that an interest in human dignity and an equal right to self-government know no artificial boundaries.

It is noteworthy, however, that human beings do use a multitude of ways to distinguish themselves from others. Racial, ethnic, cultural, linguistic, and religious differences unify persons into groups as well as separate them from one another. Within such groups considerations as various as gender, age, education, family, friendship, talents, and even tastes in food and clothing are often used to accent the differences between persons. In this regard, a vast diversity is the mark of humanity. It is against this grand backdrop of differences separating persons from one another that the idea of human dignity must be evaluated. The notion of human dignity is both vitally important and somewhat obscure, because to some considerable extent it mitigates this seemingly natural tendency to accentuate the many differences between ourselves and others. The idea of human dignity is especially important in the face of pressure to put these differences at the service of the inclination to dominate or degrade others, at times simply because they are different. Trying to understand what we have in common with others who are in so many ways quite distinct from us is a profound and difficult task. Yet, when

23. See Kenneth Karst, "Equal Protection of the Laws," *Encyclopedia of the American Constitution* ed. Leonard Levy, Kenneth Karst, and Dennis Mahoney (New York: Macmillan, 1986) 2:640–47. See also Karst, *Belonging to America: Equal Citizenship and the Constitution* (New Haven: Yale University Press, 1989), esp. pp. 52–59, 233–37.
24. Plessy V. Ferguson, 163 U.S. 537, 559 (1896).

insignificant differences provide reasons to disregard the humanity of others, human and constitutional rights anchored in a vision of human dignity offer the strongest constraint against doing so. One goal of this collection of essays is to clarify, and at times to question, this vision.

Each of the authors in this volume has already made influential contributions to moral, political, or legal theory. Their essays here cover a wide variety of topics and points of view. Various definitions of dignity and diverse proposals concerning the relation between dignity, equality, liberty, and human rights are explored. The structure of the collection leads the reader from general questions of human dignity in moral theory toward more focused questions about the role of human dignity in the understanding of particular constitutional rights. The essays by Alan Gewirth, and A. I. Melden discuss moral rights and the meaning of human dignity. Those by William A. Parent and David A. J. Richards address this concern as well as the general relationship between constitutional rights, constitutional interpretation, and human dignity. The connection between equality and dignity is discussed in essays by Bernard R. Boxill and Martha Minow. Considering the question of human dignity, constitutional interpretation, and punishment are essays by Raoul Berger and Hugo Adam Bedau. The relationship between specific constitutional liberties and dignity is investigated by Frederick Schauer, Kent Greenawalt, Louis Henkin, and Owen Fiss. The volume is dedicated to Justice William J. Brennan, Jr. It is so dedicated in recognition of his long and distinguished career and in acknowledgment of his tireless commitment to the defense of human dignity.[25]

25. The author would like to thank John Ackerman, Bill Parent, Jerold Waltman, and Lori Zink for helpful comments on earlier drafts of this essay.

I

Human Dignity as
the Basis of Rights

ALAN GEWIRTH

The close connection between human dignity and human rights has often been remarked. To take a notable example, the Universal Declaration of Human Rights promulgated by the United Nations in 1948 says in its first article: "All human beings are born free and equal in dignity and rights." The monstrous violations of human rights that have disfigured the twentieth century, epitomized by the Nazis' Holocaust and the Stalinist butcheries, have also been attacks against human dignity.

The relations between human dignity and human rights are many and complex, but one relation is primary: human rights are based upon or derivative from human dignity. It is because humans have dignity that they have human rights. This relation is stated explicitly in the preambles to the two international covenants adopted by the United Nations in 1966: "These [human] rights derive from the inherent dignity of the human person."[1] The same relation is emphasized in the Universal Declaration itself when it asserts that "everyone . . . is entitled to realization . . . of the economic, social and cultural rights indispensable for his dignity," and that these are rights "ensuring . . . an existence worthy of hu-

1. International Covenant on Economic, Social and Cultural Rights, 1966; International Covenant on Civil and Political Rights, 1966. Both are reprinted in *Basic Documents on Human Rights*, 2d ed., ed. Ian Brownlie (Oxford: Clarendon Press, 1981), pp. 118, 128. See also Declaration on Protection from Torture (p. 35) and Supplementary Convention on the Abolition of Slavery (p. 44).

man dignity."² This grounding of human rights in human dignity can be traced back at least to Immanuel Kant, who wrote that man "is obligated to acknowledge, in a practical way, the dignity of humanity in every other man. Hence he is subject to a duty based on the respect which he must show every other man." This duty of respect for human beings because of their dignity entails a correlative right: "Every man has a rightful claim [rechtmässigen Anspruch] to respect from his fellow men."³ Thus it is human dignity that justifies the duty of respect and, with it, human rights.

To understand this grounding of human rights in human dignity, we must consider three main questions: First, just what is human dignity? Second, what reasons are there for attributing dignity to all human beings equally? Third, just how does human dignity serve to ground human rights? The attempt to provide adequate answers to these questions requires recognition of some important distinctions.

TWO CONCEPTS OF DIGNITY

To get at these distinctions, let us first take note of a familiar and plausible way of relating human dignity and rights. According to this relation, a person's sense of dignity, of self-worth, is fostered or buttressed when she is in a position to claim rights against other persons. It is the ability or capacity to assert such claims that grounds human dignity. Thus, Joel Feinberg has written: "it is claiming that gives rights their special moral significance...Having rights enables us to 'stand up like men,' to look others in the eye, and to feel in some fundamental way the equal of anyone...What is called 'human dignity' may simply be the recognizable capacity to assert claims. To respect a person, then, or to think of him as possessed of human dignity, simply *is* to think of him as a potential maker of claims."⁴

Although this passage may be interpreted in various ways, I shall use it as a means of calling attention to two importantly different concepts of both dignity and rights. First, as to dignity: one concept is, broadly

2. Universal Declaration of Human Rights, arts. 22, 23 (in Brownlie, *Basic Documents*, p. 25).
3. Immanuel Kant, *Doctrine of Virtue* (Part II of *The Metaphysic of Morals*), Part II, chap. 1, sec. 2, para. 38 (Akad. ed., p. 461), trans. Mary J. Gregor (New York: Harper Torchbooks, 1964), p. 132.
4. Joel Feinberg, "The Nature and Value of Rights," reprinted in his *Rights, Justice, and the Bounds of Liberty* (Princeton: Princeton University Press, 1980), p. 151.

speaking, *empirical.* In this sense, dignity is a characteristic that is often also signified by its corresponding adjective, *dignified*; it is, variously, a kind of gravity or decorum or composure or self-respect or self-confidence together with various good qualities that may justify such attitudes. Thus, we may say of some person, "He behaved with great dignity on that occasion," or "She generally comports herself with dignity." Such dignity is a contingent feature of some human beings as against others; it may be occurrently had, gained, or lost; and, depending on the context, it may or may not have a specifically moral bearing. It is to this empirical concept of dignity that David Hume refers when he emphasizes that the "dispute concerning the dignity or meanness of human nature" is to be resolved by taking account of the comparative degrees in which various good or bad qualities are had by different humans.[5] That the passage quoted above from Feinberg also refers to this empirical sense of *dignity* is suggested by his equating dignity with the ability to "stand up like men" and "the recognizable capacity to assert claims." Such abilities and capacities are indeed valuable; but, as matters of empirical fact, they are not always had by all human beings, let alone equally.[6] Also, in this sense human dignity is *consequent upon* the having of rights and hence is not the *ground* of rights. For, on this view, one's dignity derives from the ability to make claims, in which the having of rights is said to consist. Hence, this way of relating human dignity and human rights does not meet the condition-specified above, according to which rights are grounded in dignity, and not conversely.

Let us now consider a second concept of dignity, which, following one of the United Nations documents cited above, I shall call *inherent.* In this sense, *dignity* signifies a kind of intrinsic worth that belongs equally to all human beings as such, constituted by certain intrinsically valuable aspects of being human. This is a necessary, not a contingent, feature of all humans; it is permanent and unchanging, not transitory or changeable; and, as we shall see, it sets certain limits to how humans may justifiably be treated. When the United Nations Universal Declaration of Human Rights upholds in its preamble "recognition of the inherent dignity and of the equal and inalienable rights of all members of the human family,"[7] it is to this inherent concept of dignity that it appeals.

---

5. David Hume, "Of the Dignity or Meanness of Human Nature," in his *Essays, Moral, Political, and Literary* (Indianapolis, Ind.: Liberty Classics, 1985), pp. 80–86.

6. For an interesting discussion of some important variants in the relation between what I have called "empirical dignity" and the claiming of rights, see Michael J. Meyer, "Dignity, Rights, and Self-Control," *Ethics* 99 (April 1989): 520–34.

7. Reprinted in Brownlie, *Basic Documents,* p. 21.

This is a concept that sets peculiarly stringent moral requirements. In this sense, dignity is contrasted by Kant with *price*.[8] If a thing has a price, then it can be substituted for or replaced by something else of equivalent value, where *value* signifies, as in Thomas Hobbes, a worth that is relative to a person's desires or opinions. Thus Hobbes recognizes only a certain version of the empirical concept of dignity, which he defines as "the publique worth of a man, which is the value set on him by the Commonwealth."[9] In contrast, inherent dignity cannot be replaced by anything else, and it is not relative to anyone's desires or opinions. It is such inherent dignity that serves as the ground of human rights.

In what, then, does this inherent dignity consist, and just how does it ground human rights? In addition to the relation between dignity and rights considered above, wherein having dignity is the *consequent* of having rights, we must also reject, with a view to our problem, a second relation, wherein having dignity is the *equivalent* of having rights. This relation is suggested in the following passage by Jacques Maritain: "The dignity of the human person? The expression means nothing if it does not signify that by virtue of natural law, the human person has the right to be respected, is the subject of rights, possesses rights."[10] On this view, then, the expression "*A* has human dignity" simply reduplicates "*A* has human rights"; to have the dignity just consists in having the rights.

Although this view indicates an important aspect of the relation between dignity and rights, it does not show how human dignity is the *antecedent*, the justificatory basis or ground, of human rights, as against being either their equivalent or their consequent. It is not merely that wherever there are human rights there is human dignity, or that having rights serves to buttress empirical dignity. Even if this is true, the primary relation is that persons have human rights *because* they have inherent human dignity. It is this relation, and its constituent concepts, that we must try to explain and justify.

Two Concepts of Rights

To move toward this goal, we must note that there are two concepts of rights parallel to the two concepts of dignity. One concept is *empirical*

---

8. Kant, *Foundations of the Metaphysics of Morals*, sec. 2 (Akad. ed., pp. 434–35), trans. L. W. Beck (Indianapolis, Ind.: Library of Liberal Arts, 1959), p. 53.
9. Thomas Hobbes, *Leviathan*, chap. 10.
10. Jacques Maritain, *The Rights of Man and Natural Law*, trans. D. Anson (New York: Charles Scribner's Sons, 1951), p. 65.

or *positivist*. For some person A to have a right to X in this sense means that there is social recognition and effective legal protection of A's having or doing X. A second concept is *normatively moral*. For A to have a right to X in this sense means that there is normative moral justification for A's being protected in having or doing X, as something that is his personal due or entitlement, even if such protection is in fact lacking. It is in this sense that we say that all persons have a right to freedom even if some persons, who are legally slaves or are subjected to governmentally inflicted torture, are not effectively protected in having the freedom that is the object of this right.

An initial connection between human dignity and human rights, then, is that for each the negation of the empirical mode does not entail the negation of the other, inherent or morally justificatory, mode. That all humans have inherent dignity is not disproved by the fact that some persons behave (or are treated) without empirical dignity, in that they are too raucous or obsequious or servile or lacking in self-control or otherwise "undignified." Similarly, that all persons have human rights is not disproved by the empirical fact that some persons' human rights are violated.

These distinctions also serve to buttress the point emphasized above, that the connection between the claiming of rights and the having of empirical dignity cannot provide the primary basis of human dignity. For, in the inherent sense, human dignity is not a quality that waits for its existence on the empirical fulfillment or claiming of positive legal rights; rather, it exists even in the absence of such fulfillment; indeed, it is the ground or antecedent of the rights insofar as they are morally justified, not their consequent.

SOME EPISTEMOLOGICAL PROBLEMS

These points also serve, however, to bring out the difficulties of the questions we are trying to answer here. For a further, especially important similarity between the two pairs of concepts distinguished above is epistemological. It is not especially difficult to find empirical tests for checking whether humans have empirical dignity or socially recognized rights. But it seems to be very difficult (and on some views impossible) to ascertain, or to provide justificatory arguments for the theses, that all humans equally have inherent dignity or moral rights. Especially in connection with inherent human dignity, there is an apparent absence of any empirical correlatives for it. Moreover, if inherent human dignity, as the ground of human moral rights, must belong to all humans equally, then it must be a characteristic of criminals as well as saints, of cowards as well as heroes, of fools as well as sages, of mental defectives as well as mentally normal persons, of slaves as well as masters, of subjects as well as lords, of disease-ridden invalids as well as athletes, of drug addicts as well as persons of self-control, of starving proletarians as well as well-fed capitalists, and so forth. How, in view of this vast empirical range of diverse human characteristics, can the ascription of equal inherent dignity to all human beings be justified?

We can begin to answer this question if we take note of the ways in which inherent dignity can be empirically instantiated. Let us focus on the related concept of "treating someone with dignity" (where this means to treat her *with recognition for* her dignity). Negatively, to treat someone with dignity is to exclude certain interrelated kinds of attitudes and actions. Among the excluded attitudes are contempt, blazing hatred that will stop at nothing to inflict injury, discriminatory feelings that totally disregard comparative merits of the persons concerned, and so forth. The excluded actions comprise, for example, such cruelties, whether in penal or other contexts, as rape, torture, cutting off of hands, blinding, and so forth. They also include treating persons as if they had only a "price," so that their lives, liberties, or purposive pursuits can be dispensed with through "equivalents" based on political or economic calculations, as in some types of "cost-benefit analysis." Positively, to treat someone with dignity is to accord her certain kinds of consideration: to treat her as an end, not only as a means or as an object to be exploited; to treat her with respect for her basic needs, and for herself as worthy of having these needs fulfilled. More specifically, it would not be difficult to show that the inherent dignity of human beings, because of their intrinsic worth, requires the kinds of protections embodied in the U.S. Bill of Rights and the United Nations Universal Declaration of Human Rights, including within the latter not only political and civil rights but also social and economic rights. All these modes of treatment, negative and positive, are required by the intrinsic worth of human beings in which their inherent dignity consists. But the derivation of rights from dignity must be spelled out if this relation is to be fully understood.

These considerations begin to provide an empirical content for inherent human dignity, for they specify the kinds of empirically ascertainable attitudes and actions that such dignity requires. They also take due account of the egalitarian universality of inherent dignity, for the exclusion of the negative attitudes and actions, and the opposed positive attitudes and treatments, are the moral rights of all humans by virtue of their inherent dignity, regardless of the vast array of empirical differences listed above. At the same time, however, these treatments are not *constitutive* of inherent human dignity. Humans have such dignity regardless of how they are treated; certain modes of treatment may violate but not remove their dignity. The having of the dignity normatively requires certain modes of treatment and prohibits others. Hence, these considerations begin to relate inherent human dignity to human rights, and moral rights to positivist rights, for they show that moral rights can have their effective equivalents in the legal enforcement of certain of the rights. But we are still left with the questions of what is the direct nature of such inherent dignity, what warrant there is for attributing it to all humans equally, and just how it serves to provide the justificatory ground for human rights.

NECESSARY RESPECT AND DIGNITY

One way of dealing with these questions is to reject any cognitive approach to them and to adopt a kind of emotivist position. Thus, Feinberg says: " 'Human worth' itself is best understood to name no property in the way that 'strength' names strength and 'redness' redness. In attributing human worth to everyone we may be ascribing no property or set of qualities, but rather expressing an attitude—the attitude of respect—toward the humanity in each man's person."[11] This position incurs many of the same difficulties that beset simple emotivist analyses of *good*, *right*, and other value terms. Since attitudes may vary from person to person and from group to group, the ascription of human worth or dignity would not have the universality that is assumed by the grounding of human rights in human dignity. And if the ascription of dignity to all humans, with its correlative respect, is itself "groundless," as Feinberg also suggests,[12] then no reasons can be given that serve to justify the normative necessity that is a basic feature of human rights.

None of this is meant to deny that respect is an attitude and that this attitude is an important requirement for human rights and dignity. But, parallel to our above distinctions between empirical and inherent dignity

11. Joel Feinberg, *Social Philosophy* (Englewood Cliffs, N.J.: Prentice-Hall, 1973), p. 94.
12. Ibid., p. 93.

and between positivist and moral rights, we must also distinguish between two concepts of respect, based directly on their different objects but consequently also on their different contents. *Contingent respect* consists in a favorable appraisal of variable features of human beings; like the ascription of empirical dignity, it may be justifiably accorded in some cases and withheld in others. *Necessary respect*, on the other hand, consists in an affirmative, rationally grounded recognition of and regard for a status that all human beings have by virtue of their inherent dignity.[13] It is to such necessary respect that Kant refers when he says that it is "exacted" by human dignity: "man regarded as a *person* ... possesses, in other words, a *dignity* (an absolute inner worth) by which he exacts *respect* for himself from all other rational beings in the world."[14] But even if such necessary respect is the *ratio cognoscendi* of human dignity, it cannot be its *ratio essendi*. The existence and nature of dignity cannot be constituted by respect; on the contrary, it is because humans have inherent dignity that respect is demanded or required of other persons as the recognition of an antecedently existing worth. This suggests that we must look to the ontological sphere to find human dignity as an inherent, essential characteristic of human beings. But just where should we look?

REASON AND FREE WILL AS BASES OF HUMAN DIGNITY

One famous suggestion, which goes back to the Stoics, is that the universe comprises a moral hierarchy of perfections, in which humans

---

13. This distinction is indebted to, but is more specific than, Stephen L. Darwall's distinction between "appraisal respect" and "recognition respect," in "Two Kinds of Respect," *Ethics* 88 (October 1977): 36–49. William K. Frankena holds that what he calls "moral consideration respect" (which is close to what I call "necessary respect") is indeterminate with regard to what it morally requires in the treatment of persons: "The principle that we are to respect persons in this sense says only that there are morally right and wrong, good or bad ways of treating and relating to persons, as such or for their own sakes. It does not tell us which ways of treating or relating to them are right or wrong, good or bad." "The Ethics of Respect for Persons," *Philosophical Topics* 14 (Fall 1986): 157. This, however, overlooks the kinds of determinate requirements indicated above for "treating someone with dignity." See also the important discussion of "individual human worth" and what it morally requires, by Gregory Vlastos, "Justice and Equality," in *Social Justice*, ed. Richard B. Brandt (Englewood Cliffs, N.J.: Prentice-Hall, 1962), pp. 31–72, at pp. 45–53.

14. *Doctrine of Virtue*, Part I, book I, chap. 2, para. 11 (Akad. ed., pp. 433–34; Gregor ed., p. 99).

rank just below God. As such, all humans have a certain equal "rank... in the universal chain of Being";[15] as John Locke put it, they are "Creatures of the same species and rank promiscuously born to the same advantages of Nature, and the use of the same faculties... sharing all in one Community of Nature."[16] Human dignity, in such a perspective, is to be accounted for by this theological-cosmological context, which sets the ontological status of human beings, and it consists in or derives from all humans' possession of reason or free will or both.

For various familiar reasons I shall here abstract from this theological-cosmological perspective (despite its immense historical influence). The challenge is to give a purely rational explication or justification of the attribution of equal inherent dignity for all human beings. To this purpose, I shall first focus directly on the alleged connection between human dignity and the possession of reason and free will. At least four objections can be made against this connection. The first three advert to the vast empirical range referred to above. First, since the ability to reason is distributed very unequally among human beings, how can their possession of reason serve to ground or justify the assertion of their *equal* inherent dignity? Second, since both reason and free will can be and are used for bad as well as good purposes, how can humans' possession of them account for the presumed good of human *dignity* or worth? Third, it is to be noted that human dignity is so far viewed not as directly an "objective" or ontological feature or characteristic of human beings but, rather, as supervenient on such features.[17] In this regard, "all humans have inherent dignity" is not a proposition of the same kind as "all humans have reason and free will"; instead, the former is an evaluative statement that is justified on the basis of the latter, descriptive or factual statement. But since supervenience is held to be a contingent relation, in that what supervenes is not entailed or logically necessitated by that on

---

15. Pico della Mirandola, *Oration on Human Dignity*, trans. Elizabeth L. Forbes, in *The Renaissance Philosophy of Man*, ed. E. Cassirer, P. O. Kristeller, J. H. Randall, Jr. (Chicago: University of Chicago Press, 1948), p. 233. I have rendered Pico's *De hominis dignitate* as "On *Human* Dignity" rather than "On the Dignity *of Man*" because the former is more in keeping with his intentions. It is interesting to note that although Greek and Latin have one word for the generic human being (*anthrōpos, homo*) and a quite *different* word for the specific male human being (*anēr, vir*), the main modern western languages all have the *same* word for the generic and the specific (*man, homme, uomo, hombre,* and so forth). German has the generic *Mensch* and the specific *Mann*, but the latter is far closer to *Mensch* than is *Frau*. I have found no explanation for this modern verbal masculinizing of the generic human being.
16. *Two Treatises of Government*, II, secs. 4, 6.
17. See Feinberg, *Social Philosophy*, p. 90.

which it supervenes,[18] how is the supervenience of dignity on reason and free will compatible with the alleged necessity and universality of inherent human dignity? Fourth, since human dignity is held to be the basis of human rights, which are correlative with duties or "oughts," how does the basing of dignity on *is*-statements about factual characteristics of human beings serve to generate the "oughts" of human dignity and rights?

The Dialectically Necessary Argument for the Worth of Actions

I shall now develop my answers to these questions. The argument for human dignity that I shall present here is closely related to the argument for the existence of human rights that I have worked out in much detail elsewhere.[19] I shall here use from that argument only the considerations that are directly relevant to the present problem.

To begin with, we must note that the general context of all morality (and indeed of all practice), and hence of human dignity as a moral quality, is *action* and *agency*. For all moral precepts, amid their vast differences of criteria and contents, deal directly or indirectly with how persons ought to act, especially toward one another. Some moral precepts are directly concerned with moral virtues rather than with actions; but since moral virtues are dispositions to act in certain ways, such precepts still deal indirectly with actions.

Now actions in the relevant sense—as the envisaged objects of moral and other practical precepts—may be considered either as bare actions or as actions that have general chances of success in fulfilling the purposes for which one acts (this latter because the purpose of performing an action is to succeed in fulfilling or achieving one's purpose). As such, actions and generally successful actions have two necessary constitutive conditions or generic features: *freedom* (or *voluntariness*) and *well-being* (which derives from *purposiveness*); these are, respectively, the procedural and the substantive necessary conditions of action. Freedom or voluntariness consists in controlling one's behavior by one's unforced choice while having knowledge of relevant circumstances. Well-being as

18. See R. M. Hare, *The Language of Morals* (Oxford: Clarendon Press, 1952), pp. 80–89.
19. Alan Gewirth, *Reason and Morality* (Chicago: University of Chicago Press, 1978), chaps. 1–3; Alan Gewirth, *Human Rights: Essays on Justification and Applications* (Chicago: University of Chicago Press, 1982), pp. 41–78; Alan Gewirth, "The Epistemology of Human Rights," *Social Philosophy and Policy* 1, no. 2 (Spring 1984): 1–24.

here understood, which derives from the purposiveness of action, consists in having the abilities and conditions needed for fulfilling one's various purposes. Such well-being falls into a hierarchy of three kinds of action-related goods that are needed either (*a*) as the general preconditions of actions (basic well-being, such as life and physical integrity), or (*b*) for retaining undiminished one's level of purpose-fulfillment and one's capabilities for particular actions (nonsubstractive well-being, such as not being lied to or stolen from), or (*c*) for increasing one's level of purpose-fulfillment and one's capabilities for particular actions (additive well-being, such as education and opportunities for earning wealth and income).

How does human dignity or worth enter this context of action? Most previous philosophers have tried to argue directly or assertorically, undertaking to derive the agent's possession of dignity from her necessary possession of freedom (including autonomy and unforced choice) and reason (including her knowledge of relevant circumstances and her ability to calculate from causes to effects and hence from means to ends or purposes). But such a procedure is beset by the four objections presented above. Instead of using such an assertoric method, I shall here use what I call a *dialectically necessary method*. The method is *dialectical* in that it begins not from facts about the subject matter but, rather, from statements presented as being made by agents, and it examines what these statements logically imply. The method is dialectically *necessary* in that the statements in question logically must be made or accepted by agents because of their necessary connection with the context of action. The dialectically necessary method is thus different not only from an assertoric method but also from a dialectically contingent method, which is used in most contractarian theories, and from a phenomenological method, which tries to describe what someone actually says or thinks. In contrast to these, I shall try to show that the dialectically necessary method can provide the basis for the necessary ascription of dignity to all human beings. The reason for this is that, just as we have seen that the context of action is necessarily connected with all morality and practice, so the statements elicited by the dialectically necessary method are necessarily connected with the context of action; and as we shall see, these statements include necessary ascriptions of dignity to all human beings qua actual, prospective, or potential agents. By virtue of these entailments, the use of the dialectically necessary method enables the argument to overcome the "fact-value" and "is-ought" gaps, in ways soon to be indicated.[20]

20. On reasons why the dialectically necessary method must be used here (rather than

Let us begin, then, from a statement of the following form that is necessarily attributable to every agent on the occasion of his performing some action: (1) "I do X for end or purpose E." In the present discussion we need not concern ourselves with problems about the individuation of actions or about degrees of knowledge or self-consciousness; the agent, as behaving freely or voluntarily, knows who he is and what he is doing.

At this point a conception of value and worth enters the argument. For since the agent unforcedly chooses to do X for the purpose of attaining or having E, he must think that his purpose E has sufficient *value* to *merit* his moving from quiescence to action in order to attain it—that E is *worth* acting to attain. This element of value and worth is expressed by the agent's saying or thinking (2) "E is good." Thus, an ineluctable element of worth is involved in the very concept and context of human purposive action. For such action is not merely an unordered set of episodes or events; rather, it is ordered by its orientation to a goal that, for the agent, gives it its value, its point. This is so even if the action is done for its own sake, so that it is its own goal. In either case, the goal or end has worth for the agent as something to be more or less reflectively chosen, aimed at, and achieved. And this worth is not solely instrumental; it characterizes at least some of the agent's ends themselves as he conceives and pursues them.

The goodness or worth that is here in question need not, at this stage of the argument, be moral or any other specific kind of goodness; it varies with all the various purposes that agents may have. Nor need the judgment of goodness be regarded as conclusive or definitive; it may be highly tentative or contingent, depending in part on the relation of the agent's particular purpose to other purposes or values he may have. He may, indeed, rank some purposes much higher than others, with a corresponding variation in the degree of goodness or value he assigns to them. But in all cases of purposive action there is a necessary element of valuation, of estimation of worth, that derives from the agent's unforcedly choosing to act for some end or purpose he wants to attain, even if this consists only in doing the action itself.

It will have been noted that in statement (2) above, "E is good" is put in quotation marks, as the dialectically necessary method requires. What (2) says is not that E is good *tout court* or assertorically, independently of the individual agent's standpoint (for this would surely not be justified

---

an assertoric method), see Gewirth, *Reason and Morality*, pp. 159–61; also Gewirth, *Human Rights*, pp. 20–26, and Alan Gewirth, "Why Agents Must Claim Rights: A Reply," *Journal of Philosophy* 79 (1982): 403–10.

by the antecedent). Instead, it says that E is good from the standpoint of the individual agent who acts to attain E. Thus, in the sequence from (1) to (2) the fact-value gap is crossed, but only from within the perspective of the individual agent. Nevertheless, despite this restriction, the sequence from (1) to (2) is of first importance in attaining the necessity and universality required by the argument for human dignity. For the sequence from (1) to (2) is *necessarily* attributable to *every* agent (regardless of possible contingent phenomenological variations) because it derives from the context of action from which no actual or prospective agent can permanently remove himself (except perhaps by suicide; and even then the particular steps he takes to this end would themselves embody the generic features of action). And since every human being is an actual, prospective, or potential agent, the connection with humanly attributable goods is direct.

THE DIALECTICALLY NECESSARY ARGUMENT FOR HUMAN DIGNITY

I now want to propose a way in which these considerations can be directly related to the question of human worth or dignity. As we have seen, an ineluctable element of agent-estimated worth is involved in the very concept and context of human purposive action. Now, there is a direct route from this ascribed worth of the agent's ends to the worth or dignity of the agent himself. For he is both the general locus of all the particular ends he wants to attain and also the source of his attribution of worth to them. Because he is this locus and source, he must hold that the worth he attributes to his ends pertains a fortiori to himself. They are *his* ends, and they are worth attaining because *he* is worth sustaining and fulfilling, so that he has what for him is a justified sense of his own worth. This attribution of worth to himself derives not only from the goodness he attributes to his particular actions but also from the general purposiveness that characterizes all his actions and himself qua agent. And because of this general context of agency, his attribution of worth also extends to his freedom in controlling his behavior by his unforced choice and to whatever rationality enters into his calculating the means to his ends. For he pursues his ends not as an uncontrolled reflex response to stimuli, but, rather, because he has chosen them after reflection on alternatives. Even if he does not always reflect, his choice can and does sometimes at least operate in this way.

Every human agent, as such, is capable of this. Hence, the agent is, and regards himself as, an entity that, unlike other natural entities, is not, so far as it acts, subject only to external forces of nature; he can and does make his own decisions on the basis of his own reflective understanding. By virtue of these characteristics of his actions, the agent regards himself as having worth or dignity. This attribution of worth must, at least in the first instance, be interpreted neither assertorically nor phenomenologically but, rather, as dialectically necessary, as reflecting a characteristic of human purposive action that every agent must attribute to himself or herself.

Now, this worth or dignity that the agent logically attributes to himself by virtue of the purposiveness of his actions, he must also attribute to all other actual or prospective agents. For their actions have the same general kind of purposiveness that provides the ground for his attribution of dignity to himself. It is not merely that he recognizes that *other agents* attribute dignity to themselves because of their purposiveness; in addition, *he* must attribute such dignity to each of them because of their own purposiveness, which is generically similar to his.[21] In this way, the necessary attribution of inherent dignity to all human being is dialectically established, for, as was indicated above, all humans are actual, prospective, or potential agents.[22]

The further development of the argument from (1) to (2) shows that every agent logically must hold or accept that she and all other actual or prospective agents have rights to freedom and well-being as the necessary conditions of their action and generally successful action. Since I have presented this argument in great detail elsewhere,[23] I shall not repeat

21. This universalization of the agent's dignity-attribution to other agents may be criticized by what I have elsewhere called the "individualizability" and "particularizability" objections. I have set out these objections and shown how they are to be answered in *Reason and Morality*, pp. 115–25. Brian Barry has presented a version of the individualizability objection without noting my fuller refutation of it. See Barry, *Theories of Justice* (Berkeley: University of California Press, 1989), pp. 285–88.

22. Kant writes: "The ends which a rational being arbitrarily proposes to himself as consequences of his action are material ends and are without exception only relative, for only their relation to a particularly constituted faculty of desire in the subject gives them their worth. And this worth cannot, therefore, afford any universal principles for all rational beings or valid and necessary principles for every volition." *Foundations of the Metaphysics of Morals*, sec. 2 (Akad. ed., p. 427; Beck, pp. 45–46). Kant here overlooks the point that even though the ends or purposes of particular actions are themselves particular, universality is involved, first, in the fact that all the particular purposes have worth for a single agent, who is therefore their source or locus, and second, that all other agents have the same relation to their respective purposes and the worth they embody.

23. See note 19. Although the objects of the rights are the necessary conditions of action, and the person who claims them is already an agent (so that he has these necessary

it here. The main point can be briefly put in two steps. First, if any agent were to deny that he has rights to freedom and well-being, he would contradict himself, for he would be in the position of holding that he *need not have* the necessary goods or conditions that, as an agent, he has to accept that he *must have* in order to be an agent who seeks to fulfill his purposes and thereby to attain what he regards as worth attaining pursuant to his own worth. Second, the agent must hold that he has these rights simply by virtue of being an actual or prospective agent who has purposes he wants to fulfill; hence, by universalization, he has to accept that all actual or prospective purposive agents have these rights. And since all human beings are actual, prospective, or potential purposive agents, the rights to freedom and well-being are human rights, so that, in this dialectically necessary way, the principle of human rights is given a rational justification.

This argument for the principle of human rights indicates how the rights are grounded in human dignity or worth. For it is from the worth that each agent attributes to her ends or purposes and hence, a fortiori, to herself as purposive agent that there necessarily follows the claiming of rights to the necessary conditions of acting in pursuit of those purposes. Since she must acknowledge that the rights are had by all humans equally, this also serves to impose a moral restriction on the purposes she is justified in regarding as worth pursuing, and hence, too, on her ascription of worth or dignity to herself. Thus, although the existence of human rights follows dialectically from the worth or dignity that every agent must attribute to himself, the content of that dignity is in turn morally modified by the universal and equal human rights in which the argument eventuates.

On the present account, the existence of both human dignity and human rights is viewed, not as having an independent ontological status, but, rather, in keeping with the dialectically necessary method, as agent-relative, that is, based on a rational justification that must be accepted by every agent. Since, however, agency or action is the general context of all morality and practice, it follows that the existence of human dignity, and with it of human rights, has been shown to be normatively necessary and universal within the whole relevant context.

---

conditions), the claiming of the rights is not redundant or pointless because (*a*) the agent may not have the generic abilities needed for *successful* action and (*b*) the claimant is not *always* an agent, and he claims the rights not only for his present actions but also, as a prospective agent, for his future actions. On these points, see *Reason and Morality*, p. 68.

REPLIES TO OBJECTIONS

On the basis of these considerations, I shall now try to show how we are to deal with the four objections presented above against the derivation of human dignity from humans' possession of reason and will. As for the first objection, the unequal abilities of reason among human beings do not refute the argument's conclusion about the equal distribution of human dignity and rights, for two main reasons. First, the primary ground on which every agent logically must hold or accept that he has rights to freedom and well-being is not that he possesses reason or other practical abilities, but rather that he has purposes he wants to fulfill by acting. For if he had no purposes, he would claim no rights of agency, nor would he act. And this having of purposes is equal and common to all agents, whether wise or foolish. As we have seen, it is this generic purposiveness that underlies the ascription of inherent dignity to all agents.

Second, although it is indeed true that one must use reason to follow the argument (so that in this and other ways the dialectical argument invokes the concept of a rational agent), the use of reason that enters the argument is a minimal deductive and inductive one that is within the reach of all normal human beings. Here, *normal* means having the practical abilities of the generic features of action: the abilities to control one's behavior by one's unforced choice, to have knowledge of relevant circumstances, and to reflect on one's purposes. Where human beings are not normal and rational even in this minimal sense, the attribution of dignity and rights to them must follow what I have elsewhere called the Principle of Proportionality,[24] according to which the having of rights is proportional to the degree to which humans and other entitites have the abilities of agency. But this inequality of rights is itself, in turn, based on a more fundamental equality of inherent dignity and human rights, because the unequal extents to which different humans should have the objects of various rights are grounded in an equal concern for the freedom and well-being of all humans. Just as the equality of human dignity and rights is compatible with some humans' being given more food or protection than other humans when the former have a greater need for such objects in order to sustain their basic well-being, so too the lesser freedom allowed to some mentally deficient humans is justified by an equal concern for the basic well-being and dignity of them and of all other humans.[25]

24. See *Reason and Morality*, pp. 120–28.
25. For further replies to objections about the equal distribution of human rights, see Gewirth, *Human Rights*, pp. 76–78; Alan Gewirth, "On Rational Agency as the Basis of

We must also note another way of relating human dignity to humans' possession of reason and will. Regardless of the specific extents to which they are developed in different humans, these capacities have certain generic features whose various applications—intellectual, aesthetic, and moral values—bring dignity to human life. But the basis of this dignity is the dignity inherent in all normal human beings as having these general capacities, directly reflected in their purposive actions and resulting judgments of worth. Where humans are so mentally deficient as not to have them even in minimal form, the Principle of Proportionality applies, but again with the egalitarian proviso of equal concern for dignity and rights indicated above.

The second objection concerned the compatibility of human dignity as based on reason and free will with the bad purposes to which these human capacities can be put. The criterion of "bad" here may be prudential or moral; I shall here confine myself to the alternative that this objection incorporates a moral criterion in its judgment of the agent's purposes. Such a criterion, however, does not enter the argument until the agent has universalized his ascriptions of worth and rights to himself so that they must now be attributed to all human beings equally. As was indicated before, this universal and egalitarian attribution serves in turn to modify and restrict the agent's rationally justified assessments of his purposes. Thus, to begin with, whatever the content of his purposes, the agent must attribute worth to himself in the way indicated above; but then, once the argument has established the moral restrictions that he logically must accept, these restrictions must be applied both to his purposes and to his judgments of dignity. The agent's initial ascription of worth or dignity to himself and to all other agents, based on the worth he attributes to his purposes in acting, remains in any case as an inherent and necessary quality.

We must also consider here another variant of the objection about bad purposes. The dialectical argument presented above made human dignity derivative from an agent's valuing his purposes. But may not an agent *dis*value his purposes? If he has been brainwashed or has a very low self-image from other causes, such as drug addiction or a hopeless outlook on life, he may well feel that what he wants is no good, that his purposes

Moral Equality: Reply to Ben-Zeev," *Canadian Journal of Philosophy* 12 (1982): 667–72; "Replies to My Critics," in *Gewirth's Ethical Rationalism*, ed. Edward Regis, Jr. (Chicago: University of Chicago Press, 1984), pp. 225–27; Alan Gewirth, "Why There Are Human Rights," *Social Theory and Practice* 11 (1985): 234–48.

are vile and worthless, so that, far from generating a judgment of his own worth, they may reinforce the opposite judgment.

There are two main answers to this objection. First, if he has been brainwashed or subjected to related kinds of controls over his mental functioning, then he is not an agent in the strict sense intended here, since he does not control his behavior by his own unforced choice. In such a case the principle of human rights, based on the necessary conditions of agency, requires that, so far as possible, the deleterious effects of such previously inflicted constraints on his agency be removed, so that his preexisting potentialities for agency may be actualized. Second, insofar as the person in question is indeed an agent, so that he controls his behavior by his own unforced choice, he must, as purposive, regard his purposes in acting as having *some* value for him, since otherwise he would not unforcedly choose to act as he does. It is true that agents function under many kinds of constraints, both internal and external. But these, in cases of action, that is, of voluntary and purposive behavior, do not have the combined aspects of compulsoriness, undesirableness, and threat that cause choices to be forced.[26] Hence, amid the varying degrees to which agents may value their various purposes, there persists an enduring element of valuation and hence of judgment of worth, from which the agent's judgment of his and all others agents' worth has been shown to be logically generated, regardless of possible contingent variations. This worth or dignity, moreover, is inherent because it derives from the very nature of purposive action. And it is intrinsic because, in its primary form, it is not instrumental to any other goods and because it is the basis rather than the effect of the worth that agents attribute to their purposes.

The third objection was about supervenience. It is indeed true that the attribution of dignity to human beings is supervenient on the "natural fact" of their being actual, prospective, or potential purposive agents. This supervenience, however, is not contingent but, rather, logically necessary, by virtue of the necessary connection between (a) acting for a purpose, (b) regarding that purpose as worth achieving, (c) regarding oneself as worth sustaining or preserving, (d) regarding oneself as having worth or dignity, and (e) extending this judgment to all other purposive agents.

Another way to put this point is in terms of moral realism: the doctrine that moral judgments are literally true. Applied to the attribution of

---

26. For fuller discussion of this point, see Gewirth, *Reason and Morality*, pp. 31–42, 48–63.

dignity to all human beings, this means that such attribution is literally true because it corresponds to the normative structure of action. The attribution logically must be accepted by every even minimally rational agent because it logically follows from factual statements that he logically must accept by virtue of being an agent.[27]

Fourth, the argument for human dignity and rights surmounts the "is-ought" problem because the dialectical attribution of rights, and hence of "oughts," follows logically from the agent's acting for purposes he wants to fulfill.[28]

This essay is too long to permit any full summary. What I have tried to show here is that an adequate justification can be given for the conviction, reflected in United Nations documents about human rights and elsewhere, that human dignity is the basis of human rights. The necessary conditions of human action provide the justifying grounds for the universal ascription of human dignity, and this in turn serves to justify the principle of human rights.

27. For fuller discussion, see the section "Analytic Truth and Morality" in ibid., pp. 171–87. See also *Essays on Moral Realism*, ed. Geoffrey Sayre-McCord (Ithaca: Cornell University Press, 1988). In the editor's valuable introduction (pp. 1–23), he confines "cognitivist intersubjectivism" to the thesis that spells out "the truth conditions of moral claims in terms of the conventions or practices of groups of people" (p. 18). This overlooks, however, the alternative presented in this essay, according to which the truth conditions consist not in such contingent or variable "conventions or practices" but rather in the necessary normative structure of action, including the value-claims that must be made or accepted by all humans qua agents.

28. See my essay "The 'Is-Ought' Problem Resolved," in *Human Rights*, pp. 100–127.

2

Dignity, Worth, and Rights

A. I. MELDEN

The familiar talk about the dignity and worth of the person is usually associated in the philosophical literature with Immanuel Kant's discussion of these topics in the second and third sections of *The Foundations of the Metaphysics of Ethics*. I shall begin by discussing certain features of Kant's views, for there are lessons to be learned from what he has to say, before proceeding to explore the ways in which these terms are actually employed in our moral thinking. Finally, I shall examine some of the important connections between these notions and certain viable notions of moral rights.

I

One of Kant's well-known formulations of the principle of morality is the following: "Act so that you treat humanity, whether in your own person or in that of another, always as an end and never as a means only."[1] Kant certainly intended to distinguish between the notions

I have benefited from a stimulating discussion with Robert M. Yost on the subject of dignity, and from the comments of Gerasimos Santas on a draft of this essay.

1. All quotations are taken from the readily accessible translation by Lewis White Beck (Indianapolis, Ind.: Library of Liberal Arts, 1959). For a useful discussion of what one is to understand by treating humanity "as an end," see "Humanity as an End in Itself" by Thomas E. Hill, Jr., in *Ethics* 91 (October 1980): 84–99.

of humanity and person, for it is the humanity *in* a person with which Kant is concerned. A similar distinction is to be made between Kant's use of *man* and *person* when he declares that man is not a thing. For Kant identifies the humanity of a person with the rational nature present, he believes, in all human beings, however deficient in intelligence particular human beings may happen to be. Kant thinks of the intelligence of persons as something that varies with particular persons because of the accidents of nature, whereas one's humanity or rational nature is something essential to all human beings. And we must not think that Kant identifies one's humanity with a good will; the latter, for Kant, involves the idea of a will that surmounts the pressure of our inclinations in conforming to our humanity, that is, our nature as rational beings.

It is this rational nature, according to Kant, that is priceless, having neither a "market price," which as such is replaceable by something of equal value, nor an "affective price," which, "without presupposing any need, accords with a certain taste, i.e., with pleasure in the mere purposeless play of our faculties." Our rational nature, evident as it is in our capacity to discern the causality that operates in the natural world and in the practical sphere in our capacity to set ends for ourselves and to guide ourselves in their achievement, is evident in the moral sphere, in which, guided by the moral law, we treat it—our rational nature—in our own persons or in those of others, always as an end and never as a means only, thereby discovering what our duties are. How this discovery is to be achieved is something that need not detain us here. What interests us is that this rational nature is something abstracted "from the personal difference of rational beings," and certainly from our animality. This rational nature, he tells us, is an end in itself, something that has no mere relative worth, as in the case of things with their market or affective price, but "an intrinsic worth, i.e., dignity." The worth of our rational nature is, therefore, not a worth or good *for* anything or *for* anyone; it has the worth it has simply and solely for what it is in itself; it is a worth that is wholly wrapped up, so to speak, in itself. This is what is involved in saying that the worth of our rational nature is absolute or unconditional, not relative. And it is *this* worth that Kant identifies with the dignity that can be ascribed to any human being.

It should be clear that Kant does not restrict the possession of dignity to only some human beings. For every human being is endowed with a rational nature, whether or not he or she acts habitually out of respect for the moral law.[2] For however much one's rationality may be debased, sullied, or violated by folly, stupidity, immorality, or servility, one's humanity remains unsullied, and with it one's dignity. Put paradoxically, one preserves one's dignity, however undignified one may be. And one preserves one's goodness or worth, however evil or unworthy of any respect one may be. But there is nothing self-contradictory in either sentence, for the referents of the word *one* in each of the sentences are different. In the first instance, the referent is the particular human being each of us is, with the feelings, interests, specific aptitudes, or deficiencies and the behavior that are the natural products of the accidents of our native endowments, upbringings, and fortunes or misfortunes, as the case may be. In the second, the referent is our common rational nature. Each person, accordingly, has a dual nature. What may be undignified, that is, unworthy of respect, is the flesh-and-blood individual, but what is worthy of our respect and the source of our dignity is our essential rational nature. The latter may or may not succeed in overcoming the resistance in each of us of our inclinations, but as the rational being each of us is, in respect of which each of us is a member of an intelligible or noumenal world, each one's worth and hence dignity is unsullied and intact, exerting *some* influence upon us, inadequate as this may happen to be, because of the particular persons we are. Dignity in respect of our rational nature is something that necessarily all of us *have*, even when it fails to shine through in the willingly obedient slave. For as the rational being that even a slave is, a being from whom everything has been abstracted that distinguishes any individual from anyone else, each person possesses an absolute worth as a member of an "intelligible world" at whose boundary, paradoxically enough, "all knowledge terminates."

Kant likens the person, insofar as he or she is a rational being, to a lawgiver, a sovereign as it were, in the kingdom of ends at the same time that, as the particular individual he or she is, that being is subject to the moral law that stems from that self-same rational nature. Hence it is that Kant declares that the basis of the dignity of human beings—a dignity possessed even by the servile slave—is their autonomy, their determination in moral matters by their own rational nature. But this freedom that human beings have in moral matters, that is, their self-determination or autonomy, is purchased only by their membership as rational beings

---

2. For numerous references on this point to Kant's writings, see Hill, "Humanity as an End in Itself," pp. 86–87.

in a world that transcends the bounds of sensibility and sense, a noumenal world the "incomprehensibility" of which, he declares in conclusion, we can "comprehend." Thus the freedom required by morality, in the world in which we live, is one we have only insofar as we are also members of a world we cannot possibly understand!

Recall the earlier remark that there are lessons to be learned here. One such lesson, surely, is that dignity is closely connected with worth and in some way with rationality. But we can also profit from reading Kant's account by seeing how notions like dignity, worth, and rationality, when viewed independently of their employment by agents as we find them in the world in which we live, and in the concrete situations in which they are involved, baffle us when we attempt to understand them.

Consider Kant's talk about the absolute, unconditioned good of our common rational nature, a good sundered from all possible connection with all empirically given matters of human concern or interest—Kant labels them "inclinations"—since, unlike the relative good of things with market or affective price, it is not good *for* anything or anyone.[3] Surely it is ironical to ascribe it to something—our common rational nature— by virtue of which each of us is a member of the "intelligible," that is, noumenal world, something that transcends the boundaries of our understanding. Is it even intelligible to talk about a good about which it

3. Our common rational nature, on Kant's view, is clearly distinct from the good will, for it is present in all human beings, even in those who show little or no trace of the good will. But does Kant think that the goodness of the good will, like that of our common rational nature, is absolute or unconditional? It would appear to be so. He tells us in the opening paragraph of sec. 1 of the *Foundations* that the good will is good without qualification, contrasting its goodness with, among other things, that of intelligence, courage, "health, general well-being and the contentment with one's condition which is called happiness." The goodness of these latter items is context dependent: they are good only if the will itself is good, failing which they can be positively bad. Nor is it the case, he goes on to say, that the goodness of the good will depends upon its utility in the achievement of certain ends. For even if the good will always failed us in this respect, "it would sparkle like a jewel with its own light as something that had its full worth in itself." The worth or goodness of the good will is thus intrinsic and, in the broadest sense of the term, unconditional; and Kant uses not only the expression "good without qualification" but "absolute worth," "intrinsic absolute worth," "absolutely good without qualification," and "intrinsic unconditional worth" in describing the goodness of the good will. It would appear, then, that it is not only our common rational nature but also the good will, distinct as these two are, that is said to be absolutely or unconditionally good. Nevertheless, there is a difference between the goodness of the good will and that absolute or unconditional worth of our rational nature in that the former is derivative from or depends upon that fundamental goodness of the latter, since the good will in resisting the influence of inclination is itself rational and, qua rational, unconditionally or absolutely good. It is, therefore, the alleged absolute, unconditional goodness of our rational nature, something it has per se and quite independently of any contingent matter of fact, to which we need to direct our attention.

would make no sense to speak of having more or less of it, for that would be to apply the concept of degree or quantity to it—a concept that has no application to anything that lies beyond the bounds of our understanding? And if rationality—and so, too, with the absolute worth it is said to have—is to play any role in morality, the fact that there cannot be more or less of it in anyone, or for that matter in any number of moral agents, would appear to provide no reason whatsoever for the preference, all other things being equal, we do in fact have for saving the lives of a thousand persons to saving the life of one. Since dignity is identified with the absolute worth of a person insofar as persons are rational beings—here, too, it might seem, we have it fully or not at all— there can be no room for any intelligible talk about more or less of it. But can we say even this much about it, since what is present fully is thinkably present incompletely or partially? Further, it is something that is not to be achieved or to be desired insofar as it is the dignity each person has qua rational being; what is to be achieved or desired is something that pertains to a person as the particular individual he or she is. But can we make any sense of the talk of a dignity or worth independently of any connection with our familiar human interests, of a dignity or worth as something from which all consideration of more or less has been eliminated, something that exists in its perfection (can one indeed say even *this* much?) even in scoundrels, fools, and docile slaves, something that is not even a moral desideratum, something about which it appears to make no sense to say anything about it except that only God knows *what* it is? Are we not illegitimately trading on some of the features of worth and dignity as these terms are commonly employed in the lives of human beings as we find them in *this* world, in thinking that we are making any sense when we apply them to matters that lie beyond the bounds of our understanding?

A defender of Kant will object that the terms *worth* and *dignity* are applied to our rationality, something that provides the necessary bridge between matters of human or empirical fact and matters of noumenal rationality. But will this do the trick?

Understandably, Kant himself never considers the possibility of an eminently rational but amoral human being, a being who can grasp the causal patterns that exist in the natural world, set ends for itself, and skillfully employ its understanding of the means by which these may be achieved, but nevertheless lacks any moral understanding and with it any of the familiar moral emotions. Such a being, as in the case of the sociopath, is not immoral, for the immoralist does understand well enough that what he wants and does is wrong but makes the evil he brings upon others his own good. The immoralist recognizes the impropriety of using others merely as means, or, to consider Kant's first formulation of the principle of morality, of the unfairness or injustice of employing wholly self-centered maxims of action, but does so perversely. For the amoralist, unlike the immoralist, regards all moral discourse as so much verbal chatter he has learned to mimic, thereby concealing from others his total indifference to their well-being and the risk of the havoc he may create for them during the course of their dealings with him. And to the Kantian claim that the universalization of the amoralist's maxims of conduct leads to contradiction, the amoralist's retort is, "No one else is of the slightest importance, so why consider it?" What happens to *him* is the only thing that matters, not what happens to others, and about *that* he can be brilliantly rational. The supposition of a universalized amoralism, he knows well enough, is unlikely to be realized; there will always be ready victims upon whom he can prey. And even if, imaginably, all human beings were amoralists, he, with his extraordinary intelligence, would survive. In any case, no contradiction, only practical but resolvable problems would be posed by the universalization of the amoralist's wholly self-centered maxims of conduct. Indeed—this will no doubt shock the devout Kantian—is there anything self-contradictory in the supposition of an amoralist, with a level of intellectual genius comparable to that of Kant himself, writing a *Critique of Pure Reason*?

Surely we must distinguish between mere rationality—something the amoralist has in common with other human beings—and that rationality in the sense of reasonableness that morally worthy agents as we know them display in their thought and action in the world in which all of us live. But there is no conceptual connection between the former—the rationality of the sociopath—and any notions of moral worth and dignity; *this* rationality cannot therefore provide any bridge that lends any substantive content to any notion of Kant's so-called worth and dignity. As for the rationality in the sense of reasonableness, it is appropriate to agents only as we commonly understand them in this, our everyday world.

Kant's metaphysics of ethics, which attempts to provide a basis for an enlightened common-sense morality in a noumenal world—the "incomprehensibility" of which, he tells us in the concluding paragraph of the *Foundations*, we can "comprehend"—may be testimony to his remarkable intellectual powers; but it is also testimony to the way in which familiar terms in our common moral discourse undergo radical and baffling changes when they are employed in total independence of the actual situations in which they are used, situations in which alone they do have their familiar and intelligible uses. And if we are to understand what dignity is and how it is linked conceptually with worth and rights, we would be well advised to begin by looking at the ways in which, in *this*, world, persons as we know them employ the term *dignity* and its cognates.[4] We need, as Wittgenstein put it, to bring these terms back to the language games in which they are employed, if we are to understand them.

II

It is not a trivial matter or verbal accident that there is the cognate *dignitary*, for at one time dignity was thought to be the distinctive possession of members of the nobility, and, by extension, of those members of the church who are above the rank of parish priest. More recently, of course, the application of the term *dignitary* has been widened so as to apply to holders of high offices in political and indeed other institutions such as, for example, the judiciary, universities, and even industrial organizations. In all of these cases, the connection between dignity and worth is clear; and this is brought home in the case of the ironic talk about the "worthies" in the political offices of a backwater town or village, or when it is said that one dignifies something unworthy of a reply or response by paying more attention to it than it deserves. But where without irony, levity, or jocularity one speaks of the dignity of anyone in some office, institution, class, or social organization, the person who is said to have dignity is thought to be worthy of the given position, the importance of which is taken for granted. Further, the behavior and demeanor of the persons who possess dignity are said to be dignified.

---

4. Even Kant, not in the *Foundations* but elsewhere in *The Metaphysical Elements of Justice* (Part I of *The Metaphysics of Morals*), writes, "Under positions of dignity, we must include . . . those that make the holders into members of a higher class or rank . . . —in other words, the nobility as distinct from the class of common citizens who constitute the people." I owe this reference to Michael J. Meyer's essay "Kant's Concept of Dignity and Modern Political Thought" in *History of European Ideas* 8, no. 3 (1987): 320. Here, I believe, as elsewhere in the same work in which the above quoted remark appears, Kant is speaking simply as a person of his own time, a loyal citizen of eighteen-century Prussia, as indeed he does in his dedication of *The Critique of Pure Reason*, in which he appears, to a modern reader, to be abjectly subservient to his royal patron. In the *Metaphysical Elements of Justice*, unlike the *Foundation*, dignity is tied to a conception of a social hierarchy in which members of the upper class are entitled by virtue of their dignity—their honor—to command the lower classes. But it would be futile to attempt to squeeze anything like this out of the *Foundations*.

This does not mean that the person who has dignity is always unsmiling, humorless, or austere, for there are occasions that do call for humor and the manifest enjoyment of human fellowship. Characteristically, and depending upon the circumstances of particular cases, there will be dignified forms of behavior. What is out of character with the person with dignity is the familiar back-slapping, boisterous behavior of celebrants in a barroom. Finally, persons of dignity have certain character traits: they are said to be thoughtful, and, when they decide what courses of action to take, they are resolute and confident in what they proceed to do; they maintain their customary self-respect and composure.

It would be a mistake, however, to suppose that dignity always requires some sort of institutional setting in which there are duties associated with one's office or position. One can be dignified as Nathan Hale was in facing death, dignified in responding to an attack on one's integrity or in dealing with a hostile group; but it would be incorrect to say that Nathan Hale, in acting as he did, was performing his duty as the prospective victim of a hanging, or that in preserving one's dignity as the target of vilification or verbal abuse one is performing a duty that goes with one's office as a target of such disagreeable behavior. Nevertheless, in all of these sorts of cases, as in the ones mentioned above, dignity is clearly tied to worth or merit, in the present instance in the form of desirable character traits: he or she, when appropriate, is courageous, unruffled by the unfavorable opinions of others, calm in the face of criticism, and self-confident during the course of the actions taken.

In the case of the nobility, it was once supposed that their dignity would always show itself no matter what the extremity of their misfortunes might be. A prince in beggar's clothing, it was believed, could not help manifest his dignity in his demeanor; that, it was thought, was due to his intrinsically superior noble nature. Something like this, perhaps, may be thought to be true of the bishops and princes of the church, this time because of their special relations to the Deity. But in all other cases, dignity is a desideratum, and not something invariably present in all human beings, notwithstanding Kant's claim in the *Foundations* that they have it because of an attribute—rationality—all have in common. For so far we have been concerned with human beings as we find them in this world; and whatever their natural endowments may be, they vary enormously in the extent, if any, to which they manifest, in their behavior and demeanor, any of the meritorious traits of those with dignity. The familiar talk, therefore, of the dignity that all human beings have, because, as it is sometimes said, each has infinite value, reminiscent as it is of some of Kant's remarks in the *Foundations*, may be edifying; but it is, surely, philosophically unenlightening.

III

So far there has been no mention of moral rights, nor has anything been said that even implies that there are any moral rights. If, therefore, there is any warrant for connecting dignity with moral rights, this needs to be shown; for there can be, and often is, dignity in the form of certain desirable traits of character and behavior that are intelligible independently of any consideration of moral rights. Nevertheless, conceptions of moral rights have played an important practical role in promoting human dignity, and how philosophically this can be justified is one of the matters I hope to show in this section. I begin, therefore, by asking how dignity, a moral desideratum that many *lack*, is connected with moral rights, some of which, most of us believe, all persons do in fact *have*. But first I shall consider special moral rights, a paradigm case being the right created by a promise, and then, human rights, our fundamental rights as moral agents.

A

Very often, the case of a promise is viewed from the point of view of the person under the obligation, and the philosophical question raised first by Hume and later by Prichard has been the following: How is it possible that the uttering of the words "I promise . . . " creates a moral obligation?[5] And modern utilitarians follow the lead of J. S. Mill, who in chapter V of *Utilitarianism* focuses, in his positive account of the obligation, upon the great social importance of the so-called rule of promises. Like Hume and Prichard, modern utilitarians provide us with the simple picture of a promisee who is somehow morally bound, with respect to which the notion of dignity has no special purchase any more than it has in the kinds of situations we described earlier. More recent writers like H. L. A. Hart, emphasizing the importance of the right created by a promise, have called attention to the fact that the term *obligation*, as it

5. David Hume, *A Treatise of Human Nature*, Bk.III, Part II, sec. 5; and H. A. Prichard in the essay "The Obligation to Keep a Promise," published posthumously in *Moral Obligation* (Oxford: Oxford University Press, 1949), pp. 169–79.

is employed in the philosophical literature, obscures the difference between the use of *ought* in statements about what it is that one ought to
do, as for example in statements that one ought to be kind or generous,
and the use of *obligation* where it marks a distinctive relation between,
say, promiser and promisee, more clearly stated as the obligation that
the former has *to* the latter. Here the converse of this relation is the right
that the promisee has against the promiser. And what Hart offers us in
order to represent this relation is the picture of a chain by which the
promiser is bound to the promisee, who, as right-holder, may release his
or her grip on the chain when the right is relinquished, loosen the chain
without losing his or her grip on it when the right is waived but retained,
or, finally, lose his or her grip when the right is forfeited.[6] In the situation
thus pictured the idea would appear to be that the promisee, as right-
holder, has a distinctive authority with respect to the promiser, and this,
one might think, is the locus of the dignity to be found in the situation
in which the special right and its correlative obligation have been established. And often it has been supposed, as it was by Hart, that rights and
their correlative obligations belong, as he put it, to a different "area" of
morality from the requirements of kindness, generosity, or benevolence.[7]
I shall argue that both of these ideas are mistaken.

    1. No picture, certainly not one as simple as that of a chain by which
one person limits the freedom of another, can possibly do justice to the
complex ramifications of the concept of a right and its correlative obligation. For the picture does not show why it is that a right-holder should
or should not waive the right, relinquish it, or indeed why he or she
forfeits it. Nor does it do justice to the status of the person with the
correlative obligation who should not be regarded as one who must
submit meekly to the will of the right-holder; for the promiser may have
good reason to resist the pull of the chain, that is, to refuse to meet the

    6. The figure of a chain by means of which the freedom of a person who is under an
obligation to another is thus restricted is to be found in his essay "Are There Any Natural
Rights?" *Philosophical Review* 64 (1955).
    7. This is the idea enshrined in the traditional distinction between perfect and imperfect
duties, which surfaces in a modified form in Kant's discussion in sec. 1 of the *Foundations*
and reappears much later in Prichard's "sharp distinction" between "morality and virtue
as independent, but related species of goodness" (although how they are related he does
not say) in his famous essay "Does Moral Philosophy Rest on a Mistake?" (*Mind*, n.s. 21
[1912]). And this seems to be the idea sometimes encountered in the current dispute between
consequentialists and their adversaries, that we are to take account of the good consequences
of our actions in determining their rightness or wrongness only after we have satisfied the
requirements of justice including the rights of those involved. See, e.g., Philippa Foot in
"Utilitarianism and the Virtues," *Proceedings of the American Philosophical Association*
57, no. 2 (Nov. 1983): 281–83.

obligation he or she has assumed. For to understand what is involved in having a right—and so, too, with the correlative obligation—is to understand the good reasons, sufficient or not as these may be, for waiving or relinquishing the right—and so, too, for meeting the obligation, or not meeting it, whether by deferring doing so until a more appropriate occasion arises or by refusing to do so altogether. And if, improperly or not, one does not meet one's obligation, one remains accountable to the right-holder and must understand, given the particular circumstances of the case, what one is called upon to do. So, too, with the right-holder who may not regard the right as something like a note payable on demand but must be willing to accept certain explanations and, when the other party has behaved badly, be prepared, given appropriate indications of remorse and a willingness to make amends, to forgive the wrongdoer without any sense of pride or feeling of superiority, put the incident out of his or her mind, and resume the relation of trust that had existed between them. These are some of the things that enlightened moral agents understand when they take rights and obligations into account during the course of their dealings with each other. To put it in other terms, these are some of the things that constitute the shared understanding by those who, as members of the moral community, meet the normative requirements of such membership and deal as they should with the rights and obligations that constitute the moral relations in which they stand to others. And unless there is some substantial measure of this shared understanding of persons, there could be no point to the use of promise locutions. Since there are those for whom promises are to be kept no matter what wholly unexpected and indeed unforeseeable eventualities turn up and for whom there can be neither the understanding of the need for nor the disposition to forgive those who trespass against them, there is risk involved in entering into promise transactions with them, in assuming that the considerations that lead us to deal as we do with the rights and correlative obligations established by promises will also be understood and heeded by them.

Seen in this light, it is no longer merely the moral authority of the promisee as right-holder that needs to be borne in mind, but the moral authority of the promiser who is under the correlative obligation, and who, as a member of the moral community, has his or her authority to decide how to deal with the obligation. And just as the person with the obligation has the moral burden constituted by the obligation, so the right-holder has the moral burden, constituted by his or her status as a member of the moral community, of taking due account of any of the sorts of considerations that would call for waiving or even relinquishing the right. Neither party to the transaction need be subservient to the other, and only when the normative requirements are met by either of them—willingly, confidently, and without any sense of constraint or compulsion—can there be any display of a dignity that is worthy of our admiration and respect.

2. The notion that rights together with their correlative obligations belong to a different area of morality from the one that involves considerations of the goodness of, say, benevolence, is equally mistaken. Here we need to be reminded of the point made earlier, that to understand what is involved in a right is to understand the good reasons, which may or may not be sufficient, for waiving or relinquishing a right, and for meeting or not meeting an obligation. Now in the great majority of cases issues of this sort do not arise, but there are cases in which unexpected circumstances arise, unusual and even rare as some of these may be, and in which either the right-holder or the person under the correlative obligation must, if he or she is sensible and sensitive, in the former case, waive or relinquish the right and, in the latter, refuse to meet the obligation that has been incurred. If A has promised B to do y, something without which B cannot carry out a given course of action, but wholly unexpectedly doing y would be disastrous to A while providing minor benefit to B, it would be indecent for B to stand on the right or insist that A meet the obligation. And if, to consider another case, if B, having received a promise from A, were to carry out a course of action by A's keeping of the promise at the cost of disaster to B, a fact that arises because of totally unexpected circumstances that are known only to A, it would be absurd for A to keep the promise at little cost to himself or herself unless A wished disaster to befall B.[8] And there are still many other sorts of cases in which benevolence becomes a factor in deciding whether or not a right is to be accorded or an obligation is to be met. Nor is it even true in soliciting a promise, by which a right is established and an obligation is assumed, that one always does so in order to receive

8. There is a wide variety of cases in which the normative requirements of the moral relation established when promises are made and accepted and, accordingly, rights and obligations are established, that call for waiving or relinquishing rights, or, from the points of view of the other party, for refusing to meet an obligation. In many of these cases benevolence is indeed a relevant factor in establishing that certain considerations having to do with the good or bad consequences of allowing a right to be accorded or meeting an obligation are clearly relevant. In other cases, still other considerations are relevant. See my discussion of Mill's views on the rights of promisees in *Rights in Moral Lives* (Berkeley: University of California Press, 1988), pp. 20–38.

benefits for oneself. For the solicitation may be made out of benevolence for someone other than the person who is to be the right-holder, a fact clearly shown in the case of Hart's example of a third-person promise in which A persuades B to care for A's ailing mother during A's absence on an extended trip. And it is also shown by first-person promises when, for example, a wife succeeds in persuading her husband, whose persistent indigestion is due to hurried and unwholesome lunches taken by the husband while working at his desk, to promise that he will take time out leisurely to eat nutritious food during his lunch hours.

The supposition that a right is always to be thought of as something that is self-serving, that there is no place in its grammar, to use Ludwig Wittgenstein's term, for benevolence—that it is something to be demanded, if need be, or exacted as one would a debt—is philosophical confusion nourished by a diet of special cases. It does not square with the wide variety of cases to which we must attend if we are to understand what rights are. And the same goes for the idea that also ought to be consigned to oblivion that promises, and with them the establishment of rights and obligations, are solicited only with a view to promote the goods to be enjoyed by those who are to receive the promises and have the rights these create. But if what we have said is true, it follows that considerations of benevolence, far from being independent of the attention to be paid to the normative requirements involved in the possession of rights, are conceptually involved in them.

3. In any case, the dignity to be achieved by those involved in the special relations and transitions, by virtue of which there are special rights and obligations, is a dignity to be achieved only when the normative requirements imposed upon both parties are met willingly, confidently, and unhesitatingly, when the will of neither party involved in the moral relations bows subserviently to the will of the other, and when, therefore, both of the parties are worthy of the respect they have for each other.

B

1. I turn now to the case of human rights so-called, the rights not of the few, privileged as they may be either by virtue of their social status or the special relations in which they happen to be involved with particular individuals, but of all who are members of the moral community.[9]

9. Some would regard this talk about human rights as speciesism, but this does not affect the substance of our discussion; for even if we were to concede that all or some

I use the expression "members of the moral community"—an alternative would be "moral agents"—in order explicitly to allow for the fact that some members of our species, for example, sociopaths, are individuals with whom moral relations cannot be established. We may treat these warily, even kindly when they are confined, in order to protect others from the havoc they might create, or as patients who receive the medical treatment they may need in order to recover from their affliction; but we do not consider them to be moral agents to be trusted during the course of our dealings with them. But merely in order to simplify verbal expressions and in order to conform to common usage, I shall use the expression *human rights*.

We need also to remind ourselves of the relation between human rights and the special moral rights that obtain because of the special relations of moral agents. John Stuart Mill argues for the necessary connection between justice and moral rights in chapter V of *Utilitarianism*, but none of the rights he mentions are those that traditionally were labeled "natural rights." This, however, is to make a mystery of the fact that "it is . . . unjust to *break faith* [italics his] with anyone: to violate an engagement, either express or implied, . . . at least if we have raised those expectations knowingly or voluntarily." Mill's meaning is clear: when, for example, a promise is made and accepted, there is a mutual understanding between promiser and promisee to the effect that the former will carry through with the act that has been promised, and a moral right has been created which the promisee has against the promiser. But this is to say much more, in the event that the latter deliberately "breaks faith" with the former, than that there is disappointment or inconsiderateness on the part of the wrongdoer when the course of action that depends for its success upon the keeping of the promise is brought to naught, in consequence of which the promisee is made to suffer. For this, so far, is only to call attention to the unfortunate consequence of a lack of concern for the well-being of the promisee. If this were the only thing involved in the breach of faith, the complaint of the promisee would be that the promiser had caused damage by a lack of the appropriate virtue, namely, benevolence. But the injury to the promisee is moral damage, the violation of a moral right, and the complaint is that the wrongdoer, in being accountable to the promisee, must square his or her account. And this brings into play the conceptual ramifications of the violation of a right by virtue of which the right-holder has an authority, if need be, to demand

nonhuman animals have moral rights, that would only add all or some animals, respectively, to the population of the class of moral agents. For a discussion of the claim that animals have moral rights, see my *Rights in Moral Lives*, chap. 6.

restitution, if this is at all possible, and certainly to point up the need for the remorse that is called for by the guilt incurred by the wrongdoer. But nothing of this sort is intelligible unless the recipient of the promise—the right-holder—is seen as an agent with a right freely to engage in programs of action, in the present instance to a program of action the success of which depends upon the keeping of the promise. This is true equally in the case of the right to be told the truth, for the truth is valued as it is, not merely because it satisfies some idle curiosity but also because of its practical importance to moral agents. If, for example, one carries an obviously injured child and asks a stranger for the way to the nearest hospital, and the latter, seeing what is at issue, lies, it will hardly do to say that stranger was merely inconsiderate or indifferent to the well-being of another person in deliberately giving misdirections. Clearly there is the deliberate endangering of the very life of the child and, in doing this, violating the right any child has to receive the medical help it may need. But this right is the right entailed by anyone as a human being; for if one has the human right to pursue one's interests, one has, qua child, the right to develop the capacity to pursue interests worthy of a human being, and, if in order to do so, one needs medical attention, and it is available, then one has the right to receive medical attention, a right surely violated by someone's untruthfulness in deliberately preventing one from getting the needed medical attention.

In short, there can be no special moral rights unless there are human rights. The latter are fundamental rights, rights that, so to speak, are written into our (condition as moral agents).[10] Elsewhere I have argued for the thesis that our fundamental right is the right to pursue interests, interests that define the goods, for ourselves and for others, that are achievable by, and worthy of, human beings.[11] Others have cited the right to life, freedom, and so on with the wide variety of rights listed in the Universal Declaration of Human Rights. A number of observations need to be made at this point if we are to understand the connection

---

10. In my *Rights in Moral Lives* in chap. 4, I criticize Mill's positive theory of moral rights by showing, I believe, that he cannot explain how it is possible, on his own positive account, that there is always "some assignable person," as he puts it, who suffers moral damage when a right is violated. Here I have confined myself to the contention that in omitting any mention of human or natural rights, Mill fails to render intelligible what he is insistent upon maintaining, namely, the fact that there are special moral rights involved in the making of promises. I argue in much greater detail, that a human right, i.e., the right to pursue one's own interests, is essential if there is to be a right created by a promise, in my *Rights and Persons* (Oxford: Basil Blackwell, and Berkeley: University of California Press 1977), chap. 2.

11. See *Rights and Persons*, chap. 6; and *Rights in Moral Lives*, esp. chap 5.

between our fundamental rights and the dignity and worth of human beings. First, these rights are no mere liberties with respect to which others are merely bound not to interfere. They are, rather, rights with respect to which others are under an obligation, to act, in special cases to abstain from acting, as in the case of the husband who promises his wife not to discuss politics at their dinner party. Second, the interests in question need not be self-centered, and they must not be immoral. For as members of the moral community, we are concerned with the well-being of others in addition to that of ourselves. And the interests to the pursuit of which agents have a moral right exclude the interests that, perversely, one might have in bringing evil upon others; for no one has the right to do what is wrong. Third, the possession of the right to pursue interests entails the possession of the right to life and liberty. Fourth, the interests to the pursuit of which a moral agent has a right are not only the interests worthy of a given human being, but those which they are capable of acquiring by virtue of their natural endowments. Fifth, it follows from this last point that, subject to the availability of the means required, every moral agent has a right to the kind of education and training that can develop these interests. Sixth, it follows from the fact that these are the sorts of interests to the pursuit of which moral agents have rights, that, subject again to the availability condition, moral agents have rights to medical treatment. I shall stop at this point but remark in passing that many of the rights listed in the Universal Declaration of Human Rights adopted by the United Nations General Assembly in 1948 are, like the right to education and medical treatment, implied by the fundamental human right to pursue one's interests; for a case can be made out for the claim that the right, for example, to periodic holidays with pay is, in the circumstances of an industrial society, implied by the possession of the right to pursue one's interests. For how else would it be possible to pursue these interests without the rejuvenation provided by a holiday, and how else could lower-income persons such as employees in a factory afford holidays unless they were paid for their periodic holidays?

   The assistance others need, and which we can provide, in order that they may be able to exercise the right they have to pursue interests that are worthy of human beings—for what point is there in the talk about a right they have but cannot possibly exercise?—is no mere matter of the kindness and benevolence we should display in our treatment of others; it is in fact nothing less than our meeting the obligations we have to them by virtue of the rights they have against us.

2. It was assumed, in our discussion of the relation between dignity and special moral rights such as the right conferred upon the recipient of a promise, that the normative conditions imposed by the possession of human rights are satisfied. We have now to ask ourselves what the status of dignity is in cases in which these normative conditions are *not* met.

It is sometimes said that the violation of human rights is an attack on, or the denial of, the dignity of human beings, as if this dignity somehow is guaranteed by the mere possession or even the enjoyment of one's human rights but is destroyed with their violation or denial. But this cannot be correct, since there are many who for one reason or another lack dignity, but for whom the excuse or explanation that their human rights have been violated or denied cannot be made. For many are not particularly thoughtful, resolute, and convinced of the rectitude of many of their decisions, retaining their composure as they proceed with their courses of action. And there are far too many hypocrites and scoundrels of one sort or another who have not been deprived; but we should not regard these as meritorious, however self-satisfied and self-confident they might appear to be. Nor is dignity, as we saw earlier during the course of our discussion of Kant's views, an all-or-none matter; some have it to a greater or lesser degree than others. Dignity is a moral desideratum, something that varies in degree even when there is no issue of human rights. And some are cunning scoundrels whose air of dignity serves only to mask deep character faults in no way due to the deprivation or violation of their human rights.

Further, there have been cases in which individuals have displayed genuine dignity even in the most trying circumstances that involve the violation of their human rights, as in the case of a martyr to his or her religious cause, a decent person going to an execution ordered by a tyrant, a Nelson Mandela resolute in his determination to maintain his integrity even at the cost of his freedom and well-being, or some of the poor, the sick, and the homeless who somehow manage to preserve their integrity and their dignity.

If all of this is granted, how can it be maintained that human rights are important in their bearing upon human dignity? It must be remembered, however, that the vast majority of persons are not saints—secular or religious—or heros, beings who, in circumstances of severe denials or violations of human rights, are able to preserve their dignity. Persons vary enormously in their ability to retain their composure under circumstances of deprivation and inhuman treatment. Indeed, if conditions are sufficiently extreme, it is difficult to understand how any human being can retain sanity itself. Here we need only think of some of the horrible incidents in which Jews were treated by the Nazis if they were human-like vermin; one even wonders how those who herded shrieking and weeping naked men, women, and children into gas chambers could have preserved their own sanity. But in matters that concern us here we must consider human beings as we find them, in relatively familiar circumstances with their varying capacities to retain their dignity or to achieve it when they endure deprivation, as so many do even in our own country today. And the lesson is, I believe, clear enough, that unless human rights are respected and exercised to at least a considerable degree, there is little chance, because of the stress and the deprivations from which they suffer, that many will be able to meet the normative requirements to which moral agents are subject and acquire those character traits that will enable them to conduct themselves thoughtfully, with the composure and self-confidence of those we admire and respect. It is for this reason that attention to human rights is of the first importance for the promotion of the dignity and the worth of human beings.

An appropriately final remark: consider what is involved in extreme cases in which terminally ill patients, trussed up, it might seem, by tubes and wires leading to life-support mechanisms that, for only a short time, merely prolong lives not worth living, and who want desperately to be left alone and die with dignity, instead of being treated merely as so much living lumps of flesh and bone. What greater indignity can anyone suffer than those in such conditions of extremity lying in hospital beds? But there are, of course, intermediate cases as well, in addition to this example of a peripheral but intelligible application of the term *dignity*. I say that it is peripheral because all that is involved in dying with dignity, once the life-support systems are removed, is the composure of the dying person—the welcome relief, even serenity, knowing that soon it will all be over.

3

Constitutional Values
and Human Dignity

WILLIAM A. PARENT

I

In this essay I argue that there is a distinctive conception of human dignity that is perspicuously represented as a moral status constituted by one basic right belonging to all human beings. I also try to show that dignity so conceived enjoys constitutional protection. I am not the first person to claim constitutional standing for dignity. Both the legal scholar Ronald Dworkin and William Brennan, Jr., Associate Justice of the U.S. Supreme Court, have endorsed the idea that dignity is the fundamental value underlying the U.S. Constitution.[1] Brennan has on several occasions proclaimed that "the Constitution is a sublime oration on the dignity of man, a bold commitment by a people to the ideal of libertarian dignity protected through law."[2] Several other U.S. Supreme Court justices have endorsed this view as well.[3]

But this view has yet to receive a sustained philosophical defense. I now take up the challenge, recently issued by Justice Brennan, to achieve

1. Dworkin and Brennan did so in interviews with Bill Moyers for the PBS series "In Search of the Constitution."
2. Brennan made this remark in a speech given at Georgetown University, October 12, 1985, and published under the title "The Constitution of the United States: Contemporary Ratification," in *University of California Davis Law Review* 19 (1985): 8.
3. See Jordan Paust's "Human Dignity as a Constitutional Right: A Jurisprudentially Based Inquiry into Criteria and Context," in *Howard Law Journal* 27 (1984): 145–225.

a comprehensive definition of the constitutional ideal of human dignity. I concede straightway that my effort is only a beginning—Brennan says the quest is eternal.[4] Nonetheless, my project is animated by the sincere conviction that philosophers, whose special interest lies in the investigation of ideas for the purpose of clarifying their meanings and their conceptual and logical connections, can make a unique contribution to this subject. Certainly the concept of human dignity is important enough to warrant careful philosophical study.

My central thesis is that human dignity should be understood to be constituted by a particular, especially important moral right. It is a right that secures to each and every one of us an inviolable moral status. I elaborate this thesis in section III. The question I must address first is, How are basic constitutional rights to be identified? First, of course, there are those rights that are explicitly guaranteed by the Bill of Rights or later constitutional amendments. Thus we are entitled to the free exercise of religion, to free speech, and to peaceful assembly (Amendment 1); we have the right to be secure in our persons, homes, papers, and effects from unreasonable searches and seizures (Amendment 4); we are entitled not to be deprived of life, liberty, or property without due process of law (Amendment 5)[5] and we are entitled not to be denied the right to vote on account of race or sex (amendments 15 and 19).

There are also rights that are implicitly guaranteed by the Constitution. By that I mean that they follow from a reasonable or defensible philosophical interpretation of the language that our Founding Fathers and others used in formulating the various amendments. A reasonable philosophical interpretation respects ordinary language but recognizes that the everyday, common usage of words is often plagued with inconsistency and paradox. So definitions or interpretations that depart from ordinary usage in order to enhance logical clarity and consistency are to be welcomed provided they are not so extreme as to eviscerate or destroy the conceptual identity of the very ideas under investigation. For example, we should dismiss a rendering of "freedom" that construed it as a form of coercion, but we should embrace one that helped us to eliminate contradictory claims about the freedom of disabled persons (claims hav-

---

4. "The Constitution of the United States," p. 12.

5. I am here assuming that when the First Amendment says that Congress shall make no law abridging the freedom of speech and when the Fifth Amendment says that no person shall be deprived of life, liberty, or property without due process of law, they are eo ipso establishing rights to these protections. These rights are correlative to the implicit duties imposed on government.

ing their origin in different accounts of the relations between freedom and ability) while preserving the paradigm of the slave as unfree.

There is a second dimension to logical coherence that should constrain constitutional interpretation. Our language is rich and diverse. It has evolved to produce many important and useful distinctions. These should not be ignored or flouted when one is constructing the meaning of different amendments. I have argued elsewhere, for example, that "privacy" should not be defined in terms of "liberty," since these two concepts represent distinguishable ideas with wholly distinct functions.[6] Conceptual integrity condemns interpretations that commit or allow what can aptly be called conceptual usurpation.

Logical coherence is not the only desideratum of reasonable philosophical inquiry. Sometimes our analyses are guided by certain purposes we hope to achieve. In this essay, for instance, I am setting out to construct a moral conception of human dignity. This will lead me to pass over certain common accounts of dignity which have some support in ordinary language. To be defensible, however, a moral conception must seek corroboration in paradigm cases that, by their very nature, do reflect a strong consensus about the appropriate use of *dignity*. My project will fail if I cannot draw upon such paradigms. So again, ordinary language, or more exactly paradigm cases embedded therein, properly function to constrain philosophical inventiveness.

There are also ways in which judges can confirm the existence of implicit constitutional rights. For one thing, they can claim that a moral right underlies the clear purpose of and as a result is protected by one or more explicit provisions of the text. This method or argument concerns issues of moral justification; it does not proceed via conceptual interpretation or analysis. Yet, it cannot responsibly be pursued without one's taking a position, however inarticulate, on the question of what expressions like "freedom of speech" and "due process" mean. And this position must be defensible.

Skeptics will worry about unbridled judicial discretion and tyranny by judges unaccountable to the people. But accountability is not exhausted by politics. We do hold judges responsible for their decision making by demanding that it satisfy standards of reasoning which they did not invent and which they cannot change or declare void. Judicial failure to satisfy this demand will not mean the loss of a job, but it will invite the loss of

6. See my "Privacy, Morality, and the Law," in *Philosophy & Public Affairs* 12 (1983): 269–88.

public esteem. A judge is called on to make difficult decisions. Her ability to think philosophically will be tested over and over again. For skeptics to denounce or lament this fact only serves to demean the intelligence of our judiciary.

We need to remind ourselves that the Constitution is above all else a political document that issues important moral commands to federal and state governments. It was created "in order to form a more perfect Union, establish Justice, insure domestic Tranquility, provide for the common defense, promote the general Welfare, and secure the blessings of Liberty to ourselves and our posterity."[7] It was established in the conviction, shared by Thomas Jefferson and James Madison, among others, that justice is indeed the fundamental guiding principle of government.[8]

There is a second test for confirming the constitutional standing of an implicit moral value. It asks whether the value was ever publicly endorsed by any of our Founding Fathers. In section IV, I show that human dignity was so endorsed. I also argue that it is clearly protected by several constitutional amendments and so passes the test of moral justification. In the next two sections I develop my conception of the dignity that our constitutional democracy affirms.

II

Let us begin our conceptual inquiry with Justice Brennan's views. We know that he eloquently champions dignity as a constitutional value. Indeed, he believes that its ideals are entrenched in the Constitution, and that they condemn capital punishment, segregation, and forced confessions.[9] Can we ascertain precisely how the justice conceives of dignity?

His writings suggest that he identifies it with the state of political and economic independence. At least, he seems to regard this as one dimension of dignity. His argument runs like this.[10] Until the nineteenth century, at

---

7. The words of the Preamble to the United States Constitution.

8. See, e.g., The Federalist No. 51 (J. Madison); and Jefferson's letter to P. S. DuPont de Nemours, April 24, 1816, published in James Adams, ed., *Jeffersonian Principles and Hamiltonian Principles* (Boston: Little, Brown, 1932); p. 19.

9. I recommend the following essays by Brennan: "The Constitution of the United States"; "Rededication Address: The ABA's Memorial to the Magna Carta," in *Loyola of Los Angeles Law Review* 19 (1985): 55–59; "The Bill of Rights and the States: The Revival of State Constitutions as Guardians of Individual Rights," in *New York University Law Review* 61 (1986): 535–53; "Color-Blind, Creed-Blind, Status-Blind, Sex-Blind," *Human Rights* 14 (1987): 30–35.

10. See Brennan, "The Constitution of the United States," esp. pp. 9–11.

a time when the United States was still largely an agricultural society, ownership of land provided people not just with sustenance but with the means of economic independence as well. And economic independence made political independence possible. By contrast, today "hundreds of thousands of Americans live entire lives without any real prospect of the dignity and autonomy that ownership of real property could confer."[11] Brennan also contends that even just incarceration strips a person of dignity; that the one person, one vote principle guarantees the essential dignity of each citizen to equal participation in the political process; and that government entitlement programs preserve the dignity of the least fortunate among us. All of these claims support a conceptual relation between dignity and at least certain kinds of political and economic independence.

This view, whether it is essentially Brennan's or not, confronts serious difficulties. Do we want to accept the idea that some persons by virtue solely of their political and economic standing have more dignity than others? Do we want to say that the possession of dignity depends on a whole host of natural and social contingencies like economic climate and the ability to work, which may be available to some but not all? For those of you who are undecided regarding these questions, let me pose the following scenario. You are poor, depending on welfare to survive, and you live in a state that effectively bars the poor from voting. If dignity consists of political and economic independence, we are forced to concede that you have none and thus cannot suffer further violations of it. But now suppose that you are also black and that you are constantly subjected to racist epithets and racist acts of violence. Does not such racism attack or violate your dignity? Or reverse the scenario. You are a person of great wealth and political power. But you are also a Jew, and you daily have to endure anti-Semitic propaganda and racist slurs. Is not your dignity under attack, notwithstanding the undeniable political and economic independence you enjoy? And if you are arrested just for being a Jew, wouldn't that fact, and not the condition of being in jail, capture the essence of the assault on your dignity?

My dissatisfaction with this conception of dignity cannot be formulated in knock-down, demonstrable proofs. No theory of dignity can be established with such proofs. But persuasion by the giving of reasons, the presentation of test cases, the suggestion of counterexamples, and the appeal to purposes an interpretation is justifiably meant to achieve—in

11. Ibid., p. 9.

my case, the construction of a distinctively moral idea of dignity—such persuasion, when suitably constrained by the requirements of logical coherence, exemplifies the art of philosophical argument. It leads me to believe that we can substantially improve on Brennan's views.

I need to point out, though, that Brennan does have another way of talking about human dignity. In his impassioned attack on the death penalty he frequently invokes the notion of the intrinsic worth of human beings. Thus he writes in Furman v. Georgia: "The State, even as it punishes, must treat its members with respect for their intrinsic worth as human beings. A punishment is 'cruel and unusual,' therefore, if it doesn't comport with human dignity."[12]

Unfortunately, identifying the meaning of *dignity* with "intrinsic human worth" does not help explain what dignity is. Instead, it simply renames it. We are still left with the vexing philosophical problem of understanding exactly what *intrinsic worth* means. A similar objection is applicable to definitions of *dignity* in terms of "our common humanity" or "humanity as an end in itself." Without a convincing account of these obscure ideas, we are left with high-sounding but vacuous explanations.

Joel Feinberg has forcefully set out this difficulty and made the following suggestion in response:

> "Human worth" itself is best understood to name no property in the way that "strength" names strength and "redness" redness. In attributing human worth to everyone, we may be ascribing no property or set of properties, but rather expressing an attitude—the attitude of respect—toward the humanity in each man's person. That attitude follows naturally from regarding everyone from "the human point of view," but it is not grounded in anything more ultimate than itself, and it is not ultimately justifiable.[13]

Feinberg's proposal is useful in at least two respects: it challenges us to take seriously the possibility that *dignity*, rather than denoting some intrinsic property of human beings, may have an altogether different function in our language; and it suggests that there is an important tie between dignity and respect.

Unhappily, Feinberg doesn't say much about the idea of respect except that it follows from taking up "the human point of view." But then he

---

12. 408 U.S. 238 (1972), at p. 270. See also Brennan's opinion in Gregg v. Georgia, 428 U.S. 153 (1976), at p. 227; and his "The Constitution of the United States," p. 13.

13. Joel Feinberg, *Social Philosophy* (Englewood Cliffs, N. J.: Prentice-Hall, 1973); p. 94.

fails to clarify exactly what this point of view involves. We are invited to query whether there is anything about the humanity in each person that justifies or explains it. Do we want to adopt a view that says that the practice of imputing human dignity to persons is not ultimately justifiable? Is this the only or the most convincing response to the conceded renaming difficulty? At this point in our investigation an affirmative response would be premature.

Immanuel Kant is the philosopher who, more than any other before or since, champions the idea that human dignity has essentially to do with the intrinsic worth of humanity. Does he satisfactorily address Feinberg's challenge?

For Kant, the dignity of humanity consists in its capacity for giving universal moral laws, a capacity he calls autonomy.[14] Autonomy, in turn, is the same thing as positive freedom. The person whose reason is legislative and who acts from such legislation is, then, free and autonomous. Positive freedom requires negative freedom, which Kant defines as independence from the determining causes of the sensible world.[15] The sensible world consists of all events that occur in space and time. Kant contends, and with good reason, that all such events are governed by the laws of nature. Hence we possess dignity only to the extent that our existence doesn't stand under spatial-temporal conditions and isn't governed by the laws of nature. Kant calls autonomous individuals noumenal selves,[16] and he contrasts their exalted status with the slight importance attaching to beings in the system of nature.[17]

Now, Kant concedes that the radical kind of freedom that he posits as essential to human dignity is only an idea—it cannot be proven real in ourselves.[18] I frankly doubt that we are free in this sense. On the contrary, I believe that every aspect of human behavior is determined by the same natural processes and is explicable by the same natural laws that govern the behavior of all other living things. Human reasoning, like every natural event, is the product of what Kant calls natural necessity.[19]

---

14. Immanuel Kant, *Foundations of the Metaphysics of Morals*, trans. Lewis Beck (Indianapolis, Ind.: Bobbs-Merrill, 1959); pp. 58 and 51.

15. Ibid., p. 71.

16. See Kant's *Critique of Practical Reason*, trans. Lewis Beck (Indianapolis, Ind.: Bobbs-Merrill, 1956); pp. 57 and 101.

17. See Kant's *The Doctrine of Virtue*, trans. Mary Gregor (Philadelphia: University of Pennsylvania Press, 1964), p. 99.

18. Kant, *Foundations of the Metaphysics of Morals*, p. 67.

19. Ibid., p. 65.

Of course, my skepticism concerning free will and autonomy is not demonstrably justifiable. I cannot prove that determinism is true of all human behavior. I cannot prove that we have no powers or faculties beyond those that arose with the evolution of our species over time. What I can do, though, is offer a conception of human dignity that would be persuasive and applicable to the human condition even if all of our actions and thoughts were products of prior natural events. Rather than constructing a theory of dignity on a dubious metaphysical presupposition— the existence of noumenal selves occupying an intelligible world—or on a similarly dubious practical postulate—that we must regard ourselves as belonging to such a world in order to make sense of the idea that we possess moral worth[20]—I offer a theory that makes the concept of dignity applicable to human beings considered only as members of an animal species. I argue that the human being in the system of nature is not a being of slight importance, but rather possesses a moral dignity grounded on an empirical understanding of himself and of his natural powers, limitations, and aspirations.[21] In short, I will offer a view of dignity that doesn't demean but instead elevates the status of beings who are struggling to cope in the natural world.

Some philosophers who reject Kant's approach prefer to see human dignity rest with the superiority of our biological species. Willard Gaylin, for instance, expressing his disgust with the burgeoning animal rights movement, proudly exclaims: "Well, human beings are special—a glorious discontinuity in the animal kingdom."[22] And Gaylin proceeds to enumerate five properties of our species that dignify it. Among these are the powers of conceptual thought, the capacity for technology, and the freedom from instinctual fixation. Together they make us the wonder of creation.

But what are we to say about humans who lack one, two, or all five of these abilities? Can we confidently aver that severely retarded children,

---

20. I ask the reader to judge whether it is even possible to construct an intelligible picture or conception of a noumenal self. On several occasions Kant admits that the idea is inscrutable—e.g., *Foundations of the Metaphysics of Morals*, p. 78. It is difficult to understand how we can make sense of one elusive idea, dignity, by regarding ourselves in a way that is equally incomprehensible.

21. Bernard Williams, in his important essay "The Idea of Equality," also argues that Kant's attempt to divorce the concepts of dignity and respect from all empirical characteristics is unsatisfying. Williams believes that these concepts must have an empirical basis. The essay is reprinted in his *Problems of the Self* (New York: Cambridge University Press, 1973), p. 234.

22. Willard Gaylin, "In Defense of the Dignity of Being Human," *Hastings Center Report* 14 (1984): 18–22.

say, or the technologically incompetent have no intrinsic worth? Do we want to adopt a viewpoint that makes human dignity hostage to the contingencies of natural fortune? In addition, Gaylin omits mention of the horrendous injustices that humans have perpetrated against themselves, many made possible by the very powers of conceptual thought and technological prowess he lauds. Such injustices hardly testify to our glory. Is it credible to believe that human dignity is precisely that set of powers that makes many of those horrors possible? And is it at all plausible to think that the Nazis' "final solution" violated the dignity of Jews simply because it destroyed their distinctively human powers? Is there not a significant morally relevant difference, perspicuously captured in the language of dignity, between the killing that takes place in a campaign of racist genocide and killing by accident or in self-defense?

Doubtless, a person blessed with the kinds of abilities Gaylin describes will enjoy great power among and receive much respect from her peers. But there is nothing essentially moral about this power and respect. Everything depends on how one chooses to exercise the former and earn the latter. Kant wisely recognized this.[23] If we reject the claim that might (power) makes right, why should we endorse the idea that might confers worth? The species-superiority approach fails to proffer a distinctively moral conception of dignity.

Neither does the theory according to which human dignity is essentially a matter of how we carry ourselves or present ourselves to others. It is common to say things like "she behaved with great dignity" and "he withstood the criticism with dignity." I suppose that the behavioral criteria for imputations of dignity in this sense will mostly involve matters of style—for instance, did she hold her head high, fight back the tears, look proud, stave off humiliating missteps? By these criteria someone like Fred Astaire in his dancing prime must be judged to possess great dignity (or is it that his dancing was dignified?) while the bumptious man[24] certainly has little or none. But it must be conceded that evil men like Hitler often displayed this kind of presentational dignity, at least in their public behavior. And so, for that matter, do Mafia hit men. So from a moral standpoint, this conception of dignity is wholly bankrupt.

23. See Kant's characterization of the good will in his *Foundations of the Metaphysics of Morals*, pp. 9–10.
24. Michael Meyer furnishes a forceful description of such a person in his useful essay, "Dignity, Rights, and Self-Control," *Ethics* 99 (1989): 520–34. Should we take the position that uncontrollable compulsion can strip a person of her dignity, then our unhappy addict cannot logically be said to suffer a violation of her dignity when she is unfairly subjected to contemptuous putdowns.

Moreover, it is burdened with a most serious implication. Consider the case of a person whose behavior is the model of grace and nobility. She never fails to be in total control of herself and her passions. Now, suppose that she happens to be Chinese and for this reason alone is subject to persistent verbal disparagement. The ugly words are deeply insulting to her, but they do not alter or destroy the noble, dignified way she behaves. On the presentational conception we cannot condemn the efforts at personal debasement in the language of human dignity. Yet our victim will certainly believe, and with compelling justification, that the racist attacks constitute nothing less than an unjust devaluation of her person. And isn't the concept of dignity uniquely suited to criticize unjust efforts to depreciate, demean, or disparage a human being? (I will shortly have more to say about this question.)

And permit me one last observation on the presentational view. It says that a person's dignity stands vulnerable to attack and even destruction by a multitude of natural contingencies, ranging from genuine addictions to compulsive disorders and genetic defects. Dignity in this sense is also imperiled by techniques of brainwashing, torture, poisoning, and the like. We should ask whether a conception like this is worth embracing when it apparently contravenes the long-standing idea that all humans are endowed with an equal and in some sense an intrinsic, inalienable inviolability.

III

To develop and clarify my own, original conception of human dignity, I have chosen to look at two twentieth-century events: the civil rights movement and the Holocaust. These are the kinds of paradigm cases that must figure in any defensible conception of dignity as a moral idea. (See Section I.) The language Martin Luther King, Jr., used to express his people's grievances against racist segregation bespeaks a powerful commitment to the dignity of all human beings. His famous "Letter from a Birmingham Jail" is a particularly articulate and powerful statement of the moral outrage that fueled the movement. Here is King's answer to those counseling more patience for blacks:

> I guess it is easy for those who have never felt the stinging darts of segregation to say "wait." But when you have seen vicious mobs lynch your mothers and fathers at will and drown your sisters and brothers

at whim; when you have seen hate-filled policeman curse, kick, bru-
talize, and even kill your black brothers and sisters with impunity;
when you have seen the vast majority of your 20 million Negro brothers
smothering in the air-tight cage of poverty in the midst of an affluent
nation; when you suddenly find your tongue twisted and your speech
stammering as you seek to explain to your six-year old daughter why
she can't go to the public amusement park that has just been advertised
on television, and see tears welling up in her little eyes when she is told
that function is closed to colored children, and see the depressing clouds
of inferiority begin to form in her little mental sky, and see her begin
to distort her little personality by unconsciously developing a bitterness
toward white people; when you have to concoct an answer for a five-
year old son asking in agonized pathos: "Daddy, why do white people
treat colored people so mean?"; when you take a cross-country drive
and find it necessary to sleep night after night in the uncomfortable
corner of your automobile because a motel will not accept you; when
you are humiliated day in and day out by nagging signs reading "white"
and "colored"; when your first name becomes "nigger" and your mid-
dle name becomes "boy" (however old you are), and your last name
becomes "John," and when your wife and mother are never given the
respected title "Mrs."; when you are harried by day and haunted at
night by the fact that you are a Negro, living constantly at tip-toe
stance never quite knowing what to expect next, and plagued with
inner fears and outer resentments; when you are forever fighting a
degenerating sense of "nobodiness"; then you will understand why we
find it difficult to wait. There comes a time when the cup of endurance
runs over, and men are no longer willing to be plunged into an abyss
of injustice where they experience the blackness of corroding despair.[25]

King's concern with the "degenerating sense of 'nobodiness' " and the
"depressing clouds of inferiority" experienced by black people in a racist
culture is a concern for human dignity. His condemnation of laws that
treat blacks as second-class citizens (or worse) deserving of disdainful
epithets like "nigger" is aptly characterizable in terms of "dignity." Indeed, the injustices of which King speaks are most compellingly and
convincingly condemned in the language of human dignity. After all, they
constitute a direct assault on the *worthiness* of blacks to be treated as
full citizens. So it is perfectly understandable why so many civil rights
marchers carried signs proclaiming "Equal Opportunity and Human Dignity" and "Marching in Peace and Dignity."[26]

25. Martin Luther King, Jr., "Letter from a Birmingham Jail," reprinted in Hugo Bedau,
ed., *Civil Disobedience* (New York: Pegasus, 1969), pp. 76–77.
26. See Juan Williams, *Eyes on the Prize* (New York: Viking Press, 1987).

King's famous dream was that "my four little children will one day live in a nation where they will not be judged by the color of their skin, but by the content of their character."[27] He and millions of other Americans realized, however inchoately, that it is patently unfair to devalue people solely on the basis of their race, that there is no moral justification for saying to a black person, just because she happens to be black, "You don't matter" or "Your well-being is less significant and less deserving of legal protection than white people's."

The U.S. Supreme Court has not been altogether oblivious to this special kind of injustice. In Strauder v. West Virginia, for example, a black plaintiff, indicted for murder, charged the state with a denial of his constitutional rights because it prohibited black persons from serving on grand juries. Justice William Strong, writing for the Court, said:

> The very fact that colored people are singled out and expressly denied by the statute all rights to participate in the administration of the law, as jurors, because of their color, though they are citizens, and may be in other respects fully qualified, is practically a brand on them, affixed by the law, an assertion of their inferiority, and a stimulant to that race prejudice which is an impediment to securing to individuals of the race that equal justice which the law aims to secure to all others.[28]

Strong could have made a persuasive appeal to the dignity of blacks here.

The Court should have made such an appeal in Plessy v. Ferguson, a case involving a Louisiana law that required racially segregated accommodations on passenger trains. A majority of the justices upheld the constitutionality of the law. Justice John M. Harlan, in a morally astute and now widely acclaimed dissent, argued that the statute was clearly predicated on the pernicious view that "colored citizens are so inferior and degraded that they cannot be allowed to sit in public coaches occupied by white citizens."[29] The view is pernicious because it so flagrantly assaults the dignity of black citizens.

Fortunately, the Supreme Court effectively overturned the so-called separate but equal doctrine in Brown v. Board of Education, decided some fifty-five years after *Plessy*. *Brown* involved a challenge brought by black citizens to a race-segregated public school system. Chief Justice Earl Warren, writing for a unanimous court, declared that "to separate

27. Ibid., p. 205.
28. Strauder v. West Virginia, 100 U.S. 303 (1880), at 308.
29. Plessy v. Ferguson, 133 U.S. 537 (1896), at 560.

them [black children] from others of similar age and qualifications solely because of their race generates a feeling of inferiority as to their status in the community that may affect their hearts and minds in a way unlikely ever to be undone."[30] To mark off black persons as inferiors, to regard them as less than fully human and as therefore undeserving of integrated public facilities, constitutes a brazen attack on their dignity.

I choose, as my last case reflecting judicial sensitivity to the kind of injustice constitutive of human dignity violations and as such effectively protested by civil rights activists, Heart of Atlanta Motel v. U.S. Appellant owned a large motel in Atlanta that restricted its clientele to white persons. He sued to enjoin enforcement of the Civil Rights Act of 1964 on the grounds it deprived him of liberty and property without due process of law. Justice Arthur J. Goldberg, concurring with the Court's majority, cited the Senate Commerce Committee's view, stated in public hearings, that the act's purpose was to "vindicate the deprivation of personal dignity that surely accompanies denials of equal access to public establishments."[31] The committee added, much in the spirit of King's earlier protests:

> Discrimination is not simply dollars and cents, hamburgers and movies; it is the humiliation, frustration, and embarrassment that a person must surely feel when he is told that he is unacceptable as a member of the public because of his race or color. It is equally the inability to explain to a child that regardless of education, civility, courtesy, and morality, he will be denied the right to enjoy equal treatment, even though he is a citizen of the United States and may well be called upon to lay down his life to assure that this nation continues.[32]

I am suggesting that in these segregation cases[33] members of our highest court displayed a genuine concern for the value of human dignity. They may not have articulated their opinions in the language of dignity, but their expressed outrage at the insidious government-sponsored disparagement of blacks is most clearly and persuasively formulated by direct appeal to this powerful concept. (I will shortly confirm this claim by

---

30. Brown v. Board of Education, 347 U.S. 483 (1954), at 494. For an excellent philosophical discussion of this issue, I recommend Richard Wasserstrom's "On Racism and Sexism," in his *Today's Moral Problems* (New York: Macmillan, 1985).

31. Heart of Atlanta Motel v. United States, 379 U.S. 246 (1964), at 250.

32. Ibid., at 291–92.

33. Of course, there may be other cases belonging to this group. They need not all be discussed in order to make my point.

furnishing a more precise characterization of the idea of dignity upon which I now place informal reliance.)

It is most revealing, from a philosophical standpoint, to realize that the oppression and murder of Jews under Hitler had its origin in the same kind of contemptuous attitude that marked the practices of slavery and segregation in America. The Nazis despised Jews (as well as homosexuals, the retarded, and the physically weak), and their systematic depreciation of an entire class of people should strike a responsive chord in the hearts of all people committed to the ideal of human dignity.

The physical pain suffered by the victims of racist oppression is, to be sure, horrendous enough. But for many it was of less moral significance than the shockingly insulting and outrageously disrespectful ways in which they were regarded. It is the insult and the disrespect which, on my construction, define the assault on dignity. Few have more movingly described their devastating impact than Victor Frankl, a survivor of the Nazi concentration camps. He writes:

> Beatings occurred on the slightest provocation, sometimes for no reason at all. For example, bread was rationed out at our work site and we had to line up for it. Once, the man behind me stood off a little to one side and the lack of symmetry displeased the SS guard. I did not know what was going on in the line behind me, nor in the mind of the SS guard, but suddenly I received two sharp blows on my head. Only then did I spot the guard at my side who was using the stick. At such a moment it is not the physical pain which hurts the most; it is the mental agony caused by the injustice, the unreasonableness of it all.[34]

In another incident, Frankl was doing repair work on a railroad track. When he rested for a moment, a guard threw a stone at him. Frankl observes: "That, to me, seemed the way to attract the attention of a beast, to call a domestic animal back to its job, a creature with which you have so little in common that you do not even punish it."[35] And he reiterates his conviction that the most devastating aspect of this kind of abuse is the insult it betrays.

I am reminded of how the Nazis judged Jews as they arrived in the camps by train: some were sentenced to labor, and they were sent to one side; other Jews were sentenced to death, and they were herded off in

34. Victor Frankl, *Man's Search for Meaning* (New York: Washington Square, 1984), p. 42.
35. Ibid., p. 43.

the other direction, toward the gas chambers.[36] This pernicious practice, so unjust and so barbaric that it is difficult to believe it could have happened, provides me with an archetype of the moral disrespect that marks assaults on dignity.

We can usefully identify two elements of this profound disrespect. First, its perpetrators are prone to reduce human beings to certain simple and fixed kinds, usually distinguishable by the possession of a single property like race, skin color, religion, sexual orientation, sex, wealth, intelligence, or social status.[37] Second, they are disposed to equate being different from themselves in respect to the possession of one (sometimes more) of these characteristics with being inferior to themselves.[38] So moral disrespect is marked by an arrogance founded on a perverse form of reductionism. I say, "perverse" because it purports to judge people on grounds that, in and of themselves, have absolutely nothing to do with their moral character. The bare fact that someone is a Jew or black hardly justifies the peremptory dismissal of her as an inferior, second-class, less than fully human being.

There is an important family of terms, constituting a vital part of our moral vocabulary, to which the concepts of disrespect and dignity are properly assigned. Whenever a person is arbitrarily put down, we can with perfect propriety and conviction describe the action in the language of contumely, contempt, disparagement, degradation, depreciation, disdain, debasement, or devaluation. We can also talk meaningfully in terms of vilification and use the verbs *downgrade, affront, jeer, mock, insult, deride,* and *humiliate.* Although these terms differ slightly in meaning, they all are relevant to the practice of placing less value or worth on groups of human beings for no other reason than they happen to be black, Jewish, old, female, and so forth. And it is this arbitrary, unfair devaluation that a distinctively moral conception of human dignity should be available to condemn. Such a conception ought to have a central place, alongside the idea of moral disrespect, in any theory of justice that addresses issues of merit and the ranking of human beings.

Thus far, I have not proffered a precise characterization or definition of what I will henceforth call "moral dignity." My strategy instead has

---

36. For vivid, unforgettable accounts of this and related atrocities, I recommend Claude Lanzmann's film and book *Shoah* (New York: Pantheon Books, 1985), and Alan Adelson's film and book (coedited by Robert Lepides) *Lodz' Ghetto* (New York: Viking, 1989).

37. Jean Paul Sartre sets forth a detailed phenomenological account of this reductionism is his *Anti-Semite and Jew*, trans. George Becker (New York: Schocken Books, 1970).

38. How often do I have to remind myself that being different does not automatically mean being better or worse. We should get into the habit of saying, "She's quite different, that's all," instead of "She's different, and not my equal because of it."

been to ask, what kinds of actions (or forbearances) are uncontroversially violations of dignity. In pursuing this rather oblique approach, I confess a debt to the late and great philosopher J. L. Austin. In his influential investigation of excuses, Austin wisely observed that an idea like freedom may be better understood by asking what makes us unfree rather than by straightway searching for a positive characteristic that it names.[39]

But can we say something positive about the meaning of "moral dignity"? Think back to our paradigm issues of forced segregation and the Nazi persecution of Jews. How can we most perspicuously explain the violation of moral dignity involved in them? My suggestion is that we appeal to the idea of a moral right, in particular, a negative moral right not to be regarded or treated with unjust personal disparagement. To possess moral dignity, then, is to be entitled not to be subject to or victimized by unjust attitudes or acts of contempt. It also embodies the right not to be unjustly victimized by contemptuous failures to act.

Much of the time contempt is accompanied by hate. But we should not ignore the many cases where contempt is accompanied by a condescending attitude, for example, the man who loves his wife and does everything possible to protect her in the belief that she is not his (or any man's) equal.[40] The adjective *demeaning* accurately captures the distinctive nature of these kinds of violations of dignity.

What is the function of moral rights? Why do we conceive of ourselves as possessing them? Well, one essential purpose they serve is to confer moral status. They constitute their subjects as moral beings. Negative moral rights define the ways in which their possessors may not be treated. In doing so they help construct an area or space that is to be free of gratuitous invasion. Moral dignity condemns those invasions that involve unfair personal devaluation. In doing so, it establishes a kind of moral inviolability for all human beings.[41] It furnishes each one of us, whether strong or weak, politically powerful or disenfranchised, competent or retarded, and whatever our race, religion, sex, or sexual orientation, with an indefeasible moral standing to protest (or to have protested on our behalf) all insidious attempts to degrade our persons.[42]

39. See J. L. Austin, "A Plea for Excuses," in his *Philosophical Papers*, ed. J. O. Urmson and G. J. Warnock (New York: Oxford University Press, 1979); p. 180.
40. I explore these and related questions in my forthcoming book, *On Human Dignity*.
41. In my book I argue that both embryos and patients in a persistent vegetative state possess moral dignity.
42. For more on the valuable service provided by moral rights, I enthusiastically recommend the works of Ronald Dworkin, particularly his first book, *Taking Rights Seriously* (Cambridge: Harvard University Press, 1977). Dworkin emphasizes the role of moral rights

But what does it exactly mean to claim that moral dignity is inviolable or indefeasible? Am I saying, for example, that dignity is a God-given property? I don't deny this possibility, but my conception is divorced from any such theological basis. Instead, I want to suggest a simpler interpretation, one that I believe is nearer to the common understanding of this claim. The intuitive idea is that disparaging a human being for reasons that have no relevance to the kind of person she is can never be morally justified. To possess moral dignity is to be an organism of whom this bedrock principle can meaningfully be predicated. Hence, dignity is on my conception a distinctively moral status that secures us against arbitrary contempt—its inviolability—and is not vulnerable to annulment or destruction—its indefeasibility.

Is moral dignity a universal human value? I answer that any culture with a shared understanding of the concepts that belong to the dignity family—for example, moral respect, just or fair treatment, arbitrariness, debasement, contempt, moral character—will also have a concept of dignity. Of course, this concept may not have received anything like a precise philosophical formulation. And responsible citizens of the culture may differ over the proper interpretation of "unjust debasement" in resolving particular hard cases. Furthermore, the concept of dignity may enjoy little legal protection. But the root idea, that people suffer a grievous personal wrong when they are devalued for irrelevant reasons and that we have a valid moral claim, therefore, not to be so disparaged, will occupy a place in that culture's moral ideology.

I want to make one last point about my interpretation of moral dignity. It enables us to appreciate the intimate relation between dignity and evil. "Evil" is conceptually related to "degradation," and on my view the unjust degradation of human beings marks the essence of assaults on dignity. Hence, the common belief that attacks on dignity are serious enough to warrant condemnation as morally evil is quite justifiable. And so is Rawls's claim that "what moves the evil man is love of injustice: he delights in the impotence and humiliation of those subject to him and he relishes being recognized by them as the willful author of their degradation."[43]

---

in protecting minorities. He writes, for example, that "the institution of rights is therefore crucial, because it represents the majority's promise to the minorities that their dignity and equality will be respected" (p. 205). On the view I develop, dignity is itself constituted by a moral right and thereby embodies the kind of commitment to equality central to Dworkin's jurisprudence.

43. John Rawls, *A Theory of Justice* (Cambridge: Harvard University Press, 1971), p. 439.

Let me summarize my account of moral dignity with a reminder, stated by H. L. A. Hart:

> These are in our ordinary language sentences whose primary function is not to describe things, events, or persons or anything else, nor to express or kindle feelings or emotions, but to do such things as claim rights ('This is mine'), recognize rights when claimed by others ('very well, this is yours,'), ascribe rights whether claimed or not ('This is his'), transfer rights ('This is now yours'), and also to admit or ascribe or make accusation of responsibility ('I did it', 'He did it', 'You did it').[44]

Hart's point is that the logic of our language is complex. It certainly does not serve an exclusively descriptive role. In this section, I have argued that we need to resist the temptation of thinking that *dignity* in any distinctively moral sense names or describes some property, either natural or supernatural (in Kant's terminology, noumenal), possessed by all human beings. We should also reject the claim that *dignity* functions to express an attitude or feeling (Feinberg). Instead, we should interpret the language of moral dignity as essentially ascriptive. Sentences of the form "I have dignity" and "She has dignity," when used to make moral claims, serve to ascribe the fundamental moral right not to be unjustly debased.

This interpretation of human dignity is new. It is deserving of serious consideration because it clarifies the important and intimate conceptual relation between the ideas of worth and respect. It focuses attention on the significant connection between preserving one's worth and condemning unjust personal debasement. So no one can credibly accuse me of compromising or obscuring the identity of "human dignity." My view, far from flouting ordinary language, actually draws from its richness in constructing a conception that enables us to see more clearly than ever why practices like segregation and the mass extermination of Jews (as well as sexist disparagement, gay bashing, the contemptuous dismissal of the old and sick, . . .) constitute blatant, incontrovertible attacks on the dignity of human beings.

IV

Does the moral right constitutive of the status of human dignity enjoy constitutional protection? I will concentrate first of the Fifth and Four-

44. H. L. A. Hart, "The Ascription of Responsibility and Rights," in Antony Flew, ed., *Logic and Language*, 1st ser. (Oxford: Basil Blackwell, 1952), p. 145.

teenth amendments. Among other purposes these principles prohibit the federal and state governments, respectively, from depriving citizens of life, liberty, or property without due process of law. Now, this prohibition cannot be understood to mean simply that all citizens are entitled to their day in court. After all, we should not overlook or gainsay the possibility of due process violations in the courtroom itself—recall Strauder v. West Virginia.[45] Nor is it reasonable to construe "due process" to mean simply that all citizens are entitled to decisions of government based on reasons. For there are reasons and there are reasons, and some of them may express nothing more than false beliefs or deep-seated prejudices. Are we willing to forgo due process criticism of judicial reasoning predicated on such "reasons?"

Considerations like these have led many legal scholars to propose a normative reading of the due process clause. The philosopher T. M. Scanlon expresses this interpretation with admirable clarity. He contends that the due process requirement is designed, first and foremost, to protect all citizens against arbitrary government decision making. As such, it is one of the conditions that must be met for the morally acceptable exercise of power. It "aims to provide some assurance of non-arbitrariness by requiring these who exercise authority to justify their intended actions in a public proceeding by adducing reasons of the appropriate sort and defending these against critical attack."[46]

The word *arbitrary* means "derived from mere opinion, not based on the nature of things or on facts."[47] Constitutional due process, then, condemns governmental denials of life, liberty, or property based on beliefs or feelings that have no factual support. Thus it disallows the state from prosecuting someone who happens to be black on the grounds that "only a black person could have committed such a crime," as it forbids the federal government from punishing an accused individual because "he looks like the kind of person who would commit this offense." A citizenry that cannot defend itself against such a capricious exercise of power, that enjoys no due process rights, will be ripe for exploitation.

45. 100 U.S. 303 (1880).
46. T. M. Scanlon, "Due Process," in John Chapman and J. Roland Pennock, eds., *Nomos* 17 (New York: New York University Press 1977); p. 96. Other scholars who endorse this interpretation are Charles Miller, "The Forest of Due Process of Law," in this volume of *Nomos*, p. 28 ("The idea of due process that lasts is that of individual freedom from arbitrary government imposition"); Paul Brest, "In Defense of the Anti-discrimination Principle," *Harvard Law Review* 90 (1976): 102; and Robert Rutland, *The Birth of the Bill of Rights* (Boston: Northeastern University Press, 1983), pp. 7–10.
47. *Oxford English Dictionary.*

Our Founding Fathers knew full well the extraordinary political value of establishing a government fully committed to due process. They realized, having just broken away from British tyranny, that arbitrary power was the constant enemy of freedom. They were committed to the formation of institutions that would to the greatest extent possible shield citizens from the whim and caprice of rulers infatuated with the possession of power and with the arrogance that its exercise so easily begets.[48]

In light of this historical background, it would be fanciful to suppose that the due process clause had no moral content. And given the greater powers of government today, it would be silly for us to forget or deny this fact. Justice Brennan's words bear repeating: "there exists in modern America the necessity for protecting all of us from arbitrary action by governments more powerful and more pervasive than any in our ancestors' time."[49] A person who is victimized by arbitrary treatment suffers a serious injustice. He has not received his due. He has not been dealt with fairly. So we can see that Justice Felix Frankfurter was right when he claimed that the ideal of due process pertains to our deepest notions of what is just and fair.[50] And so was David Resnick when he identified the moral basis of due process protection with the principle that individuals have the right to be treated justly by their governments.[51]

What is the relation between due process and moral dignity? The answer is obvious but extremely important. To have moral dignity is to possess the right not to be arbitrarily and therefore unjustly disparaged as a person. If I am sentenced to death or imprisoned, or if my property is confiscated, solely because a judge or jury is disdainful of my race, for example, then my moral dignity has been violated. And so has due process, which forbids precisely this kind or arbitrary abuse of power. Therefore, the due process clause of the Fifth and Fourteenth amendments serves to safeguard my dignity and the dignity of every American. The very concepts of due process and moral dignity are conceptually related through the mediating idea of arbitrariness.[52] We are now in a position

48. See, e.g., Rutland, *Birth of the Bill of Rights.*
49. William J. Brennan, Jr., "State Constitutions and the Protection of Individual Rights," *Harvard Law Review* 90 (1977): 495.
50. See Frankfurter's dissent in Selesbee v. Balcom, 339 U.S. 9 (1950), at 16.
51. David Resnick, "Due Process and Procedural Justice," in *Nomos* 17, p. 217.
52. Thomas Jefferson appreciated this connection between dignity and arbitrariness. Note, e.g., his remark that in the Europe of his day, "the dignity of man is lost in arbitrary distinctions," in Philip Foner, ed., *Basic Writings of Thomas Jefferson* (New York: Wiley 1944); p. 231. I would deny, though, that arbitrary devaluation results in the *loss* of our dignity, since we do retain the moral right not to be subject to such devaluation.

to understand and affirm Sanford Kadish's wise observation about due process, that it is concerned with preserving the dignity of the individual.[53]

I turn next to the Fourteenth Amendment's guarantee against every state that it not "deny to any person within its jurisdiction the equal protection of the laws." Obviously, this guarantee does not mean that states may draw no distinctions at all among citizens. It would be fatuous to claim that a policy providing special opportunities and benefits to the handicapped or the elderly sick violates equal protection.

It is equally silly to suggest that constitutional equality confers upon each citizen the right to be treated equally without regard to his person or character or tastes.[54] How is it possible, after all, to treat a person without regard to his person? Nor does it help to say that equality essentially means that the interests of the members of the community matter equally,[55] or that each person is as worthy as any other,[56] or that each citizen's fate is equally important.[57] The skeptic will understandably demand to know why the fate or interests of white supremacists, for example, should matter equally with those of their intended victims, or why hired murderers are as worthy as their innocent victims. Without substantial elaboration these characterizations remain empty catchphrases.

Without elaborating a full theory of constitutional equality, we can safely say this much: that arbitrary governmental discriminations are presumptively condemnable under the standard of equal protection. After all, it would be very peculiar to concede the close relation between violations of due process and arbitrary governmental action while denying any such relation between violations of equality and political arbitrariness. If the due process clause is designed to forbid injustice in the form of capricious legislative deprivation of life, liberty, or property, then it is reasonable to believe that the equal protection clause is designed to prohibit injustice in the form of capricious legislative classifications. That

53. Sanford Kadish, "Methodology and Criteria in Due Process Adjudication—A Survey and Criticism," in *Yale Law Journal* 66 (1957): 347. I want to emphasize that dignity is not the only value protected by due process. There is much arbitrary decision making that does not have to do with contempt.

54. Ronald Dworkin furnishes this formulation in the essay "Justice and Rights," reprinted in his *Taking Rights Seriously*, p. 179.

55. Ronald Dworkin, "In Defense of Equality," in *Social Philosophy and Policy* 1 (1983): 24.

56. Ronald Dworkin, *Law's Empire* (Cambridge: Harvard University Press, 1986); p. 213.

57. Ibid., p. 296.

the Constitution is dedicated to the establishment of justice supports this interpretation of our right to equal treatment.

Now, one particularly pernicious kind of arbitrary governmental discrimination occurs when laws are passed that are motivated by or betray unjustified contempt for certain groups of citizens. Think, for example, of legislation that requires blacks to sit apart from whites on public transit, or that mandates race-segregated education, or that punishes gay sodomy but permits heterosexual sodomy. Policies like these attack the moral dignity of blacks and gays. It is reasonable to think that they also violate the equal protection clause. Indeed, these are precisely the kinds of unjust laws that constitutional equality is meant to condemn. If they can survive Fourteenth Amendment scrutiny, what legislation would not?

So Justice Harlan was quite justified in claiming that the Constitution's guarantee of equality "added greatly to the dignity and glory of American citizenship."[58] The legal right to equal protection embodies the moral right not to suffer discrimination in the form of unwarranted disparagement. One can plausibly say, then, that moral dignity is a corollary of equal protection. As such, it enjoys secure albeit implicit constitutional protection.

To sum up our findings thus far, I can do no better than cite Ronald Dworkin's remark that "the rights created by the due process and equal protection clauses of the Constitution include rights that legislation not be enacted for certain reasons."[59] One such reason is unjust contempt for groups of citizens.[60] Hence, moral dignity functions as a basic and indispensable constraint on the legislative process. A government that takes dignity seriously will be a democracy in the full moral sense. That is, it will be government of, by, and for the people as a whole rather than for select majorities.[61] It will be a government in which, and under which, the respect for human beings mandated by moral dignity flour-

---

58. See Harlan's dissent in Plessy v. Ferguson, 133 U.S. 537 (1896), at 554.

59. Ronald Dworkin, *A Matter of Principle* (Cambridge: Harvard University Press, 1985); p. 66.

60. In an earlier piece Dworkin argued that each citizen has the constitutional right that he not suffer disadvantage, at least in the competition for any public benefit, because the race or religion or sect on region or other natural or artificial group to which he belongs is the object of prejudice or contempt. But does this mean the neo-Nazis or organized misogynists should not be disadvantaged in the competition for public money? What we have a right to is freedom from unjust contempt when competing for public assets. This right is subsumable under moral dignity.

61. Here again I am indebted to Ronald Dworkin for the illuminating distinction between majoritarian and communal democracy. See his "The Future of Abortion" in *New York Review of Books*, September 28, 1989, p. 48.

ishes. For it will constitute a society that "encourages each individual to suppose that his relations with other citizens and with his government are matters of justice."[62]

Is there confirmation for the thesis that human dignity enjoys implicit constitutional protection? Recall the first of my two tests: do any of the amendments to the Constitution, reasonably interpreted, protect the right? It turns out that several unquestionably do. Take for instance, the First Amendment's right to free speech. There is no question that it serves to prohibit unjust personal denigration in the form of coerced silence imposed on despised minorities. The government may not distribute free speech in ways that are arbitrarily contemptuous of individual citizens.

Similarly, the self-incrimination clause of the Fifth Amendment[63] is of particular value to those citizens who already stand vulnerable to assaults on their dignity precisely because they are most likely to be victimized by unwarranted official harassment.[64] The Sixth Amendment's guarantee of the right to a speedy and public trial by an impartial jury is obviously meant to forestall convictions based on unwarranted, prejudicial contempt for the accused. And the Eighth Amendment's proscription of cruel and unusual punishment just as obviously serves to prohibit the infliction of extraordinarily painful penalties on convicted citizens just because, for example, they happen to be black or gay. The Thirteenth Amendment's prohibition of slavery as well as the right to vote guaranteed to blacks and women under the Fifteenth and Nineteenth amendments were designed to protect the moral dignity and therewith the freedom of long-oppressed groups.

The thesis that human dignity enjoys constitutional standing also passes our second confirmation test: explicit endorsement by our Constitution's makers. In The Federalist papers Alexander Hamilton passionately writes: "Yes, my countryman, I own to you, that, that after having given it an attentive consideration, I am clearly of opinion, it is your interest to adopt it [the Constitution]. I am convinced, that this is the safest course for your liberty, your dignity, and your happiness."[65] Later he exhorts his fellow New Yorkers to take a firm stand "for our safety, our

---

62. Dworkin, *Law's Empire*, p. 32.
63. Ibid.
64. This point helps to explain Justice Earl Warren's assertion, in the celebrated *Miranda* decision, that "the constitutional foundation underlying the privilege is the respect a government must accord to the dignity and integrity of its citizens." See Miranda v. Arizona, 384 U.S. 436 (1966), at 460.
65. The Federalist No. 1, at 4 (Bantam 1982).

tranquility, our dignity, our reputation."[66] And given the nature of the British oppression against which Hamilton and his colleagues were rebelling, it is not unreasonable to impute to them a conception of dignity compatible at least with the spirit of the one I have defended in this essay.[67]

V

I have thus far argued that specific, explicitly guaranteed constitutional rights function (in part) to safeguard our moral dignity. But it is important to realize that the very institution of rights held against the government, where these rights belong equally to each and every citizen (and where the meaning of *citizen* is not left to governmental stipulation),[68] embodies the ideal of moral dignity. For it is a clarion declaration that all citizens are equal before the law, that there is no superior, dominant class of human beings,[69] that the government may not treat certain groups under its jurisdiction with arbitrary contempt by denying them protections, on morally irrelevant grounds like race or sex, that it vigorously secures to others.

My suggestion, that a bill of rights constraining the exercise of legal power against citizens is itself an affirmation of moral dignity, is not a new one. In his seminal essay "Taking Rights Seriously" Ronald Dworkin writes:

> The institution of rights against the Government is not a gift of God, or an ancient ritual, or a national sport. It is a complex and troublesome practice that makes the Government's job of securing the general benefit more difficult and more expensive, and it would be a frivolous and wrongful practice unless it served some point. Anyone who professes to take rights seriously, and who praises our Government for respecting

66. Ibid., No. 15 at 69.
67. Thus Hamilton inveighs against the ill humors and temporary prejudices that beget injustice and oppression (ibid., No. 27, at 131). Clearly one form of such oppression, all too familiar among the Framers, consisted of treatment as second-class citizens unworthy of the legal protections accorded the British people.
68. This provision is intended to rule out the kind of stipulation made in Article I, Section 2, of the Constitution, which defined blacks as 3/5 citizens for the purpose of legislative appointment.
69. I again refer you to Justice Harlan's powerful dissent in Plessy v. Ferguson, 133 U.S. 537 (1896), at 559.

them, must have some sense of what that point is. He must accept, at the minimum, one or both of two important ideas. The first is the vague but powerful idea of human dignity. This idea, associated with Kant, but defended by philosophers of different schools, supposes that there are ways of treating a man that are inconsistent with recognizing him as a full member of the human community, and holds that such treatment is profoundly unjust. The second is the more familiar idea of political equality. This supposes that the weaker members of a political community are entitled to the same concern and respect of their government as the more powerful members have secured for themselves, so that if some men have freedom of decision whatever the effect on the general good, then all men must have the same freedom.[70]

Dworkin's point is important. But if my conception of human dignity is worth embracing, then it is a serious mistake to posit, as he does, a sharp distinction between the dignity and equality of persons and to claim that the practice of rights against the government must be grounded in one or the other. For on my view, the moral demand placed on government to treat the weak (poor, sick, . . .) with the same respect that it treats the more powerful is a constitutive requirement of human dignity itself, not a principle of some separate political ideal.

In this essay I have attempted to render the idea of dignity less vague without compromising its moral power or threatening its applicability to human beings conceived solely as animals living in, and wholly governed by, the laws of nature. My conclusion is that moral dignity belongs to the family of those very great political values that define our constitutional morality.[71] Justice Brennan's belief in its preeminent status is philosophically credible. It is therefore quite fitting that in a volume dedicated to him his words should close my essay: "The Declaration of Independence, the Constitution, and the Bill of Rights solemnly committed the United States to be a country where the dignity and rights of all persons were equal before all authority."[72] We must not forget this truth, for "if we are to be a shining city upon a hill, it will be because of our ceaseless pursuit of the constitutional ideal of human dignity."[73] And finally: "If our free society is to endure, those who govern must

70. In *Taking Rights Seriously*, pp. 198–99.
71. Here I borrow from the language of John Rawls. See his "The Domain of the Political and Overlapping Consensus," *New York University Law Review* 64 (1989): 243–45.
72. "The Constitution of the United States," p. 14.
73. Ibid.

recognize human dignity and accept the enforcement of constitutional limitations on their powers conceived by the framers to be necessary to preserve that dignity and the air of freedom which is our proudest heritage.[74]

74. Ibid., p. 9.

4

Constitutional Liberty, Dignity, and Reasonable Justification

DAVID A. J. RICHARDS

American constitutionalism rests on both a political theory of legitimate government and a constitutional theory of political power. The political theory, derived from John Locke,[1] offers an account of the conditions on the legitimate exercise of any form of political power. The constitutional theory offers structures for the exercise of political power that, in light of the propensities of our political psychology, tend to render the exercise of political power consistent with the conditions of Lockean legitimacy.[2] Such a public enterprise of political and constitutional theory and political science has, of course, a rich history; and reflection on that history—so prominent in American constitutional interpretation today—notably features the attempt better to coordinate the demands of the political and constitutional theory. To name only the most dramatic example, the Reconstruction amendments play the central role they do in our constitutional understanding because they address concurrently intolerable defects in both the political and constitutional theory of the 1787 Constitution (it tolerated, indeed entrenched and protected, a form of political power—slavery—that was

1. For further development of this argument, see David A. J. Richards, *Toleration and the Constitution* (New York: Oxford University Press, 1986); and D. A. J. Richards, *Foundations of American Constitutionalism* (New York: Oxford University Press. 1989).
2. This view is defended at great and extensive length in Richards, *Foundations of American Constitutionalism*.

illegitimate and its resulting defects in constitutional structure gave powerfully effective political expression to the pathology of political power we call racism).[3] This essay examines the relationship between political and constitutional theory as a historically continuous enterprise centrally motivated by the concern to identify and give expression to values of human dignity through constitutional protections of inalienable human rights and a discourse of reasonable justification for political power appropriate to a polity that treats persons with the dignity required by respect for their moral personality. Constitutionalism is, so I will argue, a kind of generalization of the argument for the limitation of political power required by the respect appropriate to treating persons as bearers of rights, a self-correcting interpretive practice acutely sensitive to the cumulative lessons of history about both abuses of human rights and the ways in which such abuses may be corrected. My argument begins with Locke's argument for religious toleration and the political theory he generalized from that argument, and then turns to American constitutionalism itself and the conception of reasonable justifiability to all that it imposes on the exercise of political power.

The early historical focus of this essay is not of merely antiquarian interest. It is meant to be illustrative of the central motivations of American constitutionalism, namely, a historically informed reflection on both fundamental political deprivations of human rights and constitutional structures more likely to limit such abuses. A constitutional tradition, understood to be so motivated, must be critically sensitive to new insights into further such abuses and constitutionally principled ways to rectify them. The very interpretive integrity of the project of American constitutionalism thus unites a remarkably conservative and progressive public tradition of respect for inalienable human rights. The few great justices who have graced the Supreme Court of the United States throughout its long, noble and sometimes ignoble history[4] have been those, of whom Justice William Brennan was clearly one, whose interpretive practice spoke brilliantly and profoundly with such integrity to the public conscience of the American people. Will our constitutional generation, whose youth profited from such a teacher, be worthy of the interpretive responsibilities of freedom?

    3. See ibid., chap. 7.
    4. See, e.g., Don E. Fehrenbacher, *The Dred Scott Case: Its Significance in American Law and Politics* (New York: Oxford University Press, 1978).

THE ARGUMENT FOR RELIGIOUS TOLERATION

The American idea of constitutionalism rests on a normative political theory of equal inalienable rights and a constitutional theory of the constraints on political power required for those rights to be respected. Americans did not, any more than Locke, base arguments of human rights or of morality in general on history,[5] for they were quite prepared, as Locke taught them they must be,[6] to test historical political practice against objective standards of political legitimacy (including respect for rights and pursuit of the public good), and to base the right to revolution on the failures of such practice to meet these standards.[7] But Locke had taught them as well that a critical analysis of history could often clarify the ways in which corrupt abuses of power had subverted the very intellectual, moral, and political foundations of recognizing, let alone implementing, the inalienable rights of human nature. Such analysis could afford invaluable historical instruction in the need for political and constitutional principles protecting against such corruption.

Locke's argument for a principle of religious toleration illustrated this generic pattern of argument.[8] Indeed, the argument for religious toleration was taken by Americans to be a kind of model for political argument in general. Locke's critical attack on the theory and practice of religious persecution was not just on an abstract structure of argument that was demonstrably wrong, but on the pivotal historical role of this argument in the corruption of both religion and politics.[9]

5. Indeed, Locke is notable among his generation precisely for his failure to make use in his political theory of legitimacy of any appeal to the history of the ancient constitution. See, e.g., J. G. A. Pocock, *The Ancient Constitution and the Feudal Law* (Cambridge: Cambridge University Press, 1957), pp. 46, 187–88, 235–38, 348, 354–61.

6. See John Locke, *The Second Treatise of Government*, in John Locke, *Two Treatises of Government*, ed. Peter Laslett (Cambridge: Cambridge University Press, 1960), pp. 424–46. For useful commentary, see Richard Ashcraft, *Locke's Two Treatises of Government* (London: Allen & Unwin, 1987); Ruth W. Grant, *John Locke's Liberalism* (Chicago: University of Chicago Press, 1987).

7. See the Declaration of Independence in Merrill Jensen, ed., *The Documentary History of the Ratification of the Constitution*, vol. 1 (Madison: State Historical Society of Wisconsin, 1976), pp. 73–76. For useful commentary on the natural law and rights background of the Declaration and Constitution, see Carl L. Becker, *The Declaration of Independence* (New York: Vintage, 1958); Morton White, *The Philosophy of the American Revolution* (New York: Oxford University Press, 1978); Edward S. Corwin, *The "Higher Law" Background of American Constitutional Law* (Ithaca: Cornell University Press, 1955).

8. See John Locke, *Letters Concerning Toleration* in *The Works of John Locke* (London: Thomas Davison, 1823), vol. 6.

9. For a fuller analysis, see Richards, *Toleration and the Constitution*, pp. 89–98.

Locke, like Bayle,[10] thus examined the argument offered by Augustine of Hippo to justify religious persecution of heresy,[11] and he criticized Augustine's conception that there can be a politically just criterion for an erring conscience, a diabolically willful failure to accept evident religious truths. Fundamentally, Augustine's argument turned on the conviction of the truth of certain religious beliefs; but all people, however, had such a conviction of the truth of their religious beliefs. Accordingly, the argument would justify universal persecution by everyone of everyone else, which neither a just God nor the law of nature could have intended. In effect, one theological system, among others equally reasonable, was made the measure of politically enforceable truths.[12]

The crux of Locke's argument was the biased sectarian conception of enforceable rational truth that Augustine assumed, a corruptive judgment that failed to respect the just freedom of persons to exercise their inalienable right to conscience. The putatively irrational heretic was supposed, because of heresy, to be unfree, marred by a disordered will. But that judgment of unfreedom was itself corruptively biased and degraded our right to reasonable freedom of conscience: conscience was made hostage to the unreasonable judgments of others. In order to ensure respect for the right to conscience of all on fair terms, a political principle of toleration was in order that deprived the state of the power to make and enforce such sectarian judgments over conscience.

The moral nerve of the argument for the right to conscience was that persons are independent originators of reasonable claims on one another as ethical beings, and that the demands of ethics and of an ethical God could only be both known and practically effective in our lives when persons' right to conscience was appropriately respected. Otherwise, the demands of ethics would be confused with public opinion or popular taste or a tradition possibly based on what John Adams would later call

10. See Pierre Bayle, *Philosophique commentaire sur ces paroles de Jesus Christ "Contrain-les d'entree,"* in *Oeuvres diverses de M. Pierre Bayle,* vol. 2 (The Hague: Chez P. Husson, 1727) (hereinafter *Philosophique commentaire*), pp. 357–560. For a useful recent general study, see John Kilcullen, *Sincerity and Truth: Essays on Arnauld, Bayle, and Toleration* (Oxford: Clarendon Press, 1988).

11. For fuller discussion, see Richards, *Toleration and the Constitution,* pp. 86–88.

12. This was hardly a decisive refutation of Augustine's argument. As a perceptive commentator on Bayle's argument for toleration observes: "As a refutation of the Augustinian theories which in the seventeenth century gave religious intolerance its motive, or gave other motives a religious guise, Bayle's book does not really succeed. To the followers of St. Augustine some of Bayle's premises would have seemed false or arbitrary, including some which today may seem trivial and self-evident. The Augustinians were not refuted: they died out without successfully training later generations." John Kilcullen, *Sincerity and Truth,* p. 2.

"artifice, imposture, hypocrisy, and superstition."[13] This association of religious conscience with ethical imperatives was, of course, pervasively characteristic of the Judeo-Christian tradition and its conception of an ethical and personal God acting through history.[14] Locke and Bayle were religious Christians in this tradition. They regarded themselves as returning Christianity to its ethical foundations (reminding Christians, for example, of the toleration of the early patristic period)[15]—"that religious liberty," as Adams later termed it, "with which Jesus made them free."[16] Disagreements in speculative theology, which had grounded Augustinian persecutions for heresy, were, for them, patent betrayals of essential Christianity: they disabled people from regulating their lives by the simple and elevated ethical imperatives of Christian charity.

Locke's and Bayle's most acute criticism of Augustinian persecution was the focal significance of its corruption of ethics in the corruption of religion and politics, and the motivation of their arguments for the inalienable right to conscience was a new interpretation of what ethics was, one that made possible the emancipation of religion and ethics from their historical corruptions. Locke thus linked a free conscience to the autonomous exercise of the moral competence of each and every person as a democratic equal to reason in ways accessible to all reasonable beings about the nature and content of the ethical obligations imposed on persons by an ethical God,[17] and he thought of these obligations as centering on a core of minimal ethical standards reflected in the Gospels.[18] And ethics, for Bayle (as for Kant), is a vital force in one's life only when one

13. John Adams, *A Defence of the Constitutions of Government of the United States of America*, in C. F. Adams, ed., *Works of John Adams* (Boston: Little, Brown, 1851), 4:292.

14. For the distinctive force of this conception in the Old Testament's narrative style and sharp repudiation of different conceptions of divinity in surrounding cultures, see Herbert Schneidau, *Sacred Discontent: The Bible and Western Tradition* (Baton Rouge: Louisiana State University Press, 1976); Dan Jacobson, *The Story of Stories* (New York: Harper & Row, 1982); Robert Alter, *The Art of Biblical Narrative* (New York: Basic Books, 1981). On the personality of the western conception of the divine and its broader cultural significance for western ethics, politics, and science, see Denis de Rougemont, *Man's Western Quest*, trans. Montgomery Belgion (Westport, Conn.: Greenwood, 1973); and on the impersonality of India's concept of the divine, see Arthur Danto, *Mysticism and Morality* (New York: Harper, 1973), pp. 40–41.

15. See, e.g., Bayle, *Philosophique commentaire*, pp. 387–88.

16. John Adams, *A Dissertation on the Canon and Feudal Law*, in C. F. Adams, ed., *Works of John Adams*, 3:454.

17. See, in general, John Colman, *John Locke's Moral Philosophy* (Edinburgh: Edinburgh University Press, 1983).

18. See John Locke, *The Reasonableness of Christianity*, ed. I. T. Ramsey (Stanford: Stanford University Press, 1958).

independently acknowledges its principles oneself and imposes them on one's life.[19] The very point of respect for conscience, for Locke and Bayle, was to ensure that each and every person was guaranteed the moral independence to determine the nature and content of ethical obligations and that state enforcement of sectarian religious beliefs did not taint this inalienable moral freedom with speculative theological disagreements that had corrupted the central place of this democratic conception of ethics in what both regarded as true religion. On this conception, religion did not embed us in ontological and political hierarchies of being characteristic of many of the world's cultural traditions[20] but made possible, indeed emancipated, a respect for persons expressive of the dignity of their rational freedom. The right to conscience had a focal role in a just polity because it made possible the intellectual and moral foundations for reasonable self-government.

It was a decisively important fact in the distinctive formation of American constitutionalism that Americans regarded religious beliefs, properly understood, as vehicles of moral and political emancipation in this Lockean way.[21] Locke and his American posterity thus faced frontally the central puzzle for religious Christians and democrats: that a religion like Christianity (a religion for Locke of democratic equality and civility) had long been associated in the West with the legitimation of antidemocratic institutions like hereditary monarchy. Lockean Americans thus confronted the tension in traditional Christianity between a conception of radical freedom from existing roles and the coercive claims (for example, heresy prosecutions) of the Christian political community over the minds and hearts of people.[22] This critical interrogatory was particularly poignant for Locke and the Lockean American revolutionary constitutionalists a century later since they believed that a properly understood Protestant Christianity supplied the ethics of personal self-government that made possible the theory and practice of democratic self-government. How, for long millennia, could Christianity have thus betrayed its essential emancipatory purposes, degrading a just human freedom into acceptance of morally arbitrary hierarchies of religious and political privilege and power?

---

19. Bayle, *Philosophique commentaire*, pp. 367–72, 422–33.

20. Van Leeuwen notes what he calls peculiarly western anti-ontocratic concerns. See, in general, Arend Th. van Leeuwen, *Christianity in World History*, trans. H. H. Hoskins (New York: Charles Scribner's Sons, 1964).

21. See, in general, Alan Heimert, *Religion and the American Mind: From the Great Awakening to the Revolution* (Cambridge: Harvard University Press, 1966).

22. For an illuminating study of this tension from the perspective of issues of gender, see Elaine Pagels, *Adam, Eve, and the Serpent* (New York: Random House, 1988).

The American constitutional tradition chose to answer the interrogatory in a way that repudiated the alternative Erastian conception of civil religion familiar to the Founders in the classical republican tradition elaborated by Machiavelli[23] and Rousseau.[24] The challenge to all republican theorists after the ancient world was to understand whether and how republican political practice could exist in a nonpagan world—in particular, in the world of commitment to the Judeo-Christian religious synthesis. After all, the great historical examples of republican rule—Athens, Sparta, Rome, Carthage, and the like—were all pre-Christian or pagan societies, and the reawakening of interest in republican theory and practice in the Renaissance naturally posed the question whether and how republicanism could be squared with Christian commitments.

The classical republican answer by Machiavelli, Rousseau, and Marx[25] was the Erastian conception of civil religion, an established church (including, in Marx's case, its secular atheistic functional equivalent) regulated by state power to appropriately emancipatory ends. On this analysis, the great defect in the relationship of church and state since Constantine was the independence of the church from state control, and its consequent capacity to corrupt republican aims and values by theocratically defined ends. This view was naturally, though not inevitably, linked to the kind of Voltairean anticlericalism familiar to Europeans from republican Venice and Florence and the associated classical republican tradition revived by Machiavelli.[26] On this view, Judeo-Christian values, whatever their truth value, were intrinsically dangerous, and must be cabined and tamed to the ends of secular authority by the assertion of supreme secular authority over religious life on the model of Roman or Spartan civil religion. Even the political science of Montesquieu and David Hume—although not endorsing classically republican civil religion—supported Erastian established churches.[27]

Americans like Thomas Jefferson and James Madison gravitated to a

23. See Niccolò Machiavelli, *The Discourses*, ed. Bernard Crick, trans. Leslie J. Walker (Harmondsworth: Penguin, 1970), pp. 139–52.

24. See Jean Jacques Rousseau, *The Social Contract and Discourses*, trans. G. D. H. Cole (New York: Dutton, 1950), pp. 129–41.

25. See Karl Marx, *On the Jewish Question*, in *Karl Marx: Early Writings*, trans. T. B. Bottomore (London: C. A. Watts, 1963).

26. See William J. Bouwsma, *Venice and the Defense of Republican Liberty* (Berkeley: University of California Press, 1968), pp. 1–51, 417–638. For a good general study of Machiavelli's subversive attitude to Christian thought and practice, see Mark Hulliung, *Citizen Machiavelli* (Princeton: Princeton University Press, 1983).

27. For commentary on Montesquieu's Erastian conception of religion, see Thomas L. Pangle, *Montesquieu's Philosophy of Liberalism* (Chicago: University of Chicago Press, 1973), pp. 249–59. On Hume, see David Miller, *Philosophy and Ideology in Hume's Political Thought* (Oxford: Clarendon Press, 1981), pp. 117–81.

quite different constitutional conception that culminated in the religion clauses of the First Amendment[28] because they took a different view of how Judeo-Christian belief and republican values interconnected, namely, the familiar American union of equally intense personal religiosity *and* republicanism. On this view, stated by Locke, the essential moral message of Christian belief—namely, the democratic liberty and equality of all persons—was supportive of republican values of equal liberty under law but had been corrupted from its proper supportive role by Constantine's wholly heretical and blasphemous establishment of Christianity as the church of the Roman Empire. The problem was not that Constantine had opted for the wrong form of established church—one subordinating secular to religious authority—but that, as Americans like Jefferson and Madison came increasingly to see,[29] he had wedded religious to secular authority *at all*. A more radical separation of religious and political authority was required in order to preserve the integrity of each, in particular, to preserve the moral independence of conscience against which the legitimate claims of state power could then be assessed.

Americans, following Locke, thus gave prominence to the right to conscience because such historical reflection led them to believe that only the protection of conscience from sectarian corruption enabled people to emancipate themselves from the "artifice, imposture, hypocrisy, and superstition"[30] that disabled persons from knowing and giving weight to the natural rights of human nature both in religion and politics. Locke took as the central problem of politics the ways in which distortions of self-interest disabled persons from fairly adjudicating controversies over such rights, and he argued that the legitimacy of state power depended on securing greater impartiality in the enforcement of such rights.[31] The specific argument for toleration was that a legitimate state could have no power to enforce sectarian conscience because such power was corruptively biased in ways that cannot impartially enforce the right to conscience. Locke's removal of the issue from the scope of legitimate power rested on a penetrating analysis of the subversion of rationality itself by the self-deceiving excesses of a mind so impassioned by sectarian

---

28. See, in general, Richards, *Toleration and the Constitution*, chaps. 4–5.

29. Americans elaborate this principle beyond Locke, whose arguments focus on free exercise, not anti-establishment. For discussion of the ways Americans adapted and elaborated Locke's arguments, see Richards, *Toleration and the Constitution*, pp. 88–116.

30. John Adams, *A Defence*, 4:292.

31. See, in general, Grant, *John Locke's Liberalism*.

zeal[32] and deadened by oppressive custom[33] that it was incapable of any impartial or fair-minded assessment of dissenting, let alone heretical, views.[34] Toleration was thus required as a prophylaxis against an irrationalism incapable of meeting minimal demands for the reasonable justification of the power of the state.[35]

LOCKEAN POLITICAL THEORY
AND CONSTITUTIONALISM

Locke's political theory may usefully be understood as a generalization to politics of this argument for religious toleration. That argument—as we have seen—depended on the critical analysis of a historical rationale for religious persecution, namely, that the illegitimate political power of a dominant religion had been allowed to impose on society at large a factionalized conception of religious truth that sanctified unnatural hierarchies of power and privilege. Both Locke and Bayle condemned the political uses to which the argument had been put in the history of the West because it had stunted and stultified the capacities of the human mind and heart to engage the emancipatory and egalitarian moral teaching of historical Christianity. Locke, in contrast to Bayle,[36] generalized the scope of the argument to include the very legitimacy of political power. In effect, for Locke, injustices like religious persecution could not be localized to personal religion or even ethics; they undermined the general conditions for the legitimate exercise of political power by one person over another.[37]

32. See, e.g., John Locke, On the Conduct of the Human Understanding, in The Works of John Locke, 3:212, 216, 235, 267–86. On the importance of getting clear about Locke's distinctive thought about a flawed human nature, see W. W. Spellman, John Locke and the Problem of Depravity (Oxford: Clarendon Press, 1988).

33. See Locke, Conduct of Human Understanding, pp. 208, 230, 231–32, 268, 276–77.

34. See ibid., pp. 266–69, 271, 276–77.

35. I am indebted here to the discussion of Grant, John Locke's Liberalism, pp. 180–92. For a different interpretation of Locke's argument, centering on the irrationality of coercion to secure any belief at all, see Jeremy Waldron, "Locke: Toleration and the Rationality of Persecution," in Susan Mendus, ed., Justifying Toleration (Cambridge: Cambridge University Press, 1988), pp. 61–86.

36. For fuller discussion, see Richards, Toleration and the Constitution, p. 90.

37. When Locke wrote of the conditions that would justify revolution, he thus described the pertinent convictions people would entertain: "they were persuaded in their Consciences, that their Laws, and with them their Estates, Liberties, and Lives are in danger, and perhaps their Religion too." The Second Treatise of Government, pp. 422–23 (sec. 209). On the importance of the issue of religious liberty in Locke's thought about politics and revolution, see Richard Ashcraft, Revolutionary Politics and Locke's Two Treatises

The heart of Locke's political thinking was that the authority the inalienable right to conscience had in religion and in ethics carried over to politics. Parallel corruptions of power to those that had stunted and stultified the religious and moral capacities of persons carried over to people's political capacities. His political theory thus combined a normative component (respect for the inalienable human rights of persons conceived as free, equal, and rational) and a historical component (the structures of illegitimate power that had stunted our capacities to exercise religious, moral, and political freedom consistent with these rights.)

The normative component of Locke's political theory (namely, inalienable human rights) rested on the reasonable moral and political inquiry that he believed was made possible and practicable once the political force of the argument for religious persecution was circumscribed by acceptance of the argument for religious toleration. Such reasonable inquiry must be conducted, Locke had argued in his epistemology,[38] in light of experience, and reasonable inquiry into such experience demonstrably justified a theological ethics in which persons, understood to be made in God's image of rational creative freedom,[39] had inalienable rights, rights they could not surrender (for example, to conscience and to life).[40] Such rights were inalienable because, as normative claims, they secured to each and every person (understood as free, rational, and equal) the final, ultimate, and uncompromisably nonnegotiable control over the resources of mind and body essential to exercising the dignity of our rational and reasonable powers in living a complete life as independent and morally accountable creative agents.[41] Locke's theory of political legitimacy rested on working out the consequences for politics of the objective moral and political value of such rights for persons, including their right to a politics that allowed them reasonably to know and claim such rights in both their private and public lives.

Post-Lockean moral thought in Britain and America—to wit, the eighteenth-century philosophy of a moral sense[42]—often questioned the

---

of Government (Princeton: Princeton University Press, 1986), e.g., pp. 483, 487–88, 494–97, 500. See also, in general, John Dunn, The Political Thought of John Locke (Cambridge: Cambridge University Press, 1969).

38. John Locke, An Essay Concerning Human Understanding, ed. Alexander C. Fraser, 2 vols. (New York: Dover, 1959).

39. See, e.g., James Tully, A Discourse on Property: John Locke and his Adversaries (Cambridge: Cambridge University Press, 1980), pp. 3–50.

40. See, in general, Colman, John Locke's Moral Philosophy.

41. See, in general, A. John Simmons, "Inalienable Rights and Locke's Treatises," Philosophy & Public Affairs 12 (1983): 175; Tully, A Discourse on Property.

42. See, e.g., Shaftesbury, An Inquiry Concerning Virtue or Merit, in L. A. Selby-Bigge,

theological structure of Locke's argument,[43] but not on the ground of its conclusions about inalienable human rights but rather that the reasonable argument to such rights was, if anything, more direct, less intellectually circuitous, more available to all persons of common sense.[44] Locke had maintained that ethics was demonstrable but had not published any such demonstration; rather, in accord with his commitment to theological ethics, he argued that the Gospels sufficed as a practical guide to conduct.[45] The theory of the moral sense, consistent with a Lockean epistemology, filled this gap with a distinctive kind of experience available to everyone's moral sense. Although moral philosophers disagreed among themselves about emotional versus intellectual interpretations of the deliverances of the moral sense (notably, Hutcheson[46] versus Price[47]), they agreed that the moral sense justified inalienable human rights.[48] Indeed,

ed., *British Moralists* (New York: Dover, 1965), vol. 1, pp. 1–67; Francis Hutcheson, *Illustrations on the Moral Sense*, ed. Bernard Peach (Cambridge: Belknap Press of Harvard University Press, 1971); Hutcheson, *An Inquiry Concerning the Original of Our Ideas of Virtue or Moral Good*, in Selby-Bigge, ed., *British Moralists*, 1: 68–177; Hutcheson, *A System of Moral Philosophy*, 2 vols., in *Collected Works of Francis Hutcheson*, vols. 5–6 (Hildesheim: George Olms Verlagsbuchhandlung, 1969); Hutcheson, *A Short Introduction to Moral Philosophy*, in *Collected Works of Francis Hutcheson*, vol. 4; Joseph Butler, *Fifteen Sermons Preached at the Rolls Chapel*, ed. W. R. Matthews (London: G. Bell & Sons, 1969); Richard Price, *A Review of the Principal Questions in Morals*, ed. D. D. Raphael (Oxford: Clarendon Press, 1974).

43. Both Shaftesbury and Hutcheson, who shape the moral-sense theory of the age, specifically deny that the concept of ethics depends either on God's will or on divine punishment. See, e.g., Shaftesbury, *An Inquiry Concerning Virtue*, pp. 15–16, 23–24, 45–47; Hutcheson, *An Inquiry Concerning the Original of Our Ideas of Virtue or Moral Good*, pp. 71–72, 79, 85–86, 90–92, 122–23, 125. Since the experience of ethics is defined by an independent moral sense, the very content of such ethics depends on the exercise of this natural sense, in terms of which, in fact, we define our concept of a good and just God, not conversely. For both Shaftesbury and Hutcheson, the concept of ethics as linked to divine will and punishment degrades the intrinsic appeal and power both of ethical reasoning and motivation, and thus degrades the concept of an ethical god.

44. See, e.g., Francis Hutcheson, *A Short Introduction to Moral Philosophy*, pp. 24–25, 124.

45. See, in general, Colman, *John Locke's Moral Philosophy*. For Locke's central work of normative ethics, see John Locke, *The Reasonableness of Christianity*, ed. I. T. Ramsey, (Stanford: Stanford University Press, 1958). Locke's attempt to extract an essential normative ethics from a form of Bible criticism of the Gospels appears to have been immensely influential. See, for a notable example of such influence, Dickinson W. Adams, ed., *Jefferson's Extracts from the Gospels: The Papers of Thomas Jefferson*, 2nd ser. (Princeton: Princeton University Press, 1983).

46. See Francis Hutcheson, *Illustrations on the Moral Sense*; *An Inquiry Concerning the Original of Our Ideas of Virtue or Moral Good*.

47. See Price, *A Review of the Principal Questions in Morals*.

48. See, e.g., Hutcheson, *A Short Introduction to Moral Philosophy*, pp. 24–25, 124; Richard Price, *Supplemental Observations on the Naturel and Value of Civil Liberty and Free Government*, in Richard Price, *Two Tracts on Civil Liberty, the War with America,*

if anything, moral-sense theory gave more direct and robust support for an inalienable right like conscience because the failure to respect this right—for example, by religious persecution on the grounds of political enforcement of a sectarian view of religious truth—was now construed, by Jefferson among others, as a corruption of the moral sense itself.[49] Moral-sense theorists, as diverse as Hutcheson and Price, thus both used and elaborated Locke's political theory, indeed—in Britain—in the defense of the program of the radical Whig oppositionists so admired by Americans.[50]

No one of them more acutely articulated the underlying issue of respect for dignity and rights than the British moral philosopher Richard Price, who was, after Thomas Paine, the most important British defender of the American revolutionary and constitutional achievements.[51] In his *Observations on the Nature of Civil Liberty* (1776), Price articulated the emerging American political theory in the terms that "in every free state every man is his own Legislator,"[52] by which he meant institutional protections of certain basic equal liberties of all persons. He identified these liberties as physical, moral, religious, and civil, and he described them thus:

---

the Debts and Finances of the Kingdom (New York: Da Capo, 1972), p. 11. See also Price, *A Review of the Principal Questions of Morals*, pp. 178–81, 214.

49. The corruptibility of the moral sense by factual and other misbeliefs was a point made by Kames; see Henry Home Kames, *Essays on the Principles of Morality and Natural Reason*, ed. R. Wellek (New York: Garland Publishing, 1976), pp. 136–49. And for Bolingbroke, the history of intolerance exemplified such corruption of ethics, including the ethics of the Gospels, by speculative theology; see Lord Bolingbroke, *The Works of Lord Bolingbroke* (London: Frank Cass, 1967), vol. 3, pp. 373–535. Jefferson was deeply influenced by these views of Kames and Bolingbroke, which he linked to the importance of religious liberty. See Adrienne Koch, *The Philosophy of Thomas Jefferson* (Gloucester, Mass.: Peter Smith, 1957), pp. 9–39. For Jefferson's own linkage of religious persecution with moral and religious corruption, see Thomas Jefferson, *Notes on the State of Virginia*, ed. William Peden (New York: W. W. Norton, 1954), pp. 159–61; and the preface to his Bill for Religious Freedom, in Julian P. Boyd, ed., *The Papers of Thomas Jefferson, 1777–1779* vol. 2 (Princeton: Princeton University Press, 1950), pp. 545–46. In his later life, Jefferson subscribed to Joseph Priestley's views on the corruption of true Christianity. See, in general, Adams, ed., *Jefferson's Extracts from the Gospels*, pp. 14–30; Jefferson's own attempts at Bible criticism were actuated by the attempt to distinguish the gold from the dross.

50. See, for pertinent commentary, Caroline Robbins, *The Eighteenth-Century Commonwealthman* (Cambridge: Harvard University Press, 1959), pp. 185–96, 335–44.

51. See Corinne Comstock Weston, *English Constitutional Theory and the House of Lords, 1556–1832* (London: Routledge & Kegan Paul, 1965), p. 157.

52. Richard Price, *Obervations on the Nature of Civil Liberty, The Principles of Government, and the Justice and Policy of the War with America*, in *Two Tracts on Civil Liberty, the War with America, the Debts and Finances of the Kingdom* (New York: Da Capo Press, 1972), p. 6. See also Richard Price, *Additional Observations on the Nature and Value of Civil Liberty, and the War with America* (in same volume), and Richard Price, *Observations on the Importance of the American Revolution and the Means of making it a Benefit to the World* (New Haven: Meigs, Bowen & Dana, 1785).

By PHYSICAL LIBERTY I mean that principle of *Spontaneity*, or *Self-determination*, which constitutes us *Agents*; or which gives us a command over our actions, rendering them properly *ours*, and not effects of the operation of any foreign cause. —MORAL LIBERTY is the power of following, in all circumstances, our sense of right and wrong; or of acting in conformity to our reflecting and moral principles without being controuled by any contrary principles. —RELIGIOUS LIBERTY signifies the power of exercising, without molestation, that mode of religion which we think best; or of making the decisions of our own consciences respecting religious truth, the rule of our conduct, and not any of the decisions of our fellow-men. —In like manner; CIVIL LIBERTY is the power of a *Civil Society* or *State* to govern itself by its own discretion, or by laws of its own making, without being subject to the impositions of *any* power, in appointing and directing which the collective body of the people have no concern; and over which they have no controul.

It should be observed, that, according to these definitions of the different kinds of liberty, there is one general idea, that runs through them all; I mean, the idea of *Self-direction*, or *Self-government*.[53]

Price clearly did not interpret the idea, "every man... his own Legislator,"[54] to be exhausted by political liberty, for he expressly "placed *Civil Liberty* last, because I mean to apply to it all I shall say of the other kinds of Liberty,"[55] namely, that the point of civil liberty was precisely to guarantee the spheres of physical, moral, and religious liberty that he calls, equally with civil liberty, "*Self-government*," echoing Locke's justification of freedom as respect for the general exercise of the "*Reason* ... he is to govern himself by."[56]

These spheres of physical, moral, and religious liberty were understood by Price, consistent with the Lockean political theory he assumed,[57] as guarantees of moral independence—in his terms, "not effects of the operation of any foreign cause," "without being controuled by any contrary principles," "not any of the decisions of our fellow-men."[58] The idea is

---

53. Price, *Observations on the Nature of Civil Liberty*, pp. 2–4.

54. It was this phrase to which Bentham, so violent a critic of human rights, took particularly sharp objection: he wrote, for example, "Dr. Price with his self-government made me an anti-American," quoted in H. L. A. Hart, *Essays on Bentham* (Oxford: Clarendon Press, 1982), p. 61.

55. Price, *Observations on the Nature of Civil Liberty*, pp. 2–3.

56. Locke, *The Second Treatise*, p. 327 (sec. 63).

57. See, e.g., Price, *Additional Observations on the Nature and Value of Civil Liberty, and the War with America*, in *Two Tracts on Civil Liberty*, p. 25 (citing Locke against Filmer).

58. Price, *Observations on the Nature of Civil Liberty*, p. 3.

not that people form or should form their identities in a social vacuum, but the political point—at the heart of Locke's argument for religious toleration—that only what Price elsewhere called the state's "perfect neutrality"[59] among sectarian views would enable persons themselves reasonably to exercise their judgment as free and self-governing people. The scope of state power was, for this reason, limited to "the free and undisturbed possession of their good names, properties and lives,"[60] that is, general or common goods that are neutral among sectarian disagreements.[61]

It is fundamental to the Lockean conception of political legitimacy—which Price assumes—both that a state may fail to meet the minimal benchmarks that justify the power of the state and that the question of whether it has done so must be one of which "I my self can only be Judge in my own Conscience."[62] Locke, of course, understood that the right to revolution could not always be justly and effectively exercised, and he assumed that the politics of revolution would require large numbers of people to concur in their judgments about the intolerable injustice of an existing state.[63] But his conception of political legitimacy depended on inalienable human rights, rights of each and every person that could be surrendered to no other, and the judgment of whether a state's power met or flouted such rights could no more be surrendered to others than the rights themselves.[64]

Locke thought of this conception of political legitimacy as arising at two distinct stages, which correspond to two distinguishable contractualist metaphors that he employed. First, since any legitimate political community must respect the inalienable rights of each and every person subject to its power, the community of such persons must all satisfy a criterion of unanimous reasonable consent that they wish a political community to exist. In a stable existing society, Locke believed such consent must be shown by each person's actual reasonable consent to the present form of governance;[65] if such an existing society should break

---

59. Price, *Observations on the Importance of the American Revolution*, p. 21; cf. p. 29.
60. Price, *Additional Observations on the Nature and Value of Civil Liberty*, p. 12.
61. For a recent restatement of this thought, see John Rawls, "Social Unity and Primary Goods," in Amartya Sen and Bernard Williams, eds., *Utilitarianism and Beyond* (Cambridge: Cambridge University Press, 1982), pp. 159–85.
62. Locke, *The Second Treatise*, p. 300 (sec. 21). See also pp. 398 (sec. 168), 422–23 (sec. 209), 445 (sec. 242).
63. See, e.g., ibid., pp. 397–98 (sec. 168), 422–23 (sec. 209), 435–36 (sec. 230).
64. See, e.g., ibid., p. 397 (sec. 168), where Locke expressly argues that the right to revolt is a right of "the Body of the People, or any single Man."
65. See, e.g., ibid., pp. 349–50 (sec. 96), 364 (sec. 117).

down, people then must unanimously decide whether they choose to continue as a political society.[66] Second, the organization of such people into a form of government should be decided "by the will and determination of the *majority*."[67] Locke thought of majority rule in this context as the only reasonable alternative to unanimity as a *political* decision procedure that would respect equality and yet allow political communities to be formed on reasonable terms. He rejected unanimity because many people, on grounds of "Infirmities of Health, and Avocations of Business," would not attend "the Publick Assembly,"[68] and those who attended would have such "variety of Opinions, and contrariety of Interests"[69] that they would never agree. Since some political communities are, in fact, more consistent with respect for rights than a state of nature and unanimity would preclude the existence of any political community, our reasonable moral interest in having a political community that respects rights required that the decision procedure must be by majority rule. Locke's argument does not, in fact, uniquely require majority rule and might, in fact, require others (for example, as Americans were later to innovate, supermajority voting rules in constitutional conventions and amendment procedures) if they would also be superior to unanimity on the grounds Locke adduced and lead to the framing of governments that, in contrast to majority rule, are more consistent with political legitimacy, that is, that respect our inalienable human rights. Locke clearly thought of majority rule as a *faute de mieux* addressed to the narrow problem of framing constitutions, not to the substance of how those constitutions should be designed; he clearly did not believe that such majority procedures would necessarily result in frames of government that used majority rule, for the informed majority at the stage of framing the government might reasonably decide that the frame of government most consistent with respect for rights would circumscribe, if not eliminate, majority rule as a principle of political decision. Such majority rule at the stage of framing forms of government must, of course, be exercised reasonably in light of our equal rights, and its resulting frame of government, in the event it violated such rights, would be illegitimate and the justifiable object of the right to revolution.[70]

66. For useful discussion of these exegetical points, see Grant, *John Locke's Liberalism*, pp. 110–28.
67. Locke, *The Second Treatise*, p. 349 (sec. 96).
68. Ibid., p. 350 (sec. 98).
69. Ibid., pp. 350–51.
70. For illuminating commentary on these aspects of Locke's political theory, in particular his argument for majority rule, see Grant, *John Locke's Liberalism*, pp. 110–28.

Locke's political theory thus required political judgment by citizens at three stages: the judgment to join the political society as such, the judgment (if it was necessary) to frame its constitution, and the judgment to decide whether the constitution was any longer politically legitimate. The capacities requisite to such political empowerment had, in Locke's view, been stunted by the same kinds of sectarian tyrannies he analyzed in his argument for religious toleration. The political power of dominant religious groups had for millennia stultified the reasonable exercise of people's religious and ethical judgment, laying the intellectually and morally corrupt foundations of an unjust edifice of entrenched hierarchy and privilege (for example, absolute monarchy) whose power depended on the unjust disempowerment of others. The brilliance of Locke as a democratic political theorist was his deepening of this insight into a general view of the corruptions of political power and the corresponding need to rethink political legitimacy in ways that would politically constrain such power consistent with our inalienable human rights.

If Locke's theory of religious toleration addressed a history of the abusive uses of political power that undermined the intellectual and moral foundations of the exercise of the inalienable right of conscience, his political theory engaged the more general injustice of the abusive uses of political power to undermine the foundations for the exercise of inalienable rights. If much traditional religious teaching was, because supported by illegitimate religious persecution, religiously bankrupt, the same could be said for traditional teaching in politics. "Learning and Religion shall be found to justify"[71] the worst political tyrannies, "and would have all Men born to, what their mean Souls fitted them for, Slavery."[72] Locke's theory of political legitimacy was thus directed at a new conception of political argument, which would as much prohibit political imposition of sectarian religious as political argument. Political power must be justified in a way that does justice to persons who have inalienable human rights, persons understood to have dignity, that is, reasonable powers of thought, deliberation, and action, and capable and worthy of governing their lives accordingly.

Religious persecution was, for Locke, a kind of paradigm of political illegitimacy because it subverted our very capacities for thinking reasonably about essential issues of a well-lived life by the political imposition of an irrationalism that read all issues of religious truth through the

---

71. Locke, *The Second Treatise*, p. 345 (sec. 92).
72. Ibid., p. 444 (sec. 239).

Manichean lens of fixed sectarian convictions. The argument for toleration ruled out such a use of political power because such power subverted the inalienable right to conscience, undermining the intellectual and moral foundation for reasonable forms of public discussion and deliberation not hostage to fixed sectarian commitments. Locke thought of the ultimate questions of political legitimacy (including the right to revolt) as addressed to the conscience of each and every person, and the subversion of the integrity of conscience was thus, for him, an irrationalist attack on political legitimacy itself. Locke's political theory of legitimacy sought to define an alternative conception of free public reason—accessible to all, free of factionalized sectarian distortion, justifying political demands to the reasonable capacities of each and every person, whose inalienable rights to exercise those capacities were immune from political compromise or bargaining. If each person's capacities are to be respected, political power must be and be seen to be in service of a just impartiality rooted in respect for the equality of all persons.

The normative component of Locke's theory required that no legitimate political power could be exercised over our inalienable human rights because those rights are, by definition, subject to the power of no other person. The state could, however, play a normatively justifiable role if it assisted in or promoted equal respect for our rights, including the security of our right to conscience, our right to life, and so forth. In fact, in the absence of organized political power, Locke argued that each person or the persons associated with them (family, clans) has a moral right to enforce such claims, but that our historical experience had been that such enforcement was radically unjust; persons were legislatures, prosecutors, judges, and juries in their own cases, and the distortions of self-interest, bias, and vindictiveness resulted either in inadequate or excessive punishment of the guilty or punishment of the innocent.[73] The state performs a politically legitimate role when its institutions ensure a more just distribution of such punishments and of the rights and goods such punishments protect, for such a distribution better secures our equal rights and interests as persons.

Locke was, for a seventeenth-century British political theorist, remarkable for his lack of interest in historical arguments about the ancient British Constitution[74] and for his evident hostility to the reasoning of the

---

73. See, e.g., ibid., pp. 293–94 (sec. 13).
74. See, e.g., Pocock, *The Ancient Constitution and the Feudal Law*, pp. 46, 187–88, 235–38, 348, 354–61.

common lawyers of his age.[75] His theory of political legitimacy quite clearly rested on a morally independent and objective conception of justice (including equal human rights), and political arrangements were subject to criticism on grounds of that conception. But Locke brought to his political theory an acute sense of the ways in which objective moral values had been historically corrupted (for example, the psychology of religious persecution), and he used it in defining appropriate political principles (for example, the theory of religious toleration). Locke's constitutionalism equally rested on historically informed convictions about those structures of political power more likely to secure such ends of moral and political principle and even used anthropological data to define the relevance of historical change to constitutional structures.[76] He defended institutions calling for fair representation in the legislature, for example, because he construed such a constitutional arrangement as more likely to protect people's rights to property on fair terms;[77] and his defense of an inchoate doctrine of the separation of powers expressed the judgment that, at least in the later historical stages of a society (after the introduction of money),[78] division of the powers of the legislature and the executive (in which Locke included the judicial power) would tend to secure a more impartially just distribution of punishments.[79] There is no reason to believe that Locke supposed that his own appeal to "experience...in Forms of Government"[80] was exhaustive, and—in view of his strong views about the corruption of "Learning and Religion"[81] in the assessment of these matters—he invited a kind of historical and empirical inquiry, not hostage to corrupt sectarian politics, in order better to assess these matters. Later American appeals to the best political science then available are very much in the spirit of Locke's constitutionalism, and it is not surprising that, from the more informed later American

75. See, e.g., Locke, *The Second Treatise*, p. 293 (sec. 12), where Locke compares the clarity of the natural law to "the Phansies and intricate Contrivances of Men, following contrary and hidden interests put into Words"; cf. pp. 299–300 (sec. 20). See also Locke's Fundamental Constitutions of Carolina, secs. 79 and 80, which provide that all statute laws shall be null after a century, and that no comments upon the constitutions shall be permitted; *The Works of John Locke* (London: Thomas Tegg, 1823), vol. 10, pp. 191–92.
76. For pertinent commentary, see Ashcraft, *Locke's Two Treatises of Government*, p. 145.
77. See Locke, *The Second Treatise*, pp. 378–81 (secs. 138–42).
78. See ibid., pp. 356–57 (sec. 107), 359–60 (sec. 110), 360–61 (sec. 111).
79. See ibid., pp. 382–98 (secs. 143–68). Locke separates government's powers into legislative, executive (in which he includes the judiciary), and federative (foreign policy).
80. Ibid., p. 356.
81. Ibid., p. 345 (sec. 92).

perspective, Locke's one exploit in framing a written constitution (namely, The Fundamental Constitutions of Carolina)[82] should appear, as it did to John Adams, "a signal absurdity."[83]

AMERICAN CONSTITUTIONALISM

Americans needed further to develop Lockean constitutionalism in order to grapple with their political experiences in the revolution and under the early state and federal constitutions and to articulate constructive alternatives more consistent both with respect for rights and pursuit of the public interest. American constitutionalists believed, following Locke, that much traditional wisdom rested on corrupt religious and political power that had rendered people incapable of knowing and implementing the natural rights of human nature due them in politics; and they were for this reason absorbed by what they took to be the best available political science of the age because only a more impartially rigorous reflection on political psychology and comparative institutions would enable them to bring to bear on the world-historical opportunity before them the kind of reasonable impartiality adequate to their task (in particular, a deliberative perspective free of the distortions of corrupt political traditions). In effect, such deliberation would or might enable them to design constitutional structures that were, in terms of Lockean political theory, more legitimate than any the world had yet known.[84]

Each of the three great structures of American constitutionalism (federalism, separation of powers, and judicial review) should be understood as constraints on political power in service of this normative goal. The representative structure of the federal system was thus defended by Madison[85] as a way of both focusing and channeling political power in ways likely to minimize the tendencies of group psychology to oppress outsiders both by violating their rights and failing to accord appropriate weight to their interests.[86] Separation of powers divides national power

82. See *The Works of John Locke*, 10:175–99.

83. John Adams, *A Defence*, 4:463. For pertinent commentary on Locke's proposals, see Edmund S. Morgan, *Inventing the People: The Rise of Popular Sovereignty in England and America* (New York: W. W. Norton, 1988), p. 129; Maurice Cranston, *John Locke: A Biography* (Oxford: Oxford University Press, 1985), pp. 119–20.

84. See, for extensive defense of this view of the deliberative procedures of the Founders, Richards, *Foundations of American Constitutionalism*, chaps. 2, 3, 4.

85. See The Federalist No. 10 (J. Madison).

86. See, for further discussion, Richards, *Foundations of American Constitutionalism*, pp. 107–19.

in ways understood to afford more impartial deliberation on both rights in general and their applications in particular cases.[87] And judicial review immunizes from political power the violations of inalienable human rights that are, on Lockean grounds, always and in principle politically illegitimate.[88]

The most innovative feature of American constitutionalism is the conception of constitutional argument (that is, the justification and interpretation of these structures) as, in principle, quite distinct from argument in ordinary politics. Locke had, as we have seen, distinguished political legitimacy into three stages: unanimous consent to government, majority rule in the design of government, and ordinary politics within government (which might or might not include majority rule). The effect of that view would be to elide the distinction between constitutional and ordinary politics if constitutional decision was regarded as another form of majority rule in ordinary politics. American constitutionalists had learned from painful political experience that the equation of constitutionalism with ordinary legislation led to illegitimate exercises of political power: in Jefferson's acid words, "an *electoral despotism* was not the government we fought for."[89] Accordingly, they sought ways of giving constitutional argument a kind of status that would make it clearly more legitimate than ordinary politics, and both the use of a constitutional convention and the distinctive structures of American constitutionalism (in particular, judicial review) are institutional markers of the difference. In effect, constitutional argument—both for the ratification of the Constitution and its interpretation over time—was grounded in an appeal to Locke's first stage of consent: that is, that political power under the Constitution must be understood and interpreted in the way most consistent with its reasonable justification to all as respecting their rights and advancing the common interests of all alike.[90] Constitutional argument is supreme over ordinary political argument because it is more securely founded in the requirements that any exercise of political power must satisfy, in principle, to be legitimate. To the extent the Founders' implementation of this goal was radically defective, we may understand later developments (notably, the Reconstruction amendments) as efforts to render constitutional argument more consistent with its Lockean foundations, and

87. See ibid., pp. 120–25.
88. See ibid., pp. 126–30.
89. Jefferson, *Notes on the State of Virginia*, p. 120.
90. For further defense of this point, see Richards, *Foundations of American Constitutionalism*, chaps. 3, 4.

therefore more legitimate.[91] The interpretation of American constitutionalism must satisfy these demands as well.

These demands rest, as we have seen, on a historically continuous tradition of skepticism about abuses of political power. It is important to be clear that this skepticism is not about rights or the public good, but about the ways in which the coercive power of the state has historically entrenched its claims through crushing the very capacity of persons to know, understand, or give weight to their nature as bearers of rights and interests worthy of equal concern. The tradition of American constitutionalism is thus pervasively concerned with the illegitimate political force of ideas of natural hierarchy that embed human lives in structures of inequality, submission, and servility that disable them from giving weight or effect to the discourse of human rights.

That discourse enables persons to recognize and acknowledge one another as self-originating centers of value capable of bringing their powers of rationality and reasonableness to bear on the essential issues of a valuable and ethical life. Persons have value not because of a hierarchy in which they are embedded, but because of the capacities for dignity through which they find and give a rational and reasonable structure to their personal and ethical lives. They are bearers of rights because they have the capacities to originate the claims on others central to what Price properly called self-government.

American constitutional interpretation is itself a practice that holds political power to standards of reasonable justification because such justification alone addresses citizens as bearers of rights, that is, as capable of making the claims central to reasonable self-government (for example, to the rights of religious liberty, free speech, and a private life and to deliberative public argument about proper exercises of private and public power). Political power must then be justified in terms of public reasons accessible to and available to all as beings capable of epistemic and practical rationality, that is, in terms of assessments of fact consistent with reliable and publicly understood procedures of empirical investigation and in light of Price's conception of the common or general goods that all reasonably demand in order to pursue their ends, whatever they are. The idea is not that these kinds of argument occupy the whole space of value in living (they clearly do not), but that they afford the appropriate constraints on exercises of political power that must treat all persons subject to such power as reasonable and capable of self-government.

91. For defense of this view, see ibid., chap. 7.

Failure to respect this requirement bases the exercise of political power on sectarian assessments of fact or on values not reasonably available to all and thus fails to respect the reasonable judgment, the dignity, of those who do not share these assessments.

Such sectarian assessments are not, of course, necessarily either irrational or nonrational; they may possibly be quite rational in light of the particular agent's circumstances and ends. For example, beliefs about one's ultimate religious and philosophical ends may be quite rational, but not the kind of belief that is the appropriate basis for public reason. The premises of such beliefs may involve either traditions or matters of individual personality that are not broadly accessible and reasonable to all.

Sectarian religious beliefs illustrate both these features. Such beliefs are embedded in historical traditions with their own forms of inquiry, interpretation, and praxis. People are sometimes born into or otherwise naturally attracted to such traditions and reasonably find them authoritative on some moral and other questions because of the cumulative ethical and human wisdom they have often or usually exemplified for them in their lives. The authority of such traditions for them turns on a higher-order judgment of the reasonableness of its forms of inquiry, interpretation, and praxis (for example, the ethical weight given to a certain text and the tradition of interpretation and praxis centering on the text). However, the meta-judgment of the reasonableness of that tradition for some does not extend to others, who may, from their perspective, find another system of beliefs reasonable (for example, that gives different weight to the same text, and the like, or gives weight to another ethical text, and so forth, altogether). Beliefs of such sorts, based on traditions in such fundamental disagreement about such meta-judgments, lack any common basis for public reason, for the arguments in question turn on appeals to traditions that do not reasonably appeal to all.

Religious beliefs are also often practically reasonable in William James's sense of the will to believe:[92] such beliefs, not themselves epistemically irrational, are entertained largely on the basis of practical rationality—on the basis of a sense of the values of love and providential care that thus inspirit both our personal and ethical lives.[93] Such beliefs are, as James cogently argues, practically reasonable and certainly not

92. See William James, "The Will to Believe," in *Essays on Faith and Morals* (New York: New American Library, 1974), pp. 32–62.

93. This way of understanding James's argument appears in Richards, *Toleration and the Constitution*, pp. 76–78.

unreasonable, but it does not follow that they are reasonable for everyone, let alone that they would find them reasonable. Beliefs in divine love, like beliefs in human love, are often self-validating, and their force lies in the individual personalities they move and sometimes inspire. Human personalities are, however, diverse, and, in this area there is no common measure that may be reasonable for all.

Both the existence of incommensurable traditions and the play of personality render such beliefs an inappropriate basis for public reason, for the rational judgments of a particular agent cannot be the measure of public reason for all if others cannot reasonably share the premises on which the assessment is made. The test for public reasons is not the mere existence of consensus about one or another issue, for the underlying issue of legitimacy is not the good of consensus politics but treating all persons subject to political power as bearers of rights and thus justifying power to them in terms they can find reasonable in protecting their rights and their common interests. From this perspective, the rationality of religious beliefs may be conceded to be neither idle nor nonsensical; to the contrary, such beliefs are often pivotally important in sustaining human personality in living a good and ethical life. The rationality of such beliefs, however, arises at a level of personal reflection about ultimate questions of religion and philosophy about which reasonable and free people fundamentally disagree, and such beliefs—for purposes of enforcement through politics—must be distinguished from the political level of common or general goods that all persons require, whatever their differences about these more ultimate questions.

We should be clear that these distinctions derive from the basic premises of the political and constitutional project that political power be reasonably justifiable to all as respecting both their rights and their common interests. That project is motivated by a cumulative historical tradition of the abuses of political power to deny human rights, in particular, the power of politics to crush our powers of reasonable self-government. Those abuses familiarly derive from the imposition of one set of sectarian commitments on all, which fails to give weight to the reasonable judgment of those who do not share those commitments. Accordingly, as a prophylaxis against such abuses, the constitutional project must demand that the state reasonably justify its power to all, adopting, as a constraint on state power, a measure of common or general goods that all reasonable people could accept.

It is, of course, true that people may not make such distinctions among their personal ethical beliefs, indeed, may regard their ultimate religious and philosophical commitments as more fundamental than such essentially secular discourse. Political legitimacy need take no view on the etiology or structure of ethical thought as such; it only addresses the issue of how power must be politically justified in order to be legitimate. The very oppressiveness of political power—its capacity to crush the powers essential to thinking oneself to be a bearer of rights—call for constraints on that power that require its reasonable justifiability to all on terms that all can find reasonable. The argument assumes that persons, as persons, have moral powers of epistemic and practical rationality, and that all persons, as rational, can be addressed at that level of common humanity; political power, in order to be legitimate, must be addressed at that level. Only constraining political power in this way can be adequate to a constitutional project concerned to make political breathing space for the exercise of the reasonable moral powers of free people.

Requiring that political power be justifiable in this way no more unreasonably constrains ordinary citizens than it does the state.[94] It is not an unreasonable burden on religious believers, for example, that their religious views can be politically enforced only to the extent that such enforcement can be justified on independent secular grounds (the burden of justification required will, as we shall shortly see, vary with different kinds of issues). The general requirement of secular justification imposes no genetic test for the origins of views properly politically enforced at large and is hospitable to the great range of views, whatever their origins in the minds of the believer, that can be independently justified to all in the required way. Beliefs that cannot be justified in this way cannot be enforced politically at large because they impose on others beliefs they cannot find reasonable, thus failing to treat them as morally independent reasonable agents. That is not an unreasonable limitation on religious belief, but the condition of a conception of political community that treats all as reasonable. The political enforcement at large of such highly personal views raises two intolerable risks to political legitimacy.

First, as I have just suggested, such enforcement fails to take seriously others' independent judgment on these issues and thus, in a straightforward sense, insults their capacity for reasonable self-government. Indeed, such insult—if unquestioned and unquestionable—may degrade persons from their very capacity to know, understand, and give weight to the reasonable scope of their powers of self-government. The tradition of

94. For an argument suggesting that the argument does impose unreasonable burdens on religious believers, see Kent Greenawalt, *Religious Convictions and Political Choice* (New York: Oxford University Press, 1988).

American constitutionalism is built on the view that this is a very real and not a merely apparent threat, and that constitutional principles and structures must be interpreted accordingly to guard against it.

Second, such enforcement contracts the discourse of public reason to the artificially narrow range defined by one set of sectarian commitments, excluding the equally reasonable views taken by others. Such contraction degrades public reason itself from its status as public resources of inquiry and deliberation available to all to a distortively narrow sectarian conception. The history of heresy prosecutions shows that such enforcement is as corruptive of the intellectual and moral integrity of the dominant sect as it is for outsiders to the sect, for the dominant sect is itself deprived precisely of the discourse of reasonable debate and rebuttal most necessary to its continuing vitality and vindication as a reasonable tradition.[95] Such enforcement is illegitimate from the perspective of both public and private life.

For the wider society, such enforcement undermines the resources of public rationality that are fundamental to the very project of a deliberative constitutional democracy capable of bringing to bear on public issues the full range of reasonable inquiry. That attacks the very capacity of political power to be exercised in a manner consistent with the requirements of political legitimacy, namely, that it be reasonably justifiable to all as consistent with their rights and their common interests. The structures of American constitutionalism—so designed precisely to render the exercise of democratic political power consistent with the requirements of a politics of reasonable deliberation about rights and the public good— is a hollow shell if its discourse cannot bring to bear on public issues the full range of reasonable discourse about facts and values of the collective public intelligence of its polity.

Democratic constitutionalism has, from its inception, crucially depended on a critical public opinion against which the people could reasonably test whether the state had met the requirements of political legitimacy. Those tests can neither be formulated nor applied if the discourse of public reason is not allowed its full reasonable scope; such contraction of its scope further erodes the ability of political power to be, and to be seen to be, legitimate.

Such degradation of public reason denigrates private as well as public life under democratic constitutionalism. It is one of the distinctive features

---

95. See, in general, Friedrich Heer, *The Medieval World*, trans. Janet Sondheimer (New York: Mentor, 1961).

of American constitutionalism (in contrast to classical republicanism) that it gives a prominent place to private spheres of moral independence defined by the inalienable human rights that it renders immune from political power.[96] As we earlier saw, Richard Price quite properly identified these spheres as giving political space for self-government, namely, the moral competence of persons reasonably to conduct their own personal and ethical lives. The narrowing of public reason to the measure of sectarian commitments, which we already have seen to be so corruptive of a deliberative politics about human rights and the public good, has comparable effects on the private sphere of self-government. Because constitutional government places such great weight on the moral powers of free and equal persons, it must also guarantee them the fullest measure of public reason, the indispensable resources required for the reasonable exercise of those powers of moral independence.

Political issues under American constitutionalism fall into two types: those in the domain of preference, and those of principle. The former are those issues of political bargaining and compromise in which the preferences of people for various public benefits and corresponding burdens of taxation are properly registered through the political process; the latter issues relate to guarantees of basic human rights and their elaboration to all as a matter of principle. Both sorts of issue must be conducted in light of public reason, but the latter enjoy a special status under American constitutionalism.

As we have seen, the historical enterprise of American constitutionalism has been centrally preoccupied by developing constitutional structures and principles that appropriately constrain political power to allow persons to know and claim their inalienable rights of moral independence on terms of principle. That project—from its origins in the argument for religious toleration—has placed an especially demanding burden of justification by public reason on abridgments of such fundamental rights. In effect, the state may abridge such fundamental rights not by showing that some public purpose might be advanced by such abridgment, but by showing that the abridgment is indispensable to realizing some compelling secular state purpose. This heavier burden of justification is clearly required because of the prominent place such rights occupy in the political theory of legitimacy on which American constitutionalism rests and the familiar threats to such rights posed by allowing sectarian conceptions

96. For elaboration of this point, see Richards, *Foundations of American Constitutionalism*, pp. 39–49.

of value to abridge them. When such rights are at stake, it cannot suffice to abridge them on the ground of an appeal to a tradition that no longer rests on facts and values that can be reasonably justified to all.[97]

A constitutional tradition, so preoccupied by the abuses of political power to deprive people of fundamental rights, has—in light of the Reconstruction amendments—elaborated such constitutional principles to address not only failures to accord acknowledged persons their rights on terms of principle, but the degradation of whole classes of persons (for example, races) from the status of being possible bearers of rights at all. The development and elaboration of such constitutional principles illustrates the self-critical capacity of American constitutionalism to come to terms with its own betrayals of Lockean political legitimacy (the legitimation of slavery by the 1787 Constitution)[98] and to articulate doctrines adequate to the political evils thus unleashed and fostered. Consistent with the argument developed here, such doctrinal developments are naturally understood as requiring precisely the heavier burden of justification triggered whenever our tradition identifies the political tendency and temptation to deprive people of basic human rights (in this case, the morally unreasonable degradation of people on arbitrary grounds that often offer rationalizations that are viciously circular, justifying unequal treatment on the ground of facts themselves created by the moral degradation). Deprivations of rights cannot be justified on the ground of any practice (whether sectarian belief or popular racism) that fails to rest on facts and values that can be reasonably justified to all.

A constitutional theory and practice, so rooted in skepticism about the abuses of state power, must extend to contemporary generations the same kind of skepticism, that is, the closest scrutiny of alleged grounds of "traditional morality" or "natural differences" of gender or sexual preference so often used to justify what should be under American constitutionalism unjustifiable—the appeal to traditional hierarchies of domination and servility that rest on the unreasoning and unreasonable degradation of the moral powers of free and equal people. American constitutionalism is a historically continuous community of principle precisely because it demands that political power must in each generation be tested against the requirement that power is reasonably justifiable to

---

97. For further elaboration and defense of this point, see ibid., chaps. 5, 6.

98. This was a prominent theme of the abolitionist movement, whose political morality centrally motivates the Reconstruction amendments. See, e.g., Jacobus ten Broek, *Equal under Law* (London: Collier, 1965).

all in terms of respect for their rights and common interests[99] and must therefore both be sensitive and receptive to the wider scope of reasonable justification that may be required in circumstances of the expanded scope of moral pluralism today about the diverse sources of reasonable moral argument (in precisely the same way and for the same reason that moral-sense theory expanded the scope of reasonable justification from Locke's theological ethics). An unreflective majoritarian complacency about the traditional scope of human rights cannot be the measure of these demands; it may not reflect enduring wisdom but rather be a symptom of a constitutionally decadent public opinion that does not hold itself to a fair-minded and reasonable interpretation today of what rights people have.

We often think of the judiciary—with its power of judicial review—as holding public opinion to the demands of such arguments of principle. But the judiciary (like the legislature or executive) may commit the same blundering errors in the understanding and elaboration of enduring constitutional principles.[100] In an ultimate sense, American constitutionalism is the responsibility of the American people. The moral and intellectual heritage of the American people is that they have—more than any other civilized people—the cultural resources to be a community of principle, and they accordingly bear the intellectual and moral responsibility to find the judiciary (or legislature or executive) wanting when it fails to give the more reasonable and therefore more principled elaboration of the great principles of American constitutionalism. Undertaking that task, with all the moral and intellectual powers one has, not only corrects grave interpretive mistake but generates in the American people the active dignity of a people worthy of rational freedom: a people for whom the condition of legitimate political power is its accountability to the essential project of American constitutionalism, viz., to extend to all persons, no matter how despised, the inalienable rights to which all persons have a claim of principle. In short, constitutional argument—conducted at the level of historical perspective and moral and intellectual depth it requires—makes us the community of principle we have it in our grasp to be. There is an honor few peoples can even imagine, let alone seize.

American constitutionalism is for this reason both a highly traditional and highly progressive tradition of human rights: it both reflects and

99. For elaboration of this idea, see Richards, *Foundations of American Constitutionalism*, chap. 4.

100. See, e.g., ibid., chap. 6 (criticizing on such grounds the failure of the Supreme Court to extend the constitutional right to privacy to consensual homosexual relations).

stimulates the best and most reasonable public argument about issues of human rights and the public good and absorbs such argument into its conception of the proper interpretive scope of traditional structures and principles. Interpretive argument over how constitutional principles apply in contemporary circumstances inevitably ascribes to those principles the level of abstractness that allows them to be justified today in the required way, and absorbs into such interpretation the most reasonable contemporary understanding of the facts and values that are relevant to that kind of justification.[101]

These features of American interpretive practice constitute the American people as what I have called a community of principle. The intellectual and moral nerve of constitutional argument is the aspiration that political power be legitimate only when it can be reasonably justified to all as consistent with their human rights and their common interests. Reasonable arguments of principle are a requirement of the legitimacy of such constitutional argument because they require that any argument of basic human rights be extended to all to the full measure of its reasonable justification in contemporary circumstances. Constitutional argument thus addresses itself to the powers of reason of each person subject to political power, and, in so doing, is often itself the very condition of their recognizing and acknowledging themselves and others as worthy of the equal dignity to be accorded moral personality in a community of free and equal people.

101. See, for further argument along these lines, ibid., chap. 4.

5

Dignity, Slavery, and
The Thirteenth Amendment

BERNARD R. BOXILL

Several straightforward and conclusive arguments can be brought against slavery. Slavery is unjust; it unfairly restricts the liberty of the slaves; and it transgresses against their rights. It can also be demonstrated that slavery is exploitive; that it is usually cruel; that it is offensive to, and destructive of, the self-respect of the slaves; and that it tends to undermine their self-esteem, self-confidence, and self-reliance. And the evils of slavery do not fall only on the slaves. With the possible exception of the slavery of ancient Greece, slavery corrupts the slaveholders. It makes them idle, lazy, cruel, supercilious, and frivolous. Finally, as if all this were not enough, economists tell us that slavery is in most circumstances inefficient and wasteful as an economic system.

Although I endorse all these indictments of slavery, I want to explore another one here. This is not because I believe that we need another argument in order to condemn slavery. The case against slavery is clearly overdetermined. But, an examination of this further argument may help us to acquire a deeper understanding of an important moral idea—the idea of human dignity. The argument rests on the intuition that in some important sense slavery mocks the human dignity of slaves.

We know some general things about the idea of human dignity. It

I thank Jan Boxill, Bruce Silver, and the editors for reading and commenting on the manuscript, and Thomas Hill, Jr., and Lawrence Thomas for discussions on the topic over the years.

seems, for example, to be descended from the idea of dignity of social rank, and for this reason the two ideas probably have much in common. But human dignity is not the same as the dignity of social rank. The adjective *human* in "human dignity" tells us that human dignity is something persons have in virtue of their humanity, and not in virtue of their social rank. Since we are equal in our humanity, this further suggests that human dignity is something all human beings have equally and is probably related to something else human beings have equally and in virtue of their humanity—basic human rights. But this reasoning does not take us very far. It does not tell us how human dignity is related to having basic human rights, and in particular whether having human dignity is the same as having basic human rights.

Let us begin with the relation between mockery and dignity generally. Why is mockery so apt an attack on dignity? One plausible explanation is that the one claiming dignity makes certain assumptions, usually tacitly, which if true demand that one be respected and taken seriously, and mockery not only denies these assumptions but presents them as foolish, vain, and absurd. Every schoolchild knows this, almost instinctively. That is why mockery is the weapon of choice of every student who sets out to undermine a teacher's authority. And not only schoolchildren, but cartoonists, satirists, and burlesquers. They, too, understand how well mockery can not only wreck pretensions to dignity but wound dignity itself. Nor is mockery the weapon of those who cannot or dare not inflict more palpable harm. And here we may distinguish two kinds of mockery; one does its mischief by ridicule; the other by violation and contempt. In this second sense, mockery is often part of the armory of those who do inflict palpable harm. Kings have been murdered without losing their dignity as kings, and without that dignity's being called into question. But if kings are murdered contemptuously, as if they are unfit for their office, or as if the very idea of such an office is offensive to reason and to morals, if, in short, mockery is added to regicide, their dignity as kings will have been called into question. Assuming that this is correct, an exploration of the view that slavery mocks the human dignity of slaves should provide important clues to the nature of human dignity.

What does it mean, then, to say that slavery mocks the human dignity of slaves? Supposing that human dignity is related to having human rights, it may seem to mean simply that slavery violates the human rights of slaves. But this cannot be the whole story, for as our previous discussion strongly suggests, not every violation of the rights connected to an office necessarily mocks the dignity of that office. Though violation may be an apt vehicle for mockery, mockery goes beyond mere violation and expresses contempt and derision for what it violates. If, then, slavery mocks the human dignity of slaves, it must do so not simply because it violates their human rights, but because it violates those rights contemptuously, and scornfully, as if what it is alleged to violate is not only sham and worthless but patently and grotesquely so, and accordingly that its supposed violation is no real violation at all. And looking back at slavery, we see that it went beyond infringing the slaves' human rights in precisely these ways. When slaveholders beat and maimed their slaves, and worked them to death, they did so with a savagery that well expressed the contempt they felt for the idea of Negro rights. And though they might have been restrained by the admonition that they were misusing their property and thus violating their interests, they would have scornfully dismissed the remonstration that they were violating their slaves' rights. Nor was this exclusively the attitude of those directly involved in slavery like the slave overseers or the slaveholders, or more generally of the crude and unlettered. It was also the attitude of a goodly portion of the literate public, at least if we can assume that their favorite writers both reflected and helped to form their attitudes. Thomas Carlyle, for example, was one of the literary and intellectual giants of Victorian England. He was a friend of Alfred Tennyson, Charles Dickens, and John Ruskin, and at one time, of J. S. Mill. But he shared the attitude of the slaveholders. Although his remarkable "Occasional Discourse on the Nigger Question" was written specifically to discount the idea of the "Rights of Negroes," Carlyle did not deign to treat this idea as worthy of considered refutation. On the contrary, he treated it as a kind of bad joke, portraying blacks as "two-legged cattle" and lazy "pumpkin eaters," recommending a return to slavery, and a liberal use of the whip.[1]

It seems then, that slavery mocks the human dignity of slaves, not because it violates their human rights, nor because having symbolic import, it denies the idea that they have such rights, but because it denies this idea as absurd, laughable, and beneath serious consideration. If this reasoning is sound, a reasonable conjecture is that human dignity involves at least the possession of human rights. But reflection suggests that we can conjecture somewhat more than this. Remember we are supposing that slavery mocked the human dignity of the slaves not only by denying that they had human rights but by denying the very notion of their having

1. Thomas Carlyle, "Occasional Discourse on the Nigger Question," in *Critical And Miscellaneous Essays in Four Volumes*, vol. 4 (Boston: Dana Estes, n,d,), pp. 213–326.

rights as absurd, laughable, and beneath serious consideration. Consequently, assuming that these denials were lies, it seems that human dignity should involve not only the possession of human rights, but that this possession be wholly appropriate, fitting, and manifest.

Contemporary philosophers seem to have overlooked or ignored the possible significance of the idea that human beings not only possess, but manifestly possess, human rights. It is, however, a part of our traditions, enshrined in the words of the Declaration of Independence: "We hold these truths to be self-evident—that all men are created equal; that they are endowed by their Creator with certain unalienable rights." And knowing the influence of Locke on the Founding Fathers, we should not be surprised to find that he, too, believed that human beings plainly possess human or natural rights. Thus, Locke often remarked that the law of nature is "evident" or "plain,"[2] which implies, of course, that natural rights are evident or plain.

The same idea is implied in a particularly suggestive way in the famous opening sentences of his "First Treatise of Government." According to Locke, "Slavery is so vile and miserable an Estate of Man" that on first reading "Filmer's *Patriarcha*" he took it to be, "as any other Treatise, which would persuade all Men that they are slaves" "for another exercise of wit,... rather than for a serious Discourse meant in earnest."[3] This passage suggests that any attempt to persuade people that they are slaves must involve a contradiction, but it suggests more than this. On finding that a discourse involves contradiction, we do not necessarily conclude that it is not serious, or not meant in earnest, or that it is only an exercise of wit. We are inclined to do so only if the contradiction is so conspicuous and outrageous that no reasonable person could possibly miss it. In such a case, since self-contradictory discourses say nothing strictly, we infer that the author of the discourse could not have composed it to be read strictly or seriously, but as an exercise of wit perhaps, or to say something indirectly. If such an inference is correct, then in the passage cited, Locke must be saying that any attempt to persuade people that they are slaves must involve so conspicuous and outrageous a contradiction that no reasonable person could possibly miss it. But what is this conspicuous and outrageous contradiction? We know that Locke argued that Filmer's attempt failed because it contradicted the fact that all persons are born free, that is, have natural rights to freedom. Assuming that this is the

2. See, e.g., John Locke, *Two Treatises of Government*, ed. Peter Laslett (Cambridge: Cambridge University Press, 1960), Book II, chap. II, sec. 4, 5, 6, 11, 12, etc.

3. Ibid., Book I, chap. I, sec. 1, p. 141.

contradiction in Filmer's discourse, we are led to conclude that Locke must be committed to affirming that any attempt to justify slavery contradicts the claim that all persons have natural rights to freedom. But he must be committed to more than this. A discourse attempting to justify slavery may contradict the claim that all persons have natural rights to freedom, but this contradiction need not be so conspicuous and outrageous that the discourse has to be put down as an exercise of wit—even if it is true that all persons have natural rights to freedom. For suppose that this claim is true, but it is not widely known or plainly true. In that case, while those conversant with its truth would be entitled to put down a discourse contradicting it as unfortunately mistaken and misguided, they would not be entitled to put it down as an exercise of wit. Consequently, since Locke supposes that such a discourse would be put down as an exercise of wit, it seems that he must be committed to claiming that persons not only have natural rights to freedom but plainly have natural rights to freedom.

But Locke's claim that no attempt to justify slavery could be taken seriously, but had to be put down as an exercise of wit, is not generally true even among those who believe that people plainly possess natural rights to freedom. Nor could Locke have supposed that it was generally true. He himself made an attempt to justify slavery. According to Locke, those who forfeited their rights to life by some act deserving death could be justifiably enslaved, and there is not the slightest reason to believe that he wrote this as an exercise of wit.[4] But if Locke's claim is not generally true, it is at least true for a special case. It is true, I contend, that no attempt to justify *black* slavery could be taken seriously, but had to be put down as an exercise of wit. At least among those who believe that persons plainly possess natural rights to freedom and life, any such attempt would founder on the fact that it could not be plausibly claimed that black slaves had forfeited, lost, or alienated their natural rights to freedom or life. Thus, philosophers who believed in natural rights but supported black slavery saw that their position was glaringly inconsistent and so shied from discussing it.

I have Locke himself especially in mind. Although Locke was, of course, the great defender of natural rights in the seventeenth century, he had significant investments in the Royal Africa Company, which dealt in the slave trade. Further, he laid down in the *Fundamental Constitution of Carolina* that every freeman "shall have absolute power and authority

4. Ibid., sec. 24, pp. 284, 285.

over his negro slave."[5] Assuming that Locke could not have simply failed
to notice this apparently gross and glaring contradiction between his
philosophy and his business activities, and given that he was a great and
resourceful philosopher, we may be reasonably led to expect to find in
his voluminous writings some sophisticated if specious attempt to resolve
it. But there is none, at least that Locke acknowledged. Peter Laslett
suggests that Locke did make an attempt. According to Laslett, "Locke
seems satisfied that the forays of the Royal Africa Company were just
wars" and that the Negroes captured had committed "some act deserving
death,"[6] basing this claim on the fact that the "Instructions to Governor
Nicholson of Virginia," which he says Locke did "so much to draft,"
regarded "negro slaves as justifiably enslaved because they were taken
in a just war, who had forfeited their lives 'by some Act that deserves
Death.' " If Laslett is correct, Locke tried to justify black slavery by
appealing to his argument that those who had committed some act deserving of death could be justifiably enslaved. But whatever we may think
of that argument, it plainly cannot be used to justify black slavery. It
assumes that not only captured Negroes, but their descendants born in
slavery, had forfeited their lives by some act that deserves death. This is
so grotesquely self-contradictory that, on good Lockean grounds, we
should dismiss it as not to be taken seriously or as if meant in earnest,
but only as an exercise of wit.

It will be objected that the above argument shows that attempts to
justify black slavery will be put down as exercises of wit only on the
assumption that people in general and blacks in particular manifestly
have natural rights to freedom and life. But, blacks do not manifestly
have natural or human rights to freedom and life. This is because no
people, black or white, manifestly have natural or human rights to anything. If Locke believed that they do, he was mistaken. The claim that
human beings have human rights is controversial. It is a claim whose
truth can be established only by argument, but many philosophers deny
that anyone has constructed any argument that establishes its truth. Even
if they are mistaken, they are not obviously mistaken. Their doubts have
to be taken seriously because although many arguments that human
beings have human rights have been constructed, those that cannot be
rejected out of hand are abstruse, difficult, and obscure. If these arguments were simple, clear, and compelling, presumably Jeremy Bentham

---

5. *The Works of John Locke* (London: Thomas Tegg, 1823), 10: 196.
6. Ibid., note to sec. 24, pp. 284, 285.

could not have dismissed the idea of natural rights as "simple nonsense." But if the arguments that human beings have human rights are abstruse, difficult, and obscure, it can hardly be the case that human beings manifestly have human rights.

I concede the force of this argument. Consequently, I must withdraw my earlier conjecture about the nature of human dignity. I conjectured that human dignity involves the claim that human beings manifestly have human rights. But as we have now seen, this claim is false.

Let us go back to the idea that slavery mocked the human dignity of the slaves. As I have suggested, this idea implies that slavery denied, as absurd, laughable, vain, and beneath serious consideration some true claim the slaves could have made about themselves, and that this claim would have won them respect had it been acknowledged. At first it seemed that this claim was that the slaves manifestly had human rights, and I therefore conjectured that it was involved in human dignity; but, as we have seen, this cannot be the case for the claim is not true. What, then, could the claim be?

I assume that white slaveholders took it for granted that their own enslavement would have been a moral outrage because they had natural rights to freedom, and that they believed that they had natural rights to freedom because they believed that they had certain qualities which entitled them to those rights. Now, as I have argued, the enslavement of blacks was so open and defiant a violation of their natural rights to freedom that it amounted to a contemptuous denial that they had these rights. Consistency therefore required that whites also contemptuously deny that blacks had the qualities whites had which entitled them to natural rights. Yet, and this is the crux of the matter, blacks as plainly possessed these qualities as whites.

This is the claim we are seeking. As I noted, because slavery contemptuously denied that blacks had natural rights to freedom, it also contemptuously denied that blacks had the qualities which entitled whites to natural rights, and therefore presented that claim as absurd, laughable, vain, and beneath serious consideration. Further, the claim that blacks possessed the qualities which entitled whites to natural rights convicts these denials of slavery as lies for it is not absurd, or beneath serious consideration, but, I trust, manifestly true. Finally, this claim would have won blacks respect had it been acknowledged, for it was the basis on which whites claimed respect for themselves. European philosophers seem to have overlooked the importance of this point, but it was not lost on Frederick Douglass. He was drawing attention to it when he affirmed

"Commonsense itself is scarcely needed to detect the absence of manhood in a monkey, or to recognize its presence in a Negro."[7] Douglass was not making a point about biology. He was emphasizing the importance of the fact that what was distinctive about human beings, and supposedly entitled them to human rights or to special consideration, was as plain in black people as in white people. As he put it in another place, the Negro is "self-evidently a man, and therefore entitled to all the rights and privileges which belong to human nature."[8]

This argument does not assume that Europeans or any human beings manifestly have natural rights. Indeed, it does not assume that Europeans or any human beings have natural rights. It allows that arguments that people have natural rights are abstruse, complex, open to challenge at every point, and very possibly invalid, and consequently that people do not manifestly have human rights, and may not even have human rights. All it assumes is that European slaveholders believed that they had natural rights, that they based this belief on the fact that they possessed certain qualities, and that black people as plainly possessed these qualities as they did.

It may be objected that arguments for natural rights were not based on claims that were plainly true of all human beings but on claims that were obscure and controversial. For example, it may be objected that certain Europeans believed that they had natural rights because they had souls, or because God gave them these rights. Taking the first suggestion, it was possible, I imagine, for Europeans to doubt sincerely that Africans had souls; after all, the soul is immaterial, and it is easy to doubt the existence of the immaterial. But the consequences of the immateriality of souls cut both ways. If it was possible to doubt that Africans had souls because the soul is immaterial, it was for exactly the same reason equally possible to doubt that Europeans had souls. Black souls and white souls are, I conjecture, equally immaterial. Consequently, either Europeans did not believe they had natural rights because they believed they had souls, or else they had no less reason to believe that Africans had natural rights than to believe that they themselves had natural rights. And in any case, however it might have been with their very first contacts with Africans, Europeans did not for long doubt that Africans had souls.

7. Frederick Douglass, "The Claims of the Negro Ethnologically Considered," in Howard Brotz, ed., *Negro Social and Political Thought, 1850–1920: Representative Texts* (New York: Basic Books, 1966), p. 228.
8. Frederick Douglass, "Prejudice Against Color," in *The Life and Writings of Frederick Douglass*, ed. Philip Foner (New York: International Publishers, 1975), 2: 130.

Almost immediately they realized that despite the perhaps initially startling differences in physical appearance between themselves and Africans,
the latter clearly possessed the very same qualities in virtue of which they
attributed invisible and immaterial souls to themselves, and consequently
that reason demanded that they concede that Africans, too, had souls.
Very similar comments apply to the objection that Europeans believed
that natural rights were gifts from God. Whatever the merits of that idea,
since blacks manifestly possess all the qualities that make it seem fitting
and appropriate that whites have natural rights, there is clearly no merit
in the claim that God gave natural rights to whites but not to blacks.

Further, the most respectable arguments for natural rights of the period
were based not on obscure or controversial claims, but on plain indis-
putable facts about human beings. I appeal again to John Locke. According to Locke, nothing is "more evident, than that Creatures of the
same species and rank promiscuously born to all the same advantages
of Nature, and the use of the same faculties, should also be equal one
amongst another without Subordination or Subjection."⁹ Locke's conclusion in this passage, viz. that all human beings "should be equal one
amongst another without Subordination or Subjection," clearly implies
that all human beings have natural rights to freedom. But Locke does
not base this conclusion on any esoteric claim about human beings, but
on the plain fact that all human beings are of the "same species" and
have the "same advantages" and the "same faculties." And as if to make
the esoteric basis of his argument for natural rights even clearer, he
continued with an appeal to the authority of the "judicious Hooker."
"This equality of Men by Nature," Locke observes, "the judicious
Hooker looks upon as so evident in it self, and beyond all question, that
he makes it the Foundation of that Obligation to mutual Love amongst
Men, on which he Builds the Duties they owe one another, and from
whence he derives the great Maxims of Justice and Charity."¹⁰ In this
passage the basis of natural rights is unambiguously stated to be the self-
evident natural equality of human beings. Assuming that Locke cites
Hooker as corroborating his view, this leaves no doubt as to his position.

If these considerations are sound, people who supported black slavery
and believed that they themselves had natural or human rights denied
the self-evident natural equality, or what I shall call the manifest and
equal humanity, of blacks. This manifest and equal humanity includes
the use of reason, the capacity for speech and for experiencing happiness

9. *Two Treatises of Government*, Book II, chap. II, sec. 4.
10. Ibid.

and unhappiness, the liability to feel pain, the ability to see incongruity and to laugh, the sense of justice and of moral outrage, of self-esteem and self-respect, and the ability to know right from wrong which Europeans possessed, and which they thought justified their claims to natural rights to freedom, and made it utterly wrong that Europeans be enslaved. But those involved in slavery would have denied the plain fact that blacks possessed these qualities, even if they did not believe in natural or human rights. At least, this is true if they would have thought that it would be wrong for them to be slaves just because their parents were slaves, or because they were of a certain race. The crux of the argument for this conclusion is the claim I have been emphasizing all along. It is that the human qualities on which these people would base their condemnation of their own enslavement were as manifest in blacks as in themselves. This follows from the more general claim, which I cannot defend here, but which I think needs little defense, that the ultimate ground of every argument that people deserve or are entitled to any moral consideration of any sort is, at least in part, the plain facts of their humanity that I listed above. I am not denying here what has come to be known as "Hume's law," that moral judgments cannot be validly deduced from purely factual claims. I admit that any valid deduction of a moral judgment must have a moral claim among its premises. What I am insisting on is that such a deduction must also have some factual claims among its premises, and that if the moral judgment deduced is some claim to basic consideration, the factual claim among the premises will be as true about black people as about white people.

If I am right about this, no plausible case could be mounted for black slavery; indeed, if I am right, any attempt to mount a case for black slavery would involve so blatant a contradiction that in the words of Locke it would have to be put down as an "exercise of wit." Such a conclusion may seem too sweeping. Certain great philosophers argued that blacks were intellectually inferior to whites. Could their arguments be used to mount a plausible even if ultimately unsound case for black slavery? Consider, first, these arguments, if indeed we can to refer to the careless claims they recklessly strung together as arguments. David Hume's was flippant. His conclusion that "negroes" were "naturally inferior" to whites was based on a careless glance at world history, and he cavalierly dismissed counterexamples to it.[11] Kant's was worse. Kant probably never saw a black person in his life, but he confidently declared

---

11. David Hume, "National Characters," in *Essays* (London: Routledge, n.d.), p. 152, n. 1.

that "the Negroes of Africa have by nature no feelings that rise above the trifling" and, relying on the authority of Hume, concluded that "the difference between these two race of man" (Negroes and whites) "appears to be as great in regard to mental capacities as in color."[12] But even if these arguments for the intellectual inferiority of blacks were sound or even well considered, they could not have been used to justify black slavery. Thomas Jefferson, who knew far more about blacks than either Hume or Kant, was clear about this. Jefferson expressed the "suspicion" that blacks were "inferior to the whites in the endowments of both body and mind." He found that, compared with whites, blacks were "in reason much inferior, as I think one could scarcely be found capable of tracing and comprehending the investigations of Euclid."[13] But though this conclusion led him to question the wisdom of emancipation, this was not because he believed that black inferiority justified black slavery, but because he believed black inferiority would make the emancipated slaves a burden on the society. And it did not take a Jefferson to see that black inferiority did not justify black slavery. Everyone saw this. If black inferiority justified black slavery, then white inferiority justified white slavery. But Europeans were no longer prepared to accept such an idea.

It is for these reasons that although many notable European philosophers of the period supported, or failed to oppose, black slavery and—if we can judge from their passing remarks—were also very likely racists, none seriously endeavored to justify black slavery. Such an endeavor would have been doomed to obvious self-contradiction. Lesser lights did concoct arguments for black slavery, but these arguments were ludicrously bad. Montesquieu's parody of these arguments accurately estimates their intellectual weight. Europeans have a right to enslave blacks, Montesquieu laughs, because "these creatures are all over black, and with such a flat nose that they can scarcely be pitied" and "prefer a glass necklace to that gold which polite nations so highly value."[14]

There is, however, an anomaly. With apparently great seriousness, Aristotle constructed elaborate arguments for ancient slavery. What was it about black slavery that prevented modern philosophers from following his lead? Was black slavery more obviously wrong than ancient slavery?

12. Immanuel Kant, *Considerations of the Feelings of the Beautiful and the Sublime* (Berkeley: University of California Press, 1960), pp. 110, 111.
13. Thomas Jefferson, "Notes on the State of Virginia," Query XIV, in *Writings* (New York: Library of America, 1984), pp. 266, 270.
14. Baron de Montesquieu, *The Spirit of the Laws*, trans. Thomas Nugent (New York: Hafner Publishing, 1965), pp. 238, 239.

I do not see how the latter question can be answered in the affirmative. Insofar as ancient slavery supposed that people could be born into slavery, or that people could be enslaved just because they were of a certain race or nationality, it was as self-evidently unjustifiable as black slavery. If this reasoning is sound, then Aristotle's arguments for slavery should be as transparently bad as the arguments for black slavery Montesquieu parodied, but this does not seem to be the case. I do not mean that Aristotle's arguments are persuasive or even plausible! They are embarrassingly and uncharacteristically bad, involving Aristotle in painfully obvious contradictions, as for example, where he both denies and affirms the possibility of friendship between master and slave. Still, they do not have the ludicrous quality of arguments for black slavery. Why is this so? Besides the obvious fact that Aristotle wrote when slavery was widely accepted, whereas black slavery emerged when the world was turning against slavery, a considerable part of the answer to this question lies in the physical differences between Europeans and Africans. In Black slavery, where the slaves differed from their masters in manners and conspicuously so in physical appearance, elaborate efforts at justification proved unnecessary. Although the physical differences were superficial—literally skin deep—they were striking enough to be made the basis of an unreasoning prejudice and transparently bad arguments sufficed to distract the slaveholders from their monstrous contradictions. On the other hand, whereas in Aristotle's time, slaveholder and slave tend to be more similar in manner, custom, and especially physical appearance, the slaveholders, or their ideologues, are compelled to resort to elaborate argument to prevent themselves from acknowledging the plain truths they are committed to denying.

Apparently, what is self-evidently the case need not always be acknowledged, and people adopt a variety of strategies to help them to ignore, or to choose not to see and acknowledge, the plain contradictions that the clash between their behavior and their principles often commits them to. There is nothing surprising about the use of such strategies. The concept of self-evidence allows that people can fail to see what is self-evident, though it supposes that they are normally culpable for such failures. This is how Locke used that concept. Although, as we have seen, he maintains in the "Second Treatise" that the Law of Nature is "plain and intelligible to all rational creatures," he also allows that people may be "ignorant for want of study of it."[15] And in his *Questions Concerning*

15. *Two Treatises of Government*, Book II, chap. IX, sec. 124.

the Law of Nature, he suggests that this ignorance is always to some extent deliberate, and culpable. Thus, after insisting that "reason is granted to all by nature" and that "there exists a law of nature knowable by reason," he maintains that "it does not follow necessarily from this that it is known to each and all, for some make no use of this light, but love the darkness and would not be willing to reveal themselves to themselves."[16]

Now Locke was, of course, explaining how people can manage to avoid acknowledging self-evident principles of reason, while the claim I am urging here is that the slaveholders avoided acknowledging the plain fact that blacks possessed the same humanity as whites. But his observation applies to the latter case, too. People employ various strategies to avoid acknowledging plain facts. In the case of the modern slaveholders, the plain humanity of blacks had to be denied, but the pretentious and specious arguments of Aristotle were not a feasible way to do this. The times ruled this out as a strategy. As Douglass observed, but he was right only for the modern period, "Slavery cannot endure discussion."[17] This left mockery, and in both of its forms. Thus, on the one hand, there was contemptuous, scornful violation, the denial of a plain fact by rejecting it as beneath consideration. And on the other hand, there was the vulgar ridicule of Carlyle.

Slavery then told the blatant lie that Africans did not possess the very features Europeans possessed and in virtue of which they claimed moral immunity to slavery. That is, slavery openly lied when the truth was plain for everyone to see. Now, it is bad enough when ordinary people openly contradict themselves, and knowingly deny the plain truth. We find this disconcerting and bewildering, for contradictions say nothing, and we must therefore wonder what the self-contradictor is up to. But the "murder of the truth"[18] we are now considering was committed by those who were powerful, and able to enslave and abuse those they slandered and libeled. Should the slaves have engaged their masters in discussion? Their masters would not have listened to them because doing so would have conceded that the slaves were human, and in any case the masters were deaf to argument. Their embracement of contradiction proved this. At

---

16. John Locke, *Questions Concerning the Law of Nature* (Ithaca: Cornell University Press, 1990), p. 109.

17. Frederick Douglass, "The Folly of Our Opponents," in *The Life and Writings of Frederick Douglass*, 1: 115.

18. The phrase, which comes from Camus, is cited by Joel Feinberg in "Non-Comparative Justice," in *Rights, Justice, and the Bounds of Liberty* (Princeton: Princeton University Press, 1980), p. 293.

best, the slaves could only futilely point to the obvious facts their masters perversely choose to deny, knowing ahead of time that this is futile. Faced with an anti-Semitism impervious to argument, Shylock, we may recall, could ask only rhetorical questions, "Hath not a Jew eyes? Hath not a Jew organs, dimensions, senses, affections, passions?" to point to the humanity that he plainly shared with his persecutors, but that they seemed to deny. What were the slaves to think? That their masters were incredibly immoral and even irrational? Although this was in fact the case, it was not altogether easy to believe because the masters ruled. Should the slaves have believed, then, that they were not manifestly equal in their humanity to their masters?

Even if the slaves never abandoned the well-founded conviction that their humanity was as plain as that of their masters, slavery certainly mocked that conviction by its scornful and contemptuous rejection of the very idea that it had to justify itself. And this mockery continued as long as slavery lasted, and was of a scale and depth sufficient to shake, perhaps, the slaves' confidence in their manifest equal humanity. For slavery was not one of those intermittent violations that we can learn to live with without losing faith in what we think we are. It was a pervasive violation that at every moment of the slaves' lives blared out the brazen lie that they did not as plainly as their masters share in that humanity that is the ultimate foundation of all moral claims. Frederick Douglass recalled that as a child he kept asking himself, "Why am I a slave?" and "Why are some people slaves and others masters?" and that he was perplexed and troubled by the questions, and dissatisfied by the answers he was given. If what I have been saying is true, he could reasonably have felt nothing else. Now, Douglass never gave up trying to make sense of things, and he eventually found the sobering answers to his questions; but I do not doubt that some, perhaps many slaves, less capable or fortunate than Douglass may have ceased to believe in the plain evidence of their eyes and escaped thereby into insanity.

Now, I started with the intuition that slavery mocked the human dignity of the slaves, and I have argued that it mocked the slaves' sense that they were manifestly equal in their humanity to their masters. It is therefore a plausible conjecture that human dignity is nothing but a sense that we are as manifestly human as others, and consequently that we are entitled, without the slightest equivocation or hesitation, to any basic moral consideration they assume for themselves. And our nontheoretical ideas about dignity tend to confirm that conjecture. Notice, for example, that we associate dignity with calm, reserve, and an economy of words and gestures. These are the attributes of a person who is confident that her nature and status are clear, and consequently that she does not have to prove anything. On the other hand, we associate frenzy, futile argument, preening, and pointless self-assertion with a loss of dignity, and these are the attributes of a person who, even if confident of his status, fears that others will overlook it. Finally, this conception of dignity enables us to understand why those with the greatest human dignity, Socrates on trial for his life, for example, or Jesus before Pontius Pilate, disdain excessive argument even when others are obviously preparing to violate their most basic rights. For what is there to argue about? After the details are established, the only relevant consideration, their equal humanity, is already clear to everyone. Nor can we suppose that their reticence is only sullenness or resignation or, even less, acquiescence in injustice, for tacitly, but unmistakably, it accuses the violators of denying the obvious truth and disgracing themselves.

I do not think that it is necessary to say much about the value of human dignity so conceived. If I am right, it is inestimable. Given that our plain humanity is the ultimate ground of every basic moral claim, the person who has human dignity will take it for granted that—without any question, hesitation, or need for the merest argument—he is entitled to every fundamental moral consideration any society assumes for its members. Anyone who doubts the value of this feeling has never had it challenged. A person who lacks it, who is made to feel that he needs to prove that he deserves the consideration all others simply assume on the basis of their plain humanity, cannot play his proper part in his society. Instead, he will spend his life trying to prove that he, too, being plainly human, deserves the same consideration as anyone else. And his frantic self-assertion, his furious efforts to force others to acknowledge freely that his manifest humanity is indeed manifest, may make him dangerous. If James Baldwin is right, Bigger Thomas, the protagonist of Richard Wright's *Native Son* who commits murder and rape, manifests this possibility. As Baldwin observes in "Everybody's Protest Novel," "the tragedy of Bigger Thomas" is that "he admits the possibility of his being subhuman and feels constrained, therefore to battle for his humanity."[19]

On my account then, human dignity not only may be affronted, insulted, and ridiculed, it can also be lost, though always at some cost to sanity. This means that the duty to respect and affirm human dignity involves definite and specific obligations. It is not enough that we treat

19. James Baldwin, *Notes of a Native Son* (New York: Bantam Books, 1972), p. 17.

others as equals. If we are to respect and affirm their human dignity, we should do so without question or hesitation, as a matter of course, and as if the alternative were unthinkable. In abolishing slavery, the Thirteenth Amendment thus abolished one frightful challenge to the human dignity of black people in America and paved the way to their full participation in the society. But other lesser, though perhaps more intractable, challenges persist, for example, racial discrimination. James Baldwin said once that the black American often cannot *believe* that white Americans are treating him the way they do. What is this refusal to believe, but reason's recoil from a blatant lie?

6

Equality and the Bill of Rights

MARTHA MINOW

Equality is not mentioned in the Bill of Rights. The Constitution awaited
the Reconstruction amendments, and most notably the equal protection
clause of the Fourteenth Amendment, for this concept to acquire explicit
attention. Nonetheless, an implicit commitment to equality imbues many
of the first ten amendments. I suggest that making sense of the Bill of
Rights depends upon recognizing this commitment. The rights announced
here are announced for all and invite challenges to political and social
practices that interfere with the equal application of those rights. Any
constitution dedicated to individual liberty and dignity for all cannot
protect these ends without pursuing this commitment to equality.

Perceiving the centrality of equality is not the standard interpretation
of the Bill of Rights. Equality as a dimension of the Bill of Rights did,
however, surface in the public eye as a fine point in legal debate during
the Senate confirmation hearings on Judge Robert Bork's unsuccessful
nomination to the Supreme Court. As someone maintaining that due
process, properly understood, creates fewer constraints than the Supreme
Court has announced, Judge Bork faced a particularly difficult question
in his attitude toward Bolling v. Sharpe.[1]

There, the Supreme Court relied on the due process clause of the Fifth

---

1. 347 U.S. 497 (1954). See Robert H. Bork, *The Tempting of America* (New York:
The Free Press, 1990), pp. 82–84.

Amendment to invalidate racial segregation in public schools of District of Columbia. The case addressed the technical difficulty of applying the decision in Brown v. Board of Education[2] to the District, which is not a state and therefore is not governed by the Fourteenth Amendment's equal protection clause. In applying the Fifth Amendment's due process guarantee to acts of the federal government to the schools of the District, the Supreme Court announced an important connection between the notions of equality and due process. The Court reasoned there that "the concepts of equal protection and due process, both stemming from our American ideal of fairness, are not mutually exclusive... discrimination may be so unjustifiable as to be violative of due process."[3] Life, liberty, and property can be so jeopardized by practices of discrimination that essential requirements of lawful process are undermined. For example, the basic ground rule of fairness—treating like cases alike—depends upon a stringent guard against discriminations based on factors irrelevant to the treatment at hand. Moreover, treating people badly on the basis of traits, such as race, beyond their control interferes with perceptions of fairness as well as equality. This is what the Court recognized in Bolling v. Sharp; the court interpreted the Fifth Amendment to reflect both historical developments that occurred long after its adoption and the struggle since the mid-nineteenth century to articulate constitutional intolerance toward racial discrimination. Like other dimensions of the Constitution, its ideals acquire meaning through continuing historical struggles over interpretation in changing times.

The basic commitment to equality is not, however, something added onto the Bill of Rights. The due process provision of the Fifth Amendment shares with the guarantees of orderly legal procedures throughout the Bill of Rights a demand for equal treatment before the law. People who are guilty as well as people who are innocent are equally assured the protections of probable cause, a warrant, and the rule against unreasonable searches and seizures under the Fourth Amendment. Race, age, sex, class, sexual orientation, or any other trait must make no difference here. Similarly, the Fifth Amendment's assurances of a grand jury for capital

---

2. 347 U.S. 347 (1954). The Fifth Amendment does not use the language of equality, but it does state that "no person shall... be deprived of life, liberty, or property, without due process of law." U.S. Const. amend. V.

3. 347 U.S., at 499. The Court has since reasoned that the due process clauses of the Fifth and Fourteenth amendments impose the same norms of equal treatment as those embedded in the equal protection clause. Buckley v. Valeo, 424 U.S. 1, 93 (1976) ("Equal protection analysis in the Fifth Amendment is the same as that under the Fourteenth Amendment").

offenses and its ban against double jeopardy apply to everyone. The Sixth Amendment's guarantees of speedy and public criminal trials, with advance notice, right to be heard, right to confront adverse witnesses, and powers to subpoena favorable witnesses apply equally to all criminal defendants.[4]

The jury guarantees of the Sixth and Seventh amendments[5] and the Fifth Amendment assurance that no "private property be taken for public use, without just compensation" each proscribe inequality in the relationships between each individual and the community. The jury system grants each litigant the opportunity to be judged by the same process afforded someone else in the same circumstances. As a process that selects as fact finders a group of individuals who are not professional judges, the jury system not only supplies a quality of fresh attention but also implicitly recognizes an equality between litigant and decision maker. The jury guarantees additionally create the opportunity for individuals to take turns in the jury box and, by rotating, extend the power to serve in judgment to an expansive group. Jury guarantees thus remind defendants and civil litigants that they are evaluated by people who are like themselves, peers situated on the same plane of worth in society. That the definition of who may serve as a juror itself has undergone considerable change demonstrates the power of equality as an evolving corrective ideal.[6] Continuing debates over what counts as a representative jury in terms of racial and gender composition establish equality as a critical tool for improving the quality of justice.[7]

Another dimension of equality as a pivotal principle governing relationships between individuals and the group appears in the Fifth Amend-

---

4. Through the idea that the Fourteenth Amendment incorporates at least some of the prior amendments, the Court has interpreted these provisions to apply to the states as well as to the federal government. Pointer v. Texas, 380 U.S. 400 (1965).

5. "In all criminal prosecutions, the accused shall enjoy the right to a speedy and public trial, by an impartial jury of the State and district wherein the crime shall have been committed," U.S. Const. amend. VI; "In suits at common law, where the value in controversy shall exceed twenty dollars, the right of a trial by jury shall be preserved," U.S. Const. amend. VII.

6. Strauder v. West Virginia, 100 U.S. 303 (1879) (equal protection violated when black defendant was convicted by a jury that barred blacks as members); Taylor v. Louisianna, 419 U.S. 522 (1975) (systematic exclusion of women from state jury duty held unconstitutional). Moreover, potential jurors cannot be excluded on racial grounds through the use of peremptory challenges. See Batson v. Kentucky, 476 U.S. 79 (1986).

7. Some would argue that the Eighth Amendment's ban against cruel and unusual punishment prohibits the death penalty where applied with disproportion to poor people and to members of racial minorities (see Furman v. Georgia, 408 U.S. 238, 314 [1972] [Marshall, J., concurring], or to defendants whose victims were white (see Randall Kennedy, "McCleskey v. Kemp: Race, Capital Punishment, and the Supreme Court," *Harvard Law Review* 101 [1988]: 1388).

ment's just compensation clause. It has often been interpreted as a guard against group exploitation of an individual in order to achieve goals asserted even in the name of principles toward general good.[8] The clause represents a demand for redistributing the costs of governmental actions between those more fortunate and those less fortunate not only in cases where the government's taking of land affects some and not others, but also in the preexisting allocation of resources.[9] Through just compensation, the government reallocates funds gathered by taxing everyone in order to spread the burden of particular collective actions. No one should be forced to bear an unequal share of public costs; community needs are to be shared equally both because this is fair and because this acknowledges the worth and capacity of each in helping to meet collective needs.

Thus far, it may seem that the commitment to equality in the Bill of Rights only takes the form of assuring every individual the same rights assured others. Sometimes, however, differences among people may mean that similar treatment produces different results. Notably, wealth differentials may make the availability of a particular right carry very different meanings, if its exercise requires expenditures that some people simply cannot afford. For this reason, it is especially significant that the Supreme Court interpreted the Sixth Amendment's pronouncement that criminal defendants shall "have the Assistance of Counsel" to yield a right to counsel in criminal proceedings, even for those who cannot afford to pay an attorney.[10] Otherwise, the right to an attorney would divide—and treat unequally—those who could pay for one and those who could not.

The Court has been less committed to establishing a right to equality through noncriminal matters in legal representation regardless of ability to pay. Yet, neither has the Court been content to conclude that the Constitution imposes no guarantee of counsel for those who cannot pay in a noncriminal setting. As a result, the Court has called for a case-by-case review assessing the need for counsel when an individual faces transfer from a state prison to a mental hospital,[11] and when an individual risks termination of parental rights.[12]

8. See Frank Michelman, "Property, Utility, and Fairness: Comments on the Ethical Foundations of 'Just Compensation' Law," *Harvard Law Review* 80 (1967): 1165.
9. See Joseph Sax, "Takings and the Police Power," *Yale Law Journal* 74 (1964): 36; Joseph Sax, "Takings, Private Property and Public Rights," *Yale Law Journal* 81 (1971): 149; Laurence Tribe, *American Constitutional Law*, 2d ed. (Mineola, N.Y.: Foundation Press, 1988), p. 607.
10. Gideon v. Wainwright, 372 U.S. 335 (1963).
11. Vitek v. Jones, 445 U.S. 480 (1980) (plurality would provide counsel for a convicted felon facing transfer from state prison to mental hospital, while Justice Powell would assure assistance but not necessarily from a lawyer).
12. Lassiter v. Dept. of Soc. Services, 452 U.S. 18 (1981).

Why has there been this ambivalence about the meaning of equality in the provision of legal representation beyond the criminal context? Surely a basic reason is the Court's reluctance to issue a ruling that will require the expenditures of moneys to hire attorneys, moneys the courts themselves do not command. But given the requirement of court-appointed counsel in criminal cases, where requested by the defendant, this concern is clearly one of degree, not kind.

The Court similarly has been hesitant to treat access to court as a basic right that must be distributed equally. The Supreme Court rejected the claim that a statutory fee limitation for attorneys representing veterans violated the First Amendment by curtailing individual rights to pay attorneys, even while admitting that this claim would produce a wider pool of talent.[13] Nor has the Court been willing to treat a minimum filing fee for bankruptcy as an impermissible monetary barrier to litigants seeking access to court.[14] Still, some building blocks for a constitutional right of equal litigation opportunity do appear in the Court's decisions. A state may not restrict access to divorce litigation on the basis of litigants' ability to pay court fees and costs;[15] nor may a state structure its criminal appeals process to discriminate on the basis of poverty or ability to pay for the appellate stages.[16]

Perhaps the Court's failure to pursue equality more fully in elaborating the rights to counsel and to judicial access in noncriminal matters reflects a concern that recognizing differences between people in order to assure equality would require so much redistribution as to threaten basic freedoms. If the price of equal access to court and free legal counsel for those who cannot afford to pay is a substantial increase in taxes, shifting costs to people who are not seeking to use the courts or hire counsel at public expense, then some people may object that their own freedoms and choices are curtailed. A tension between freedom and equality is often treated as the reason for limiting equality.

In other contexts within the Bill of Rights, however, the Supreme Court has addressed potential tensions between freedom and equality, and over time it has concluded that freedom requires equality as a prerequisite. Thus, the First Amendment's religion clauses may once have seemed to

13. Walters v. National Association of Radiation Survivors, 473 U.S. 305 (1985).
14. See United States v. Kras, 409 U.S. 434 (1973).
15. Boddie v. Connecticut, 401 U.S. 371 (1971).
16. Griffin v. Illinois, 351 U.S. 12, 18 (1956). This decision applies only to the direct appellate process, not to collateral or discretionary review.

call for a strict wall between the government and religion, but the Court has increasingly articulated the need for governmental accommodation of individuals whose religious beliefs and practices collide with dominant institutional practices. In order to preserve individual freedom to exercise religion, the government must recognize these religious differences and restructure social institutions to spread the costs that the individuals would otherwise bear themselves. Thus, the Court has required states to make unemployment benefits available to individuals who become unemployed because of collisions between their religions and their employers' practices—and the result is that the larger society has to help bear the costs of those collisions.[17] Similarly, the Court has permitted public schools—and at times has required them—to accommodate individuals when the school programs interfered with religious beliefs and practices.[18]

Behind these all these rulings is a central, though again implicit, commitment to equality: members of all religions are protected by the First Amendment, not just those whose religions coincide with the rules produced by employers, state unemployment commissions, and public schools. Even the claim to treat all persons the same way cannot salvage practices that in effect impose a special burden on adherents of a given religion. The First Amendment's commitment to equality directs courts to examine the unspoken assumptions running through societal institutions. Those institutions may so reflect the needs and interests of members of majority groups that a member of a minority religion will be burdened even when treated the same as anyone else. Routine practices may not take minority practices into account. Similar treatment, such as denying unemployment benefits to someone who refused to work on Saturday, carries very different meanings for individuals whose refusal stems from observance of a religious Sabbath than it does for others whose religious Sabbath is Sunday, or who refuse Saturday work for non-religious rea-

---

17. Hobbie v. Unemployment Appeals Comm'n, 107 S. Ct. 1046 (1987); Thomas v. Review Board, 450 U.S. 7007 (1981); Sherbert v. Verner, 374 U.S. 398 (1963). But see Employment Division v. Smith, 110 S. Ct. 1595 (1990).

18. See also Wisconsin v. Yoder, 406 U.S. 205 (1972) (requiring the state to exempt Amish people from the compulsory education laws as applied to high school students); Zorach v. Clauson, 343 U.S. 306 (1952) (upholding program of released time for prayer conducted off public school premises). The state can prohibit the use of public schools for prayer, e.g., Ill. ex rel. McCollum v. Board of Education, 333 U.S. 203 (1948); Abington School Dist. v. Schempp, 374 U.S. 203 (1963), but the state cannot refuse to let religious groups use facilities that are open to other groups. See Widmar v. Vincent, 454 U.S. 263 (1981).

sons. The member of a minority religion may require the accommodation mandated in order to exercise religious freedoms equally enjoyed by members of the majority. If this accommodation taxes the rest of the community to help defray the cost, such cost-sharing is justified by the commitment to equality. The burdens of religious difference are not to be borne solely by those in the minority.

Similarly, the First Amendment's protections for freedom of association advance goals of equality in free speech and assembly. Freedom of association received a boost from judicial decisions approving collective litigation efforts on behalf of racial justice.[19] Where tensions between freedom of association and equality emerge, the Court has ruled that equality must prevail. Thus, the Supreme Court has rejected formulations of free association advanced by parents who sent their children to racially segregated private academies.[20] Similarly, the Court denied claims of freedom of association preferred to shield all-male clubs from state laws against sex discrimination.[21] At the same time, equality does not command identical treatment of associations created for expressive purposes. Acknowledging the different political postures of dissident movements and majority movements, the Supreme Court has rejected governmental efforts to force disclosure of group membership where anonymity is critical to the survival of the group.[22]

Some judicial opinions, and some commentators, have expressed a powerful conception of free expression that requires equality as a key element of the First Amendment's guarantee of free speech.[23] By treating restrictions based on the content of speech as the most noxious, the Court

19. NAACP v. Button, 371 U.S. 415, 430–31 (1963).
20. Runyon v. McCrary, 427 U.S. 160 (1976).
21. Roberts v. United States Jaycees, 468 U.S. 609 (1984); Rotary International v. Rotary Club of Duarte, 107 S. Ct. 1940 (1987).
22. Talley v. California, 362 U.S. 60 (1960); NAACP v. Alabama *ex rel.* Patterson, 357 U.S. 449 (1958). See also Shelton v. Tucker, 364 U.S. 479 (1960) (invalidating a state statute requiring teachers in state-supported schools as condition of employment to file an annual list of every organization to which they belong or made contributions). The Court has not abandoned earlier decisions that allowed states to obtain the names of members of the Ku Klux Klan and Communist party, for public safety reasons: New York *ex rel.* Bryant v. Zimmerman, 278 U.S. 63 (1928); and Communist Party of the United States v. SACB, 367 U.S. 1 (1961). To reconcile these cases with those in which membership may be shielded from public disclosure, one may more usefully look to changing historical understandings and attitudes than to a considered judgment about the differences between groups. Future litigation may challenge differential treatment of groups for disclosure purposes.
23. The most comprehensive and thoughtful statement of this conception appears in Kenneth Karst, "Equality as a Central Concept in the First Amendment," *University of Chicago Law Review* 43 (1975): 20.

has demonstrated a basic commitment to treating all expression as equal. For example, a government may not forbid expression through picketing with one exception made for issues involving a labor dispute, for this exception selects for approval some expression based on its content while forbidding expression about another topic.[24] No individual or class of expression is more or less valuable as a form of expression than any other; each idea and each speaker deserve the same constitutional protection.

In practice, however, the Court has not always followed this conception. It has permitted some distinction between political and commercial speech,[25] according lesser protection for commercial speech. Moreover, the Court has permitted greater restrictions of speech that may pose harms to particular listeners or bystanders.[26]

Yet, these apparent departures from the general assertion that the government must not discriminate against any kind of speech significantly acknowledge that speech itself may discriminate against some kinds of people. Speech itself may undermine the goals of equality, and especially the goal of respect for the dignity of each individual. That protected dignity—so pervasive in the rights of due process, confrontation of witnesses in criminal prosecutions, trial by jury, and protection against cruel and unusual punishment—marks a constitutional sensitivity to degradation either committed or tolerated by the state.

Human dignity is so important that it serves not only as a foundation for many constitutional rights but also as a significant constraint on the scope of other rights. Thus, child pornography and obscenity may so degrade those depicted that it contributes to and exacerbates the mistreatment and abuse of some children and adults in the broader society. This is an argument advanced by advocates of city ordinances providing for individual claims against pornographic materials that subordinate people through the depiction of violence conjoined with sexual activity.[27] This is also an argument pursued by college and university communities regulating discriminatory harassment. College campuses began to adopt

24. Police Dept. of Chicago v. Mosley, 408 U.S. 92 (1972). See Kenneth Karst, "Justice Marshall and the First Amendment," *The Black Law Journal* 7 (1979): 26, 35–36.

25. See Lehman v. Shaker Heights, 418 U.S. 298 (1974).

26. See New York v. Ferber, 458 U.S. 747 (1982) (child pornography); Young v. American Mini Theatres, Inc. 427 U.S. 50 (1976) (permitting zoning restrictions against near-obscenity).

27. See generally Catharine MacKinnon, "Pornography, Civil Rights, and Speech," *Harvard Civil Rights–Civil Liberties Law Review* 20 (1985): 1; Cass Sunstein, "Pornography and the First Amendment," *Duke Law Journal* (1986): 589.

regulations after finding posters defaced with racist references, racially abusive jokes broadcast over a university radio station, and other acts offensive to members of racial minorities, women, homosexuals, or other historically stigmatized groups.[28]

Both the pornography ordinances and the campus regulation of discriminatory harassment can be, and have, been challenged as unjustifiable incursions on freedom of expression.[29] Yet the assertion of a constraint on free expression should be the beginning, not the end, of a First Amendment analysis. The question here, as always, is whether the constraint is justifiable. Freedom for some to express hate toward historically stigmatized groups is inconsistent with the other constitutional values, including freedom from stigma assigned by group membership. It is the most serious violation of an injunction to respect persons to permit the assignment of any person to a status of less respect or regard than anyone else, simply on the basis of traits beyond the individual's control. Such degradation can inflict psychic wounds and also impose tangible and material harms.[30] Impositions of stigma so often reflect fear of people who are different, but also fear of elements within one's self.[31] Thus, in permitting degradation, the community—as well as the legal system—degrades itself. In permitting stereotypes, the community, and the law, undermines the dignity of all persons because everyone's humanity is at stake when anyone's is denied. If freedom of speech is interpreted as a license for some to stigmatize others, then the community itself is implicated in the cause of degrading some of its members.

Is this what the Bill of Rights, taken as a whole, means to accomplish? This question, and others like it, will draw judicial attention as courts continue to consider ostensible tensions between freedom and equality.

28. See generally Mari Matsuda, "Public Response to Racist Speech: Considering the Victim's Story," *Michigan Law Review* 87 (1989): 2320.

29. See, e.g., American Bookseller Ass'n v. Hudnut, 771 F.2d 323 (7th cir. 1985), aff'd mem., 475 U.S. 1001 (1989); Doe v. University of Michigan, 721 F. Supp. 852 (E.D. Mich. 1989). Such changes, I believe, must be assessed contextually. See Martha Minow, "Adjudicating Differences: Conflicts among Feminist Lawyers," in *Conflict among Feminists*, ed. Marianne Hirsch and Evelyn Fox Keller (New York: Routledge, 1990), pp. 149–63;; Martha Minow, "Speaking and Writing against Hate," *Cardozo Law Review* 11 (1990): 1393. If threats to free expression are increasing, even well-founded restrictions may be unwise. Often, human dignity may be enhanced by more not less, discussion about degrading speech. But such degradation itself may at times impair the possibilities of *equal* expression, as when it has the effect of silencing or discrediting some speakers.

30. See Kenneth Karst, *Belonging to America: Equal Citizenship and the Constitution* (New Haven: Yale University Press, 1989), pp. 25–26.

31. See Charles Lawrence, "The Id, the Ego, and Equal Protection: Reckoning with Unconscious Racism," *Stanford Law Review* 30 (1987): 317; Martha Minow, "Justice Engendered," *Harvard Law Review* 101 (1987): 10.

The danger of governmental suppression of speech is serious enough to raise doubts about the wisdom of any rule accepting stigmatizing or degrading speech. Yet, the actual injuries to individuals and to society as a whole from expressions of hate in turn violate basic commitments to the equality and dignity of all.

The problem is not simply a conflict between the freedoms assured by the First Amendment and notions of equality present elsewhere in the constitutional tradition. The conflict arises with the recognition that the free expression guaranteed by the First Amendment is guaranteed for all; this commitment to equality represents the ground rule within which anyone's freedom is protected. The freedom of expression means freedom for all to express themselves. Analysis under the First Amendment itself requires considering whether the space occupied by hate and harassment impermissibly interferes with the freedom of each person to think and engage in expression. Ours is a constitution protecting ordered liberty, for only with some restraint can there be room for the exercise of any liberty. Consider whether harassment of someone on the basis of her sex or her race represents the kind of liberty to be protected or the kind of interference with liberty justifying restraint. Verbal teasing, abusive labeling, unwelcome sexual overtures, and pranks interfere with the victim's ability to work and to think, as well as to enjoy a sense of dignity and respect.[32] Whatever answer the courts give to particular lawsuits challenging regulations of harassment, pornography, and hate-speech, judges, lawyers, and litigants will continue to struggle over how society must share the costs of difference in order to fulfill the vision of freedom and equality embedded in the Bill of Rights. The point is not a conflict between the First Amendment and other social purposes. The tension built into the First Amendment reflects simultaneous commitments to freedom and equality, because the freedom to be protected is a freedom for everyone.

Elizabeth Cady Stanton, a feisty and tireless advocate for women's equality during the nineteenth century, joined with Susan B. Anthony and others in 1848 to write the Seneca Falls Declaration.[33] They took the Declaration of Independence as their model in enunciating a set of objections to the treatment of women by law and by society, and they launched a series of reform movements that secured equal treatment for

32. See Regina Austin, "Employer Abuse, Worker Resistance and the Tort of Intentional Infliction of Emotional Distress," *Stanford Law Review* 41 (1988): 1.

33. See Ellen Carol DuBois, *Feminism and Suffrage: The Emergence of an Independent Women's Movement in America, 1848–1869* (Ithaca: Cornell University Press, 1978).

women in laws governing contracts, property, and, ultimately, suffrage. Stanton struggled to frame arguments throughout her lifetime that could convey the meaning of equality and human dignity while acknowledging differences between men and women. Late in life she wrote that the fundamental question about equality was not whether differences between groups mattered, but whether each person could recognize how one's own solitude in the world is mirrored by the solitude of others.[34] In the face of physical difficulties, the search for identity and meaning, and the confrontation with death, each individual is at some level alone. The courage in each solitary person's encounter with life's travails deserves the acknowledgment of the community. She thus highlighted a set of paradoxes: We are equal in our very uniqueness and mutually dependent in our universal isolation. The fundamental theme of equality, thus, cannot be severed from any genuine commitment to acknowledging the freedom and dignity of the individual. Stanton's reminder about the solitude of each person can inspire continuing struggles to breathe life into the commitments to equality, freedom, and dignity in the Bill of Rights.

34. Hearing of the Woman Suffrage Association, *Hearings Before the House Committee on the Judiciary,* 47th Cong., 1st sess. (1892), pp. 3–4 (address of Elizabeth Cady Stanton, President, National Woman Suffrage Association).

7

Justice Brennan, "Human Dignity," and Constitutional Interpretation

RAOUL BERGER

The judge "is not a knight errant roaming at will in pursuit
of his own ideal of beauty or goodness."
—BENJAMIN N. CARDOZO

It has long been the practice of German scholars to celebrate the contributions of a renowned colleague by tendering him a sheaf of essays as
a *Festschrift*—festival writings. In that spirit we honor Justice William
Brennan, Jr., for his dedication to freedom. Mine is a dissonant note,
not because I do not share his generous social aspirations, but because
his approach to constitutional interpretation disquietingly substitutes his
personal predilections for the historical limits on delegated powers.
Expression of my differences may be the less constrained because he said
of those who differ with him that they "feign self-effacing deference to
specific judgments of those who forged the original social compact" that
is "arrogance cloaked as humility. It is arrogant to pretend that...we
can gauge accurately the intent of the framers."[1]

   The writer has in part drawn on an article published in *Boston College Law Review* 29
(1988): 787–801.
   1. Brennan, Address, Georgetown University, Washington, D.C., Oct. 12, 1985, reprinted in *The Great Debate Interpreting Our Written Constitution* (Washington, D.C.:
Federalist Society, 1986), p. 14. Those who may think my strictures too severe should
consider Leonard Levy's scathing indictment: "Brennan's humanistic activism runs amok
and he evinces an arrogance beyond belief.... He believes that the ban on cruel and unusual

Justice Brennan's most ringing pronouncements were made in the frame of death penalties, on the issue whether they were barred by the cruel and unusual punishments" clause of the Eighth Amendment. The "fundamental premise" of the clause, he insists, is "that even the most base criminal remains a human being possessed of some potential, at least, for human dignity." "Death," he said, "stands condemned as fatally offensive to human dignity."² He handsomely acknowledged that his "is an interpretation to which a majority of my fellow Justices [7]—not to mention it would seem, a majority of my fellow countrymen [70 percent] ...does not subscribe.... On this issue, the death penalty, I hope to embody a community striving for all, although perhaps not arrived."³ His "perhaps" is out of tune with what the *New York Times* recently noted: "Opponents of the death penalty, acknowledging the overwhelming public, political, and legal support for the death penalty, are saying that they expect it to be a long time before public attitudes can be changed."⁴ Plainly, the people do not share Justice Brennan's conception of what "human dignity" requires. He is not content merely to express a pious hope but, departing from the usual dissenters' practice of accepting a ruling, dissents in case after case,⁵ so that he would embody his own predilections in the Constitution—were he in the majority.

---

punishments embodies uniquely 'moral principles' that prevent the state from inflicting the death penalty because it irrevocably degrades 'the very essence of human dignity.' What makes this humane opinion so arrogant is that Brennan knows that the Fifth Amendment three times assumes the legitimacy of the death penalty as does the Fourteenth Amendment (no denial of life without due process). Moreover, he also understands that the majority of his countrymen and his fellow Justices disagree with his opinion, yet he holds it, he said, because he perceives their interpretation of the text 'to have departed from its essential meaning' making him 'bound, by a larger constitutional duty to the community, to expose the departure and point toward a different path.' No one has a right to veto the Constitution because his moral reasoning leads him to disagree with it in a particular case. Brennan and Thurgood Marshall corrupt the process and discredit it." Leonard Levy, *Original Intent and the Framers' Constitution* (New York: Macmillan, 1988), pp. 372–73. "The Constitution rests on a political theory of limited government that deserves public defense and judicial fidelity. It is disregard of that substantive principle that discredits Justice Brennan's brand of judicial activism." Richard Epstein, "Needed Activist Judge for Economic Rights," *Wall Street Journal*, November 14, 1985, p. 32.

2. Brennan, Address, in *The Great Debate*, p. 24; Furman v. Georgia, 408 U.S. 238, 305 (1972). Recently Judge Frank Easterbrook observed, "When we observe that the Constitution... stands for 'human dignity' but not rules, we have destroyed the basis for judicial review." Easterbrook, "Approaches to Judicial Review," in *Politics and the Constitution: The Nature of and Extent of Interpretation* (Washington, D.C.: American Studies Center, 1990), p. 29.

3. Brennan, Address, in *The Great Debate*, p. 24.

4. *New York Times*, August 19, 1985, p. A-13.

5. The "refusal by some judges to quit dissenting, long after they have failed to have

The philosopher Sidney Hook decried those "who know better what basic needs *should* be, who know not only what those needs are but what they require *better* than those who have them, or should have them."[6] The theory that governments "can identify what people would *really* want were they enlightened" was rejected by Lord Annan, then vice chancellor of the University of London, for that would justify the State "in ignoring what ordinary people say they desire or detest."[7] In the hands of a zealot such views can lead to a Robespierre, who maintained that "if Frenchmen would not be free and virtuous voluntarily, then he would force them to be free and cram virtue down their throats."[8]

It needs to be said forthrightly that Justice Brennan's view has no constitutional warrant. The words *cruel and unusual punishment* were borrowed from the English Bill of Rights of 1689. For one hundred years thereafter, a crowded catalogue of offenses—some trivial indeed—remained punishable by death, both in England and the colonies.[9] Justice Brennan himself observed "when this country was founded...the practice of punishing criminals by death was widespread and by and large acceptable to society."[10] When the Eighth Amendment added the cruel and unusual punishment clause in 1789, the companion Fifth contemplated that one could be deprived of life after a due process proceeding.[11] Justice Brennan's resort to "human dignity" would therefore nullify the Fifth Amendment's permission to employ death penalties. And the draftsmen of the Eighth Amendment enacted the Act of April 30, 1790, which

---

their way on an issue, contributes to an impression that they write on a clean slate." Thomas Lewis, in Symposium, "Constitutional Scholarship: What Next?" *Constitutional Commentary* 5 (1988): 23–24.

6. Sidney Hook, *Philosophy and Public Policy* (Carbondale: Southern Illinois University Press, 1980), pp. 28, 29.

7. "Introduction" to Isaiah Berlin, *Personal Impressions*, ed. Henry Handy (New York: Penguin, 1981), p. xvii.

8. Crane Brinton and R. L. Wolff, *A History of Civilization* (Englewood Cliffs, N.J.: Prentice-Hall, 1955), 2:115.

9. Justice Brennan notes Archdeacon William Paley's justification in 1785 of the "English 'Bloody Code' of more than 250 capital crimes." McGautha v. California, 402 U.S. 183, 281 (1971). As late as 1813 Lord Ellenborough inveighed against repeal of the death penalty for the theft of a few shillings. Furman v. Georgia, 408 U.S. 238, 246 note 9 (1972).

10. Furman v. Georgia, 408 U.S. 238, 305 (1972).

11. Sanford Levinson considers it a "devastating" fact that "both the Fifth and Fourteenth Amendments specifically acknowledge the possibility of a death penalty. They require only that due process of law be followed before a person can be deprived of life." Levinson, "Wrong but Legal?" *Nation*, February 26, 1983, p. 24849. Edward J. Erler comments on Brennan's exaltation of "human dignity" that it "flies in the face of the literal language of the Constitution itself." Symposium, supra note 5, p. 52.

made a number of offenses punishable by death,[12] thus evidencing their understanding that death penalties had not been barred.

Nothing in the history of the Fourteenth Amendment indicates an intention to abolish the states' rights to impose death penalties. The Court declared in 1885 that the amendment was not "designed to interfere with the power of the State, sometimes termed its police power, to prescribe regulations, to promote . . . good order of the people."[13] Capital punishment, Justice Brennan recognized, "has been employed throughout our history."[14] Until recent times a perfervid opponent of death penalties, Hugo Bedau, acknowledged, "An unbroken line of interpreters held it was the original understanding and intent of the Framers of the Eighth Amendment . . . to proscribe as 'cruel and unusual' only such modes of execution as compound the simple infliction of death with added cruelties,"[15] such as "burning at the stake, crucifixion."

To do Justice Brennan justice, he did not invent the "human dignity" formula; that distinction belongs to Chief Justice Earl Warren. In a loss of citizenship case he stated, "The basic concept underlying the Eighth Amendment is nothing less than the dignity of man."[16] But Warren was at pains to "put to one side the death penalty as an index of the constitutional limit on punishment. . . . [T]he death penalty has been employed throughout our history, and in a day when it is still widely accepted, it cannot be said to violate the constitutional concept of cruelty."[17] Nothing daunted, Justice Brennan invoked "human dignity" to strike down death penalties, overlooking that "all punishment affronts human dignity."[18]

English and early American law cared not a whit for "human dignity." So, Blackstone, the oracle of the common law, wrote that some punishments "fix a *lasting stigma* on the offender" by slitting the nostrils or branding the hand or cheek; other punishments "consist principally in their *ignominy* . . . such as whipping . . . the pillory, the stocks, and duck-

12. Chapter 9; 1 Stat. 115, 119.
13. Barbier v. Connolly, 113 U.S. 27, 31 (1885). For more extended discussion see Raoul Berger, *Federalism; The Founders' Design* (Norman: University of Oklahoma Press, 1987), pp. 158–63.
14. Furman v. Georgia, 408 U.S. 238, 282 (1972).
15. Hugo Bedau, *The Courts, the Constitution, and Capital Punishment* (Lexington, Mass.: Lexington Books, 1977), p. 35.
16. Trop v. Dulles, 356 U.S. 86, 100 (1958). Warren had been anticipated by Justice Felix Frankfurter in Louisiana *ex rel.* Francis v. Reisweber, 329 U.S. 459, 468 (1947).
17. Trop v. Dulles, 356 U.S. at 99.
18. Polsby, "The Death of Capital Punishment? Furman v. Georgia," *Supreme Court Review* 1972: 19.

ing stool."[19] Lord Camden, who had been chief justice of the Court of Common Pleas, referred in the course of the debates on Fox's Libel Act to the punishments that might "be inflicted . . . fine, imprisonment, loss of ears, whipping or any other *disgrace.*"[20] Such punishments were common in colonial and early American law.[21] "Ignominy" and "disgrace," not respect for "human dignity," were the earmarks of punishment.

Justice Brennan entertains an expansive view of individual rights that was not at all shared by the Founders. As Alexander Hamilton pointed out, the Constitution was "merely intended to regulate the general political interests of the nation" rather than "every species of personal and private concern."[22] Alpheus Thomas Mason justly concluded that "in the Conventions and later, states rights—not individual rights—was the real worry."[23] "The original Constitution," wrote Zecheriah Chafee, "did very little to protect human rights against the State."[24] In his enumeration of "rights" that were "secured," Hamilton listed the privilege of habeas corpus, the prohibition of bills of attainder and ex post facto laws, of titles of nobility (a threat to republicanism), and the circumscribed treason provisions.[25] When the Founders came to spell out individual rights in the Bill of Rights, the list was meager indeed. Four amendments are concerned with the criminal process, another with civil suits; the others safeguard freedom of speech and religion, the right to bear arms, and a ban on quartering soldiers in private homes.[26]

The "human rights" fashioned of late by the Court are judicial fab-

19. 4 W. Blackstone, Commentaries 377 (1765–1769).

20. Quoted by Justice Gray in Sparf & Hansen v. United States, 156 U.S. 51, 136 (1895), dissenting opinion.

21. A. M. Earle, *Curious Punishments of Bygone Days* (Irvine, Calif.: Reprint Service, 1896).

22. The Federalist No. 84, at 539 (Modern Library 1937).

23. A. T. Mason, *The States Rights Debates: Anti-Federalists and the Constitution* (New York: Oxford University Press, 1964), p. 75.

24. Zecheriah Chafee, *Three Human Rights in the Constitution of 1787* (Lawrence: University of Kansas Press, 1968), p. 90. Justice Brennan notes, "The original Document, before addition of any of the amendments, does not speak primarily of the rights of man, but of the abilities or disabilities of government." Brennan, Address, in *The Great Debate*, p. 18.

25. The Federalist No. 84, at 556.

26. Voltaire, who resided in England in 1726–1728, wrote, "The laws of England . . . have restored to every man his natural rights. . . . These rights are: full freedom of person and property; to speak to the nation though his pen; to be judged in criminal matters by a jury of free men; to be judged in any matter only according to precise laws; to profess in peace whatever religion he prefers." Quoted by Will and Ariel Durant, *The Age of Voltaire* (New York: Simon and Schuster, 1965), p. 247.

rications without constitutional warrant. For this we have the Court's own word. In the recent sodomy case, Bowers v. Hardwick, Justice White observed that despite the procedural implications of the due process clause language, the Court has read substantive restrictions into due process and recognized "rights that have little or no support in the constitutional language." The Court refused "to discover new fundamental rights embedded in the Due Process Clause," explaining that "the Court is most vulnerable and comes nearest to illegitimacy when it deals with judge-made constitutional law having little or no cognizable roots in the language or design of the Constitution." Otherwise, he stated, "the judiciary necessarily takes to itself further authority to govern the country without express constitutional authority."[27] Respect for "human dignity" clearly is spun out of thin air; it is an evangelistic exhortation rather than a constitutional mandate. And it would transform the judicial function from inquiry into what the law *is* into what a given judge considers it *should* be.

Ultimately, the judicial claim finally to say what the law *is* derives from the necessity of interpreting the Constitution. So we may begin by asking what does *interpret* mean? In 1755 Dr. Johnson's famous *Dictionary of the English Language* defined *interpret* as "To explain; to translate; to decipher . . . to expound."[28] So it remains today: the *Oxford Universal Dictionary* defines *interpret* as "To expound the meaning of . . . to elucidate; to explain."[29] To explain is not to rewrite or to formulate a new definition. Invariably the Founders discussed the judicial role in terms of "expounding" the Constitution.[30] Commenting on the exclusion of the Justices from a Council of Revision that would share the President's veto, Edward Corwin correctly concluded that the Framers acted on the principle "that the power of *making* ought to be kept distinct from that of *expounding* the law."[31] That principle was rooted in the common law, and the courts recognized it again and again. Francis Bacon cautioned judges "to remember that their office is . . . to interpret law, and not to

---

27. 106 S. Ct. 2841, 2844, 2846 (1986). For citations to activists who agree that there is no constitutional warrant for the "human rights" created by the modern Court, see Raoul Berger, "Michael Perry's Functional Justification for Judicial Activism," *University of Dayton Law Review* 8 (1983): 466.

28. 2d ed. (1755), vol. 1.

29. 3d ed. (1964).

30. For citations to "Expounding the Law," see Raoul Berger, *Congress vs. The Supreme Court* (Cambridge: Harvard University Press, 1969), p. 409.

31. Edward Corwin, *The Doctrine of Judicial Review* (Magnolia, Mass.: Peter Smith, 1963), p. 42.

make it."[32] James Wilson, second only to Madison as an architect of the Constitution, instructed a judge to "remember that his duty and his business is, not to make the law, but to interpret and apply it."[33] In Luther v. Borden, Chief Justice Taney emphasized that "it is the province of a court to expound the law, not to make it."[34] This principle lies at the heart of the separation of powers, as Chief Justice John Marshall perceived: "The difference between the departments undoubtedly is, that the legislature *makes*, the executive executes, and the judiciary *construes* the law."[35] Today jurisprudes engage in vast labors to ascertain what *interpretation* means,[36] notwithstanding that for centuries judges experienced no such difficulties. Whatever the resulting hair-splitting definition may be, one thing it plainly does not mean—"making" law. Justice Brennan's view that the cruel and unusual punishment clause outlaws death penalties as an affront to "human dignity" manifestly exemplifies judicial law "making."

Yet another instance of judicial law "making" is furnished by the one man, one vote decisions under color of the Fourteenth Amendment in which Justice Brennan participated.[37] Section 2 of the amendment reduces state representation in the House of Representatives in proportion as blacks are denied the franchise. Discriminate if you will, but at a price. Under a time-honored rule of construction, mention of this particular sanction excludes all others.[38] The legislative history leaves no doubt on this score. Senator Jacob Howard, who with Elisha Washburne "had been the only Republicans to hold out for black suffrage to the end, all the others proved willing to abandon it,"[39] said that "the second section leaves the right to regulate the elective franchise with the States, and does not meddle with that right."[40] He is confirmed by the Report of the Joint

32. Francis Bacon, *Selected Writings* (New York: Modern Library, 1955), p. 138.
33. James Wilson, *Works*, ed. Robert McCloskey (Cambridge: Harvard University Press, 1967), 2:502.
34. 48 U.S. (7 How.) 1, 41 (1849).
35. Waymen v. Southard, 23 U.S. (10 Wheat.) 1, 46 (1835), emphasis added. Chief Justice Morrison R. Waite reiterated that the Court's "province is to decide what the law is, not to declare what it should be." Minor v. Happersett, 88 U.S. (21 Wall.) 162, 178 (1874).
36. Raoul Berger, "New Theories of Interpretation: The Activist Flight from the Constitution," *Ohio State Law Journal* 1 (1986).
37. E.g., Reynolds v. Sims, 377 U.S. 533, 558 (1964).
38. T.I.M.E. v. United States, 359 U.S. 464, 471 (1959); United States v. Arredondo, 31 U.S. (6 Pet.) 691, 725 (1832).
39. M. L. Benedict, *A Compromise of Principle* (New York: Norton, 1975), p. 170; J. R. James, *The Framing of the Fourteenth Amendment* (Urbana: University of Illinois Press, 1956).
40. A. Avins, *The Reconstruction Amendments' Debates* (New York: Ben Franklin,

Committee on Reconstruction, which drafted the amendment. "It was doubtful... whether the States would consent to surrender a power they had always exercised," and therefore the committee decided to "leave the whole question with the people of each State, holding out to all the advantage of increased political power as an inducement to allow all to participate in its exercise."[41] Such reports in the legislative history of statutes carry great weight.[42] Where Justice Brennan dismisses out of hand the attempt to "gauge accurately the intent of the framers," Justice John Marshall Harlan, his distinguished colleague, declared that the one man, one vote doctrine flew "in the face of irrefutable and still unanswered history."[43] Justice Brennan explains that "recognition of the principle of 'one man, one vote' as a constitutional one redeems the promise of self governance by affirming the essential dignity of every citizen in the right to equal participation in the democratic processes,"[44] thereby nullifying the judgment expressed in the Fifteenth, Sixteenth and Twenty-Sixth amendments that federal jurisdiction over suffrage required enactment by the people, never mind the demands of "human dignity."

Brennan's derisive reference to those who "feign self-effacing deference to specific judgments" of the Framers gives short shrift to the centuries-old respect for the "original intention" of the law *makers*. The "non-originalist interpreter," wrote Walter Benn Michaels, "isn't interpreting an old text, but either writing a new one or imagining that someone else has written it."[45] The "originalist" interpreter, on the other hand, maintains that the text is to be read in light of the explanations furnished by

---

1967), p. 220. 1967). Subsequently Howard stated, "We know very well that the States retain the power, which they have always possessed, of regulating the right of suffrage in the States. It is the theory of the Constitution itself. That right has never been taken from them; no endeavor has been made to take it from them; and the theory of this whole amendment is to leave the power of regulating the suffrage with the people or Legislatures of the States, and not to assume to regulate it by any clause of the Constitution." Ibid., p. 237.

41. Ibid., p. 94.

42. Wright v. Vinton Branch, 300 U.S. 440, 463 (1936); United States v. Wrightwood Dairy, 315 U.S. 110, 125 (1942).

43. Oregon v. Mitchell, 400 U.S. 112, 202–203 (1970), dissenting in part. Activist Louis Lusky wrote that Harlan's demonstration is "irrefutable and unrefuted." Lusky, "Book Review," *Hastings Constitutional Law Quarterly* 6 (1979): 406. Michael Moore considers that difficulty of ascertaining intention is only a "problem of evidence, of verifying just what intention a person has on a given occasion. The surmountability of these problems is shown by the law of crime, torts, and contracts, where we presuppose the existence and discoverability of the real intention of the individuals all of the time." Moore, "A Natural Law Theory of Interpretation," *Southern California Law Review* 58 (1985):350.

44. Brennan, Address, in *The Great Debate*, p. 22.

45. W. B. Michaels, "Response to Perry and Simon," *Southern California Law Review* 58 (1985): 678.

the draftsmen of what they intended to accomplish. That view, wrote a nonoriginalist, Thomas Grey, "is one of great power and compelling simplicity ... deeply rooted in our history and in our shared principles of political legitimacy. It has equally deep roots in our formal constitutional law."[46]

"Interpretation" and "original intention" have long been closely allied. In the seventeenth century John Selden reduced the common-law doctrine to an aphorism: "A man's writing has but one true sense, which is that which the Author meant when he writ it."[47] This did not envisage a psychoanalytical search of his mind but rather contemporary *proof* of what he intended to accomplish.[48] That is the counsel of common sense. It is the essence of communication that a writer should be permitted to explain what his words mean;[49] the reader may not insist that he knows better than the writer what the writer means. To maintain the contrary, as Judge Frank Easterbrook observed, is to assume that "it is the readers rather than the writers who matter."[50] As long ago as the end of the thirteenth century, Chief Justice Frowicke, a fifteenth-century sage, recounted, the judges asked the "statute makers" whether "a warrantie with assetz shulde be a barre [in the Statute of Westminster] & they answered that it shulde." And so, Frowicke continued, "in our own dayes have those that *were the penners* & devisors of statutes been the grettest lighte for the expocision of statutes."[51] Such was the invariable practice

46. Thomas Grey, "Do We have an Unwritten Constitution?" *Stanford Law Review* 27 (1975): 705.
47. John Selden, *Table Talk: Being the Discourses of John Selden, Esq.* (Salem, N.H.: Ayer, 1696), p. 10.
48. Writing circa 1587, Lord Chancellor Hatton said, "When the intent is proved, that must be followed ... but whensoever there is a departure from the words to the intent that must be well proved that there was such meaning." Christopher Hatton, *A Treatise Concerning Statutes or Acts of Parliament; and the Expocision Thereof* (London: Richard Tonson, 1677), pp. 14–15.
49. John Locke understood this full well: "When a Man speaks to another, it is, that he may be understood; and the end of Speech is, that those Sounds, as Marks, may make known his *Ideas* to the Hearer. That then which Words are the Marks of, are the *Ideas* of the Speaker: Nor can any one apply them, as Marks, immediately to anything else, but the *Ideas*, that he himself hath: For this would be to make them Signs of his own Conceptions, and yet apply them to other *Ideas*; which would be to make them Signs, and not Signs of his *Ideas* at the same time; and so in effect, to have no Signification at all." John Locke, *An Essay Concerning Human Understanding*, ed. Peter H. Nidditch, (Oxford: Clarendon Press, 1975), p. 405. For this reference I am indebted to Dr. Gary McDowell.
50. Frank Easterbrook, "The Influence of Judicial Review on Constitutional Theory," in *A Workable Government?: The Constitution after 200 Years*, ed. Burke Marshall (New York: Norton, 1987) p. 173.
51. *A Discourse Upon the Expocision and Understandings of Statutes*, ed. S. Thorne (San Marino, Calif.: Huntington Library, 1942), p. 152.

across the centuries.[52] Small wonder that Chief Justice Marshall stated that he could cite from the common law "the most complete evidence that the intention is the *most sacred rule* of interpretation."[53] Writing in 1939, Jacobus TenBroek said that the Court "has insisted, with almost uninterrupted regularity, that the end of constitutional construction is the discovery of the intention of those persons who formulated the instrument."[54]

It is the current fashion to ask whether the Founders intended us to be guided by their intent. Given Marshall's view that "intention" is "the most sacred rule of interpretation," we are entitled to require, as he stated on another occasion, that "a principle never before recognized"—that is, abandonment of "intention"—"should be expressed in plain and explicit terms."[55] Not a shred of evidence that the Founders meant to depart from the long-settled practice is to be found in the constitutional history. A number of factors testify to the contrary.

1. The Framers worked against the background of common-law practices. As said by the Court, they "were born and brought up in the atmosphere of the common law and thought and spoke in its vocabulary. ... When they came to put their conclusions into the form of fundamental law ... they expressed them in terms of the common law."[56] Thus they employed habeas corpus, bills of attainder, trial by jury, treason, and the like. Madison stated in the Virginia Ratification Convention that "where a technical word was used, all the incidents belonging to it necessarily attended it."[57] In the words of Justice Joseph Story, the common law "definitions are necessarily included, as much as if they stood in the text

---

52. The "rule of reference to the intention of the legislators . . . was certainly established by the second half of the Fifteenth century"; S. Chrimes, *English Constitutional Ideas in the Fifteenth Century* (New York: American Scholar Publications, 1966), p. 293. Samuel Thorne concluded, "Actual intent . . . is controlling from Hengham's day to that of Lord Nottingham [1678]." *A Discourse*, p. 60, n. 126.

53. *John Marshall's Defense of McCulluch v Maryland*, ed. G. Gunther (Stanford, Calif.: Stanford University Press, 1969), p. 167. See also infra text accompanying note 75.

54. Jacobus TenBroek, "Use by the Supreme Court of Extrinsic Aids in Constitutional Construction: The Intent Theory of Constitutional Construction," *California Law Review* 27 (1939): 399.

55. United States v. Burr, 25 F. Cas. 55, 165 (C.C.D. Va. 1807) (No. 14,693).

56. *Ex parte* Grossman, 267 U.S. 87, 108–109 (1925). Chief Justice Marshall stated, "So far as the meaning of any terms, particularly terms of art, is completely ascertained, those by whom they are employed must be considered as employing them in that ascertained meaning." United States v. Burr, 25 F. Cas. 55, 159 (C.C.Va. 1807) (14,693). See also infra text accompanying note 81.

57. Jonathan Elliot, *Debates in the Several State Conventions on the Adoption of the Federal Constitution*, 2d ed. (New York: Ben Franklin, 1836), 3: 531.

of the Constitution."[58] That rule was obviously meant to be binding. In The Federalist No. 78 Hamilton declared, "To avoid an arbitrary discretion in the courts, it is indispensable that they should be bound by strict rules and precedents."[59] There is no reason to conclude that the Framers regarded the "common law terms" rule with more favor than the "sacred" rule of "intention." It is the nonoriginalists who have the burden of proving that the Founders gave them the privilege of jettisoning these rules of interpretation, the presuppositions they brought to the task of drafting. Against them stands Justice Story, who emphasized that the rules of construction provide a "fixed standard by which to measure its [the Constitution's] powers."[60]

2. The Framers resorted to a written constitution, said Marshall, in order to "define and limit" the power they delegated. And he asked, "To what purpose are powers limited, and to what purpose is that limitation committed to writing, if those limits may, at any time, be passed by those intended to be restrained?"[61] "Such a Constitution," Philip Kurland observed, "could only have a fixed and unchanging meaning, if it were to fulfill its function."[62] It does violence to the presupposition of a "fixed" Constitution to assume that the Framers did not intend us to be bound by their intention—that "sacred" rule.[63]

58. United States v. Smith, 18 U.S. (5 Wheat) 153, 160 (1820). When Justice Brennan remarks, "We have very little evidence of the Framers' intent in including the Cruel and Unusual Punishments Clause," Furman v. Georgia, 408 U.S. 238, 258 (1972), he overlooks the established presumption that they used the terms because they intended them to have their common-law meaning, which required no explanation. See supra, note 56; infra, text accompanying note 79.

59. (Mod. Lib. 1936), at 510. If "the sense in which the Constitution was accepted and ratified by the Nation," wrote Madison, "be not the guide in expounding it, there can be no security for a consistent and stable [government], more than for a faithful exercise of its powers." James Madison, *The Writings of James Madison*, ed. G. Hunt (New York: G.P. Putnam's Sons, 1900–1910), 9:191.

60. Joseph Story, *Commentaries on the Constitution of the United States*, sec. 899, 5th ed. (Durham, N.C.: Carolina Academic Press, 1905), p. 305.

61. Marbury v. Madison, 5 U.S. (1 Cranch) 137, 176 (1803).

62. Philip Kurland, *Watergate and the Constitution* (Chicago: University of Chicago Press, 1978), p. 7. Justice William Paterson, who had been a leading Framer, said, "The Constitution is certain and fixed. It contains the permanent will of the people." Van Horne's Lessee v. Dorrance, 2 U.S. (2 Dall.) 304, 308 (C.C.D. Pa. 1785). "The Constitution is a written instrument. As such its meaning does not alter. That which it meant when adopted it means now." South Carolina v. United States, 199 U.S. 437, 448 (1905). See also Hawke v. Smith, 253 U.S. 221, 227 (1920).

63. "In framing an instrument, which was intended to be perpetual, the presumption is strong, that every important principle introduced into it is intended to be perpetual also." Ogden v. Saunders, 25 U.S. (12 Wheat.) 210, 355 (1827), Chief Justice Marshall and Justice Story dissenting. Justice Story wrote that the Constitution "is to have a fixed, uniform, permanent construction. It should be...not dependent upon the passions or parties of

3. James Wilson urged that the Journals of the Convention be preserved because "as false suggestions may be propagated it should not be made impossible to contradict them."[64] In other words, "false" interpretations could be rebutted by resort to the intention of the Framers. George Washington, president of the Convention, cited to its Journals in 1796.[65] So, too, Abraham Baldwin, Caleb Strong, Charles Pinckney, and Pierce Butler, Framers all, referred to discussions in the Convention.[66] In the Ratification Conventions those who had been delegates to the Federal Convention were frequently called upon to explain provisions of the Constitution.[67] All of which indicates that the Founders themselves looked for guidance to the Framers. How can we conclude that they absolved us from respect for that intention?

Beyond doubt, the Framers of the Fourteenth Amendment, which in the eyes of judicial activists has come to represent the Constitution, intended us to be bound by their intention. Thus, Senator Charles Sumner, the most extreme advocate of Negro rights, stated to the Framers that if the meaning of the Constitution "in any place is open to doubt, or if words are used which have no fixed signification [for example, equal protection], we cannot err if we turn to the Framers, and their authority increases in proportion to the evidence they left on the question."[68] This was the view of the Reconstruction Congress. Rejecting an appeal by women for a statutory grant of suffrage under the Fourteenth Amendment, a unanimous Senate Judiciary Committee Report dated January 1872 stated that a "construction which would give the phrase . . . a meaning differ[ent] from the sense in which it was understood and employed by the people when they adopted the Constitution, would be as unconstitutional as a departure from the plain and express language of the Constitution."[69]

Much has been made of Madison's statement that "the only authoritative intentions were those of the people of the State as expressed

---

particular times, but the same yesterday, today, and forever." Joseph Story, *Commentaries on the Constitution*, vol. 1, sec. 426, p. 326.

64. Max Farrand, *The Records of the Federal Convention of 1787* (New Haven: Yale University Press, 1911), p. 648.

65. 5 Annals of Congress 760–761 (1796).

66. Baldwin, in Farrand, *Records*, 3: 369–70; Strong, in ibid., p. 247; Pinckney, in ibid.; Butler, in ibid, pp. 249–50.

67. For citations see Raoul Berger, "Original Intention in Historical Perspective," *George Washington Law Review* 54 (1986): 327, n. 228.

68. Cong. Globe, 39th Cong., 1st sess. (1966): 677.

69. Avins, *The Reconstruction Amendments' Debates*, p. 571.

through the Conventions which ratified the Constitution."[70] For, he explained, "as the instrument came from [the Framers] it was nothing more than the draft of a plan, nothing but a dead letter, until life and validity were breathed into it by the voice of the people, speaking through the several State Conventions."[71] But he also regarded the Framers' debates as "presumptive evidence of the general understanding at the time of the language used."[72] Even disputable presumptions "hold good until they are invalidated by proof."[73] The Ratifiers, to be sure, may be regarded as the more authoritative spokesmen where their views conflict with those of the Framers. But on important issues their views coincide, thus lending credence to those of the Framers. Most of the provisions, however, were not discussed by the Ratifiers, who were immersed in a debate about some large issues. Why should the people be shut off from the explanations their agents, the draftsmen, had made in fashioning the "limited" Constitution? The Framers also represented the people, who appointed them through the instrumentality of their representatives, the state legislatures. Certainly the Ratifiers did not consider the views of the Framers as out of bounds. To the contrary, they frequently called upon the Framers in their midst to explain some of the provisions of the Constitution.[74] Madison himself cited to the Framers.[75] As president, Jefferson pledged to read the Constitution in accordance with the "meaning to be found in the explanation of those who advocated it."[76] Very early the practice was recognized by the Supreme Court—the construction "must necessarily depend on the words of the Constitution; the meaning and intention of the *convention which framed* and proposed it for adoption and ratification to the conventions . . . in the several states . . . to which this court has always resorted in construing the Constitution."[77]

It remains to take account of Justice Brennan's view of due process; he postulates "the patent ambiguity of the terms 'due process of law—' "[78] an assumption history contradicts. From earliest times it meant the

70. Letter from Madison to M. L. Hurlbert (May 1830), reprinted in *Letters and Other Writings of James Madison* (Philadelphia: J. B. Lippencott, 1865), 4:73, 74.

71. 5 Annals of Cong. 776 (1796).

72. Cong. Globe, 39th Cong., 1st sess. (1966): 677.

73. Bouvier's Law Dictionary.

74. Supra, note 67.

75. For citations see Berger, supra note 67, at 327–28.

76. C. P. Paterson, *Constitutional Principles of Thomas Jefferson* (Salem, N.H.: Ayer, 1953), p. 70.

77. Rhode Island v. Massachusetts, 37 U.S. (12 Pet.) 657, 721 (1838)(emphasis added).

78. Brennan, "The Fourteenth Amendment," Address, New York University Law School, August 6, 1986, pp. 13–14 of mimeographed copy.

(judicial) process that is due, as Hamilton declared on the eve of the Convention: "The words 'due process' have a precise technical import, and are only applicable to the process and proceedings of the courts of justice; they can never be referred to an act of legislature."[79] Charles Curtis, an admirer of judicial revisionism, nevertheless considered that the meaning of due process of law in the Fifth Amendment "was as fixed and definite as the common law could make a phrase.... It meant a procedural due process."[80] Of due process we may say, as did Chief Justice Marshall in speaking of "treason": "It is scarcely conceivable that the term was not employed by the Framers of our Constitution in the sense which had been affixed to it by those from whom we borrowed it."[81] That was how it was understood by Hamilton.

But for a couple of "aberrational" cases,[82] that was the accepted meaning, left unchanged by the Fourteenth Amendment. John Bingham, draftsman of the amendment, said that its meaning had been settled "long ago" by the courts.[83] The phrase, Hurtado v. California stated, was used in the Fourteenth "in the same sense and with no greater extent" than in the Fifth.[84] Brennan's reliance on *Hurtado* is mistaken. There the issue was whether California could prosecute a criminal offense by an information filed by a prosecutor rather than by grand jury indictment. Noting that the Fifth provided both for due process and indictment by grand jury, whereas the latter was absent from the Fourteenth, the Court declined to read a grand jury requirement into the due process of the Fourteenth Amendment. The gratuitous dictum that judicial *procedure* was not frozen in ancient patterns was hardly an invitation to employ due process in order to control substantive *legislation*. That was a generic alteration of a later day, when the Court, to quote Justice Brennan, was "shield[ing] the excesses" of "expanding capital from governmental re-

79. *Papers of Alexander Hamilton*, ed. Harold Syrett and Jacob Cooke (New York: Columbia University Press, 1962), 4:35. Justice Story wrote that due process means "being brought in to answer... by due process of the common law. So that the clause in effect affirms the right of trial according to the process and proceedings of the common law." Story, *Commentaries on the Constitution*, vol. 2, sec. 1789.

80. Charles Curtis, "Review and Majority Rule," in *Supreme Court and Supreme Law*, ed. Edmond Cahn (Westport, Conn.: Greenwood Press, 1954), p. 177.

81. United States v. Burr, 25 F. Cas. 53, 159(C.C. Va. 1807) (No. 14,693). See also supra note 56.

82. J. Ely, *Democracy and Distrust* (Cambridge: Harvard University Press, 1980), p. 18. For detailed discussion see Raoul Berger, "The Scope of Judicial Review and Walter Murphy," *Wisconsin Law Review* (1979): 361.

83. Cong. Globe, 39th Cong., 1st sess. (1866): 1089.

84. 110 U.S. 516, 535 (1884).

straints."[85] Since then the Court has repudiated the practice, referring to "our abandonment of the use of the 'vague contours' [?] of the Due Process Clause to nullify laws which a majority of the Court believed to be economically unwise."[86] This abnegation, however, did not extend to "social" legislation, a differentiation without textual basis. Justice Hugo L. Black regarded resort to substantive due process as "no less dangerous when used to enforce the Court's views about personal rights than about economic rights."[87] As Justice Felix Frankfurter declared, the "Constitution does not give us greater veto power when dealing with one phase of liberty than another."[88] Justice Brennan notes that the Fourteenth Amendment lay "substantially dormant as a document of human freedom until at least the 1930's,"[89] so we must assume that the modern Court has drunk more deeply of the Pierian Spring than did its predecessors, notwithstanding that "constructions by contemporaries" of the Constitution carry great weight because, Justice William Johnson explained, they had "the best opportunities of informing themselves of the Framers of the Constitution, and of the sense put upon it by the people when it was adopted by them."[90]

But Justice Brennan considers that "the ultimate question must be, what do the words of the text mean in our time? For the genius of the Constitution rests not on any static meaning it might have in a world that is dead and gone, but in the adaptability of its great *principles* to cope with current problems and current needs."[91] But the "principles" were articulated in "words"; change the meaning of the "words" and you change the "principles."[92] Brennan is welcome to give words that *he* employs a new meaning, but he may not saddle the Framers with *his* meaning. In more decorous diction he affirms that the Founders "may not rule us from their graves," thus repudiating the Constitution, text and all, while he purports to speak in its name.

85. Brennan, "Fourteenth Amendment," p. 3.
86. Ferguson v. Skrupa, 372 U.S. 726, 731 (1963).
87. Griswold v. Connecticut, 381 U.S. 479, 522 (1965), dissenting opinion.
88. Board of Education v. Barnette, 319 U.S. 624, 648 (1943). Judge Learned Hand considered that "there is no constitutional basis for asserting a larger measure of judicial supervision over liberty" than over property. Learned Hand, *The Bill of Rights* (New York: Macmillan, 1962), pp. 50, 51.
89. Brennan, "The Fourteenth Amendment," p. 19.
90. Ogden v. Saunders, 25 U.S. (12 Wheat.) 213, 270, 290 (1827).
91. Brennan, Address, in *The Great Debate*, p. 17.
92. Jefferson commented that the words in a written constitution designed to limit delegated power were meant to "bind" down our delegates "from mischief by the chains of the Constitution." Elliot, *Debates in the Several State Conventions*, 4: 543.

Judicial revision of the Constitution for benign purposes is not its own justification. Addressing a judge's resort to his "individual sense of justice," Cardozo wrote, "That might result in a benevolent despotism if judges were benevolent men. It would put an end to the rule of law."[93] I would commend to Justice Brennan the words of his illustrious colleague, Justice Harlan:

> when the Court disregards the express intent and understanding of the Framers, it has invaded the realm of the political process to which the amending power was committed, and it has violated the constitutional structure which it is its highest duty to protect.[94]

93. B. N. Cardozo, *The Nature of the Judicial Process* (New Haven: Yale University Press, 1921), p. 136. Lord Mansfield stated, "Whatever doubts I may have in my own breast with respect to the policy and expedience of the law . . . I am bound to see it executed according to its meaning." Pray v. Edie, 99 Eng. Rep. 1113–14 (1786).
94. Oregon v. Mitchell, 400 U.S. 112, 203 (1970), dissenting in part.

8

The Eighth Amendment, Human Dignity, and the Death Penalty

HUGO ADAM BEDAU

"The basic concept underlying the Eighth Amendment is nothing less than the dignity of man."
—CHIEF JUSTICE EARL WARREN,
IN TROP V. DULLES (1958)

Even the vilest criminal remains a human being possessed of common human dignity."
—ASSOCIATE JUSTICE WILLIAM J. BRENNAN, JR.,
IN FURMAN V. GEORGIA (1972)

I

Human dignity is perhaps the premier value underlying the last two centuries of moral and political thought. But were we to measure its importance by the prominence accorded it in the writings of moral philosophy or in the texts and documents of constitutional law, we might well reach the opposite conclusion. Explicit reference to and reliance upon the value of human dignity as such plays no more than a minor role (with one conspicuous exception, to be noted below) in the writings of classic modern western moral theory. Similarly, human dignity also plays no explicit role in the federal Constitution and the Bill of Rights. What other conclusions can one reach when the term *human dignity* (as well as equivalent phrases and synonyms) nowhere appear in these constitutional texts and when there are no treatises (or even chapters in them) of any influence explaining the nature of human dignity and stressing its importance?

For several reasons, it is useful to notice a certain parallel between the status of human dignity in our constitutional texts and the role of two other values, autonomy and privacy, which have also become important and familiar in modern moral thinking. Autonomy and privacy, unlike human dignity, are among the values prominently analyzed and advocated in recent moral and social theory.[1] They are also values whose importance in contemporary constitutional interpretation could hardly be exaggerated.[2] Yet, like *human dignity*, the words *autonomy* and *privacy* nowhere appear in the Constitution or the Bill of Rights. The omission of explicit reference in our constitutional texts to these values has led some commentators to doubt whether any of them are recognized and protected by our fundamental law.

Conceding the absence of these terms, the constitutional interpreter can proceed in one of three main ways. The first is to conclude straightaway that since the terms nowhere appears in the texts, the values to which they refer are not recognized as such in our constitutional law. On this view, the Constitution and Bill of Rights are indifferent to human dignity, neither protecting and advancing it nor thwarting and retarding it. If human dignity is to be protected and advanced, it must be by congressional legislation, or by the sovereign states, or by private persons and their organizations—but not by the federal courts claiming to interpret our constitutional law. The silence of constitutional law leaves no alternative (of course, the Constitution could be amended to introduce explicit recognition of the value of human dignity, but that is another matter).

A second interpretative response is to argue that the values *dignity*, *autonomy*, and *privacy* name are recognized by the Constitution, albeit implicitly, because other terms and values expressly incorporated into the Constitution amount to implicit recognition of these particular values.

1. On autonomy see, e.g., John Christman, ed., *The Inner Citadel: Essays on Individual Autonomy* (New York: Oxford University Press, 1989); Gerald Dworkin, *The Theory and Practice of Autonomy* (Cambridge: Cambridge University Press, 1988); and Laurence Haworth, *Autonomy: An Essay in Philosophical Psychology* (New Haven: Yale University Press, 1986). On privacy see, e.g., Ferdinand D. Schoeman, ed., *Philosophical Dimensions of Privacy: An Anthology* (Cambridge: Cambridge University Press, 1984); J. Roland Pennock and John Chapman, eds., *Privacy: Nomos XIII* (New York: Atherton Press, 1971).

2. Roe v. Wade, 410 U.S. 113 (1972); Eisenstadt v. Baird, 405 U.S. 438 (1972); Griswold v. Connecticut, 381 U.S. 479 (1967).

On this view human dignity is inextricably if only tacitly (and perhaps elusively, obscurely) intertwined with values the Constitution plainly recognizes. If this is true, then one of the abiding tasks of the federal judiciary, as well as of the other branches, is to protect and promote human dignity just as though there were language in the Constitution and Bill of Rights expressly commanding such concern.

The third style of interpretation agrees with the first, that the terms in question do not appear in the texts, but argues that their absence creates only a presumption against constitutional protection of the values so named. Moreover, this is a rebuttable presumption, precisely as the second position implies. Whether in regard to the value of human dignity the presumption is overcome is simply a question of what we may infer from the available evidence. In this particular case, according to the third position, we must conclude that the evidence is insufficient to tell one way or the other.

One might object to the foregoing set of alternatives on the ground that it fails to take into account two centuries of congressional legislation, executive and administrative orders, as well as actions by the several states, all of which has been subjected to review and criticism by the federal courts in light of the Constitution and the Bill of Rights; all this history (so the objection goes) sheds considerable light on the role of human dignity (as well as of autonomy and privacy) in our constitutional thinking and practice. But the objection is misplaced. Whatever edification we obtain by taking these developments into account, it cannot create additional basic options. Such historical evidence can only reinforce or undermine one or more of the three basic positions already identified. It cannot by itself create additional basic options to these three.

What is true about the place of human dignity under the Constitution and the Bill of Rights in general is true with particular reference to the Eighth Amendment. The language of the amendment reads in its entirety:

> Excessive bail shall not be required, nor excessive fines imposed, nor cruel and unusual punishments inflicted.

Obviously, in this language there is no explicit reference to human dignity. Either, therefore, the amendment is indifferent to this value, or it tacitly and indirectly supports it (perhaps by expressly and directly supporting other values inextricably related to human dignity). Or we simply cannot tell anything conclusive about the status of human dignity under the Eighth Amendment.

In the ensuing discussion I intend to defend a version of the second alternative, and I propose to argue roughly as follows: Principles invariably defend values and often do so without expressly mentioning the values being defended. What is true of principles in general is true of the Eighth Amendment and the value of human dignity. The laws and practices forbidden as "cruel and unusual punishments" are punishments that violate certain values. Indeed, such punishments are forbidden *because* they are an affront to these values. We cannot make sense of the prohibition without acknowledgment of the underlying values; we cannot accept the prohibition without tacitly embracing the values it protects. The values in question are inseparably connected with human dignity. This can be seen once we analyze the essential concepts—human dignity and cruel and unusual punishment. The connection becomes more plausible once we notice other constitutional provisions in which there is unmistakable evidence of a concern to protect human dignity even though that value is nowhere explicitly mentioned.

Let us suppose a convincing line of reasoning that embodies and advances the foregoing position can be developed. What do we find when we take this argument and confront it with the practice, authorized by state and federal statutes, that a defendant convicted of a certain crime may be punished by being sentenced to death and executed—the death penalty? Elsewhere it has been argued that when one thinks about the death penalty in this nation today and evaluates it in light of all the relevant facts and moral principles, one must conclude that it is an unjustified punishment.[3] The best (if not the only) way to express this conclusion in constitutional language is to affirm the judgment that the death penalty is a cruel and unusual punishment in violation of the Eighth Amendment. Yet the role of the value of human dignity in such a judgment is obscure. One reason for this obscurity is that arguments against the death penalty mounted by philosophers not preoccupied with constitutional interpretation typically fail to allot any explicit role to human

3. On recent criticism of the death penalty by moral philosophers see, e.g., Stephen Nathanson, *An Eye for an Eye: The Morality of Punishing by Death* (Totowa, N.J.: Rowman & Littlefield, 1987); Jeffrey H. Reiman, "Justice, Civilization, and the Death Penalty: Answering van den Haag," *Philosophy and Public Affairs* 14 (1985): 115–48; Richard A. Wasserstrom, "Capital Punishment as Punishment: Theoretical Issues and Objections," *Midwest Studies in Philosophy* 3 (1982): 473–502; Jeffrie G. Murphy, *Retribution, Justice, and Therapy* (Dordrecht: Reidel, 1979), pp. 223–49; and my *Death Is Different: Studies in the Morality, Law, and Politics of Capital Punishment* (Boston: Northeastern University Press, 1987), and "How to Argue About the Death Penalty," in Michael R. Radelet, ed., *Facing the Death Penalty* (Philadelphia: Temple University Press, 1989), pp. 178–92.

dignity, relying instead on other values. Another reason is that arguments against the death penalty mounted by jurists prefer to focus solely on the explicit language of the Bill of Rights, prececent cases, and related discourse—in which, as we have noted, little or no mention is made of human dignity as such—rather than on abstract values at best tacitly expressed. So at least two questions naturally arise. First, how is explicit connection to be made between the value of human dignity and the Eighth Amendment? Second, does explicit reliance on the constitutional recognition and protection of the value of human dignity really strengthen the argument against the death penalty?

II

Let us begin by noticing that norms, including principles, are designed to guide conduct in order to secure respect for, and discourage indifference to, certain values typically held dear by those who issue, authorize, endorse, or enforce the norms. The point of normative requirements, prohibitions, and permissions is incompatible with viewing them as value-neutral imperatives. Suppose someone were to say, "Don't violate principle P—but if you do, that's all right, it doesn't matter." Unless the person who says this rejects (or is indifferent to) principle P, the utterance is essentially unintelligible. Its unintelligibility derives from the conflict between the conduct required (or forbidden) by P and the indifference expressed toward that conduct's performance by the very person who insists on P. Such a conflict presupposes the implicitly value-laden character of P.

Very well, then; norms are not value neutral. But must they expressly mention the values that they are intended to defend or protect? Let us look briefly at a few examples.

Take first an example from the Bible, the commandment "Thou shalt not kill." No one would deny that this prohibition arises from a recognition of the value of (innocent) human life; the killing prohibited is the killing of human beings, not other living things; and the kind of killing is usually understood to be confined to murder. Yet no such phrase as *human life is valuable* appears in the commandment. If an argument is needed to persuade that this commandment protects a value that it does not mention, here is one: It makes little sense to prohibit the murder of every person (as the commandment does), to treat murder as a sin against God or as a crime against the person, unless it matters whether people murder other people. Now it cannot matter unless what murder invariably destroys—the life of a person—is *valuable*. (We may ignore here the further question whether only a realist and objectivist account can make sense of such a value.) The universality of the condemnation of murder implicitly but unmistakably recognizes the universality of the value of human life.

Take as a second example language from the Bill of Rights, the portion of the Fifth Amendment that reads: "n or shall [any person] be compelled in any criminal case to be a witness against himself." No competent interpreter of the Bill of Rights would deny that this language establishes a constitutional *right* to be silent under accusation of a crime, even though the term *right* nowhere appears in the text quoted. More than that, this right has constitutional status because of the *value* of the interest it protects—the value of according finality to the accused's own judgment on whether, when testifying under oath, it is in his best interest to be silent or to give testimony against himself. But no such value is expressly mentioned at all in the language of the amendment. Nevertheless, if this value is ignored or repudiated, the purpose of the right itself is undermined; by the same token, refusal to grant the right makes the prohibition pointless.

Take finally an example from social philosophy, the maxim derived from Louis Blanc and made famous in Karl Marx's slogan: "From each according to his abilities, to each according to his needs." This slogan is generally understood to express a principle of distributive *justice*, and to assert it implies acceptance of justice as a *value*, even though the term *justice* is nowhere used in formulating the maxim. Yet it would be wrong to argue from omission of that term that the Blanquist slogan does not express, and is not intended to express, a principle of justice. Again, if argument is needed, here is one. First, the slogan can be reformulated (without loss or addition to its content) in order to make good this omission, so that it reads in revised form: "Justice requires that property and services be provided to persons according to their needs and taken from them according to their abilities." If it is objected that this reformulation begs the question, one can reply by explaining how the slogan in its original form derives whatever force it has by implicitly asserting that fairness requires placing one person's needs and another's abilities in a recriprocal relationship, and that fairness and justice are conceptually or semantically intertwined. If this, too, is unconvincing, then one might argue more elaborately to the effect that the best interpretation of Blanc's intentions in formulating this slogan is to see it as a principle or maxim of justice.[4] These tactics apart, it is clear that the point of the slogan is to advocate practices that secure certain values; in the absence of commitment to those values, asserting the slogan is pointless.

Here, then, are three different norms—different in origin, in content, and in kind—each of which protects a value it does not expressly mention. (For those with a taste for semantics, this is but a special case of the general truth that it is not necessary for a sentence to *use* a given term T in order to *mention* what T refers to.) What has been illustrated with these three examples could be confirmed in countless other cases. There is no general objection, therefore, to the view that the Eighth Amendment, through its language prohibiting "cruel and unusual punishments," aims to protect a value or values it does not mention, and that human dignity is, or is one of, these values. (Notice that I have not tried to provide a general criterion to enable us to tell in any given case what particular value[s] a given norm is intended to protect when the norm makes no explicit mention of the relevant value[s].)

III

We are now in a position to face the question whether in fact there is good reason to agree with Chief Justice Earl Warren in Trop v. Dulles when he claimed (recall the epigraph) that the value of human dignity is centrally relevant to a correct understanding of the constitutional prohibition against cruel and unusual punishments. Is it really true that we must have eventual recourse to this value in order to make sense of the constitutional prohibition? Or is it possible that our Constitution prohibits cruel and unusual punishments as a matter of fundamental rights but without regard to whether doing so protects or respects human dignity? Could one truly declare, for example, "I don't care a fig about human dignity, but of course I respect the constitutional prohibition against cruel and unusual punishments"? Could it be true to say, as some in effect have, "The prohibition of cruel and unusual punishments certainly protects some fundamental albeit implicit values, but human dignity isn't one of them—talk about human dignity, at least in connection with the eighth amendment, is empty rhetoric and arrant nonsense"?[5]

4. See the discussion of the Blanquist-Marxist slogan as a "precept of justice" in John Rawls, *Theory of Justice* (Cambridge: Harvard University Press, 1971), p. 305.

5. This is how Raoul Berger dismisses reference to human dignity in the interpretation of the Eighth Amendment; see his *Death Penalties: The Supreme Court's Obstacle Course* (Cambridge: Harvard University Press, 1982), p. 118.

The straightforward way to answer these questions requires several steps. First, we need to identify the complex of beliefs, values, and norms that constitute human dignity. Second, we need to understand cruelty and unusualness as they are found in punishments. Third, we need to see what values (presumably, those connected with human dignity) the prohibition against cruel and unusual punishments can be understood to protect. Finally, we need to specify the definitions, empirical generalizations, and "mediating maxims"[6] that connect the language of the amendment with the concepts and values in question. All this is much easier said than done, and easier done with than without any tacit bias (for or against particular kinds of punishments) that tends to prejudge the outcome of the inquiry.

The territory we are about to explore is terra incognita, so far as recent and contemporary philosophy is concerned. For (as noted at the outset) philosophers have shown little or no direct interest in the concept of human dignity, in alternative elaborations of this concept, or in the history and role of this concept in modern moral and political theory. In recent decades moral philosophy has been dominated by reliance on and interest in other values, depending on whether one is a consequentialist (where the values are human feelings, desires, interests, preferences, needs, welfare, or utilities) or a deontologist (where the values are human rights, duties, obligations, or principles). Philosophers have ignored what (if anything) an emphasis on human dignity adds to moral theory and how it is to be integrated with the factors that have captured their attention.

One route, perhaps the safest one to take, in exploring the concept of human dignity is to approach it historically. The concept of human dignity abruptly comes on stage in moral theory two centuries ago in the philosophy of Immanuel Kant.[7] There are, of course, versions of this idea that predate Kant.[8] It may well be that the Kantian idea of human dignity is nothing more than a secular counterpart to the biblical notion of the sanctity of human life, according to which our dignity is established by

---

6. I borrow this term from Joel Feinberg; see his *Harm to Self* (New York: Oxford University Press, 1986), p. xvi, and his *Harm to Others* (New York: Oxford University Press, 1984), pp. 187–88.

7. Immanuel Kant, *Grounding for the Metaphysics*, trans. James W. Ellington (Indianapolis, Ind.: Hackett Publishing, 1981), pp. 40–45; and *The Metaphysical Elements of Justice*, trans. John Ladd (Indianapolis, Ind.: Bobbs-Merrill, 1965), pp. 98, 132 n.

8. See especially the essay (ca. 1486) by Pico della Mirandola, "Oration on the Dignity of Man," in Ernst Cassirer, P. O. Kristeller, and J. H. Randall, eds., *The Renaissance Philosophy of Man* (Chicago: University of Chicago Press, 1948), pp. 223–54.

having been "created in the image" of God.[9] Be that as it may, it is thanks largely to Kant that contemporary moral theory has a concept of human dignity to work with.

Emphasizing a Kantian conception of human dignity is especially appropriate in the present context, since Kant's own retributive defense of the death penalty is based on his belief that respect for human dignity requires the death penalty for murder and other grave crimes.[10] If a Kantian conception of human dignity can nonetheless be shown to be consistent with, and perhaps even support, moral condemnation of the death penalty, it will be implausible to object that the emphasis on this (rather than some other) conception of human dignity has distorted and biased the analysis in favor of the desired outcome.

Although Kant nowhere set out a full-dress account of his conception of human dignity, it is clear from what he did write that there are half a dozen or so important things about human dignity that must be kept in mind if the nature of this value is to be understood.

First, referring to a person's dignity is another way of referring to a person's *worth*. (Our word *dignity* comes from the Latin *dignitas*, and the usual German translation of *dignitas* is *Würde*. *Würde* is usually translated into English as "worth," but English translators of Kant generally render *Würde* as "dignity.") A person's worth must be kept distinct from other attributes of the person, in particular the person's merit or value or usefulness. Above all, a person's dignity, in the sense of that term here, is not to be seen as a result or product of decent conduct, virtuous behavior, moral rectitude, or respect for the moral law. Rather, it is to be seen as a result of the *capacity* for such conduct.

Second, persons vary from one to another and from situation to situation in their merit, value, and usefulness. These variations are owing to variable environment, genetics, luck, effort, skill, and so forth. But persons do not vary in their dignity or worth. Their dignity or worth is a kind of value that all human beings have *equally* and *essentially*. The deepest, least empirical, way in which to express the moral egalitarianism of persons is by reference to their inherent dignity. Hence human worth

9. See Herbert Chanan Brichto, "The Hebrew Bible on Human Rights," in David Sidorsky, ed., *Essays on Human Rights: Categories, Issues, and Jewish Perspectives* (Philadelphia: Jewish Publication Society of America, 1979), pp. 215–33, esp. at pp. 217–18.

10. On Kant's defense of the death penalty, see Tom Sorrell, *Moral Theory and Capital Punishment* (Oxford: Basil Blackwell, 1987), pp. 129–46. For an argument that Kant's defense of the death penalty was faithless to his own idea of human dignity, see Stephen Schwarzschild, "Kantianism and the Death Penalty (and Related Social Problems)," *Archiv für Rechts- und Sozialphilosophie* 71 (1985): 343–72.

or dignity is invariably described as "intrinsic" or "inherent," to contrast it with value that is instrumental, contingent, extrinsic, or circumstantial. Third, human dignity is intimately related to human *autonomy*. An autonomous creature is a self-activating, self-directing, self-criticizing, self-correcting, self-understanding creature. Autonomous creatures do not merely have and pursue ends, they create them and thereby confer value on those ends. Autonomy is typically contrasted with heteronomy. (The distinction was popularized a generation ago in a study of the American national character in which the autonomous person was contrasted with those whose heteronomy took the form either of "adjustment" or of "anomie.")[11] At the extreme, a person surrenders his or her autonomy (and dignity) by becoming another's slave. More typically, a person violates the autonomy (dignity) of another when the one exercises patronizing or condescending supervision and control over the other, or (worse yet) manipulates the other by using force or fraud in order to achieve some good or end chosen without regard to the other's welfare or capacity for autonomy. Such patronizing or manipulative behavior is insulting, undignified, an affront to the other person's status as a person.[12]

Fourth, our dignity is inseparably connected to our *self-conscious rationality*, our capacities to evaluate, calculate, organize, predict, explain, conjecture, justify, and so forth, and to prize and appraise things and situations, and thus to choose not only the means to our ends but the ends themselves. Irrational or nonrational creatures cannot or do not exercise these capacities, and so their autonomy is slight to nonexistent. In lacking self-conscious rationality, a creature lacks dignity; only rational creatures can have that.

Finally, human dignity provides the basis for equal human *rights*. All and only creatures with rights (not merely positive legal rights, but the rights that sound moral theory confers) have dignity. We should not be surprised, therefore, to find in the preamble to the Universal Declaration of Human Rights (1948) explicit reference to "the inherent dignity . . . of all members of the human family" and to "the dignity and worth of the

11. See David Riesman, *The Lonely Crowd: A Study of the Changing American Character* (New Haven: Yale University Press, 1950).

12. Perhaps the best known recent attack on the notion that persons have "dignity" is to be found in B. F. Skinner, *Beyond Freedom and Dignity* (New York: Alfred A. Knopf, 1971), pp. 44–59. Skinner never explains what dignity is, but it is clear that he attacks it because it is implicated with "autonomy," and he is convinced that human autonomy is an illusion. For reasons to conclude that Skinner's arguments utterly fail to establish this conclusion, see D. C. Dennett, "Skinner Skinned," in his book, *Brainstorms: Philosophical Essays on Mind and Psychology* (Montgomery, Vt.: Bradford Books, 1978), pp. 53–70; and my review essay, "Beyond Skinner," *Worldview*, April 1972, pp. 45–48.

human person" as part of the rationale for universal human rights. These rights are the sword and shield that secure our interests and our sense of our own worth in the political arena. Equal human rights is a necessary consequence of equal human worth and dignity. Whatever inequalities (socioeconomic, psychological, physical) may arise owing to the natural lottery or to the contingencies of our social environment, they do not efface, override, or undermine our equal human rights.[13]

Thus, the (Kantian) idea of human dignity involves and consists of a certain cluster of interrelated attributes, which together confer on persons a certain *status*. This status is constituted by the equal worth and capacity for autonomy and rationality of all persons, a status not shared with other things or even other creatures. It is reflected above all in the equal human rights that all persons enjoy. In virtue of this status, persons deserve certain kinds of treatment and not other kinds, whether from each other or from lawful authority. We show that we recognize the worth of persons, whether in ourselves or in others, by the *respect* we accord them.[14] Finally, we may say that human dignity is tacitly alluded to whenever at least one of its constitutive concepts—worth, equality,

---

13. Probably the best-known current version of this essentially Kantian position is to be found in John Rawls, *Theory of Justice*. But human dignity as such plays little explicit role in the pages of this book. It is somewhat more evident in the equally Kantian moral theory of Alan Gewirth; see his *Human Rights: Essays on Justifications and Applications* (Chicago: University of Chicago Press, 1982). Gewirth argues against trying to "derive" any human rights from human dignity (see pp. 27–30.), and I agree with his objection that such a "derivation" is circular. That Kant's conception of human dignity as presented in his own writings is not beyond criticism is shown by Joel Feinberg in his *Harm to Self*, pp. 94–97.

14. Kant's belief that the value of human dignity requires society to adopt the death penalty for murderers has many sources, one of which turns on what it is to respect another's dignity: I respect another's dignity as a chooser of ends, as a rational agent, only if I treat that person according to the rationale ("maxim") of that person's own actions. Consider the person who chooses to be a murderer; he acts on the rationale that when it suits his purposes, he may kill other persons, disregarding their status as ends in themselves. Therefore, to respect his dignity I must treat him according to the same rationale and authorize or endorse his being murdered in turn (i.e., lawfully put to death).

The major premise of this argument is the chief source of trouble. First, this premise does not follow logically from the idea of human dignity as I have presented it in the text above. Second, even if one's dignity is expressed in being a chooser of ends and rationales for action, and that one's dignity is equally well expressed no matter what ends or rationales one chooses, it does not follow that my respect for the dignity of another is expressed only if I act toward him as he would act toward me (or some third party). Finally, since Kant agrees of course that the rationale of action chosen by the murderer is a paradigm of immorality ("using other persons merely as a means to one's own ends"), it is extremely difficult to see why someone else who wishes to act morally toward and respect the dignity of others *must* authorize or endorse the murder of someone for no better reason than the fact that the latter is himself a (convicted) murderer.

autonomy, rationality—is mentioned or when its expressive concept—equal human rights—is invoked.

Whether the constitutional prohibition against "cruel and unusual punishments" protects human dignity is thus to be decided by the extent to which this prohibition is made more intelligible by being understood as a norm reflecting the equal worth of persons and their equal human rights—despite the fact that the persons in question may also be the duly authorized subjects of deserved punishment.

Although our Bill of Rights omits all use of the language of "autonomy" and "dignity" and "equal worth," it does not omit the use of the language of "rights" and related ideas. It is useful to recall that the Bill of Rights *explicitly* refers to this or that "right" in five of its ten amendments (viz., amendments 1,2,4,6, and 7), as well as to "other... rights" not expressly named (Amendment 9). Other amendments unmistakably indicate that considerations of individual or personal rights provide the background of the explicit provisions. For quartering troops, the householder's "consent" is required (Amendment 3); this requirement entails that the householder has a *right* to deny entry. Any punishment or lawful deprivation must be imposed by "due process of law" (Amendment 5); this entails that the person has a *right* to such procedures. To these provisions we may add the later prohibition of slavery and peonage (Amendment 15) and above all the guarantee to all "persons" of "equal protection of the laws" and of "due process of law" (Amendment 14). It is these two later amendments that explicitly establish the equality of all persons before the law, a legal status that makes most sense only if it is presupposed that all persons are of equal worth insofar as the law is concerned, whatever their variable merits and usefulness may be, and whatever their socioeconomic or political status. (As the argument unfolds below, there will be occasion to return to the important provisions of the Fourteenth Amendment mentioned here.)

This explicit language in the Bill of Rights and later constitutional amendments resonates so handsomely with Kant's views that one might almost think the two, concurrent in their historic origins in the last decade of the eighteenth century, had a common source. Indeed, in a sense they did; both are products of the Age of Enlightenment in which the liberating ideas of the Renaissance and Reformation were consolidated in European moral and political philosophy. If, therefore, we mean by *human dignity* roughly what Kant meant by it—and if this is not what we mean, then it is difficult to give any very exact sense to the term—it is virtually impossible to argue that the Bill of Rights and the Constitution as a whole are indifferent to human dignity. We cannot argue that although our constitutional law certainly acknowledges various equal human rights, it has no interest in the value of human autonomy or the worth of human persons or—in a phrase—in human dignity. And it would be more than surprising if the Eighth Amendment prohibition against cruel and unusual punishments stood apart in this regard from the rest of the Bill of Rights and the Constitution as subsequently amended. After all, as we have seen, the Eighth Amendment must be intended to defend *some* values, or else its prohibitions would be arbitrary and to that extent make no sense. So what values does cruelty in punishment flout, fail to acknowledge, ignore? What rights, if any, would cruelty in punishment violate, repudiate, or nullify? And precisely why does the death penalty amount to an affront to human dignity?

IV

In his thoughtful opinion in Furman v. Georgia Justice William J. Brennan, Jr., proposed four "principles" designed to connect human dignity with the Eighth Amendment prohibition of cruel and unusual punishments. On behalf of these principles he advanced two claims. First, they are "recognized in our cases and inherent in the Clause" forbidding cruel and unusual punishments. Second, when taken in conjunction with the relevant empirical facts, these principles suffice to permit a "judicial determination whether a challenged punishment comports with human dignity."[15]

Justice Brennan's elucidation of these principles was a bold and original contribution to constitutional interpretation. Hitherto, in the slender and somewhat scattered string of cases decided by the Supreme Court on Eighth Amendment grounds,[16] no judicial opinion had endeavored to offer any interpretative structure—bridging principles, definitions, sufficient or necessary conditions, empirical generalizations—to supplement and interpret the blunt and abstract language of the amendment.[17] Yet

15. Furman v. Georgia, 408 U.S. 238 (1972), at 270.
16. See Larry Charles Berkson, *The Concept of Cruel and Unusual Punishment* (Lexington, Mass.: D. C. Heath, 1975), pp. 9–16.
17. The contribution by constitutional commentators to the analysis of human dignity in the setting of the Eighth Amendment has, so far, been slight; see, e.g., Gerald H. Gottlieb, "Testing the Death Penalty," *Southern California Law Review* 34 (1961): 268–81, esp. at pp. 277–78; Malcolm E. Wheeler, "Toward a Theory of Limited Punishment II: The Eighth Amendment after *Furman*," *Stanford Law Review* 25 (1972): 62–83, esp. at pp. 67–71;

some such structure is necessary if the Court is to evaluate and decide the constitutional status of actual punishments imposed by law. To say this is not to foreclose the question whether the structure proposed by Justice Brennan is the only or the best one. Nor is it to imply that a close scrutiny of the Court's opinions in the precedent cases would reveal all and only the principles he cited to be tacitly at work. Nor, finally, is this to imply that Justice Brennan was right when he concluded that given his four principles and the relevant facts, one must conclude that the death penalty violates the Eighth Amendment prohibition of cruel and unusual punishments. (It would require a detailed study—inappropriate here—of the reasoning by the majority of the Court in later capital cases, beginning with Gregg v. Georgia, to show the subsequent status in the Court's own reasoning of each of Brennan's four principles. In this connection it is worth noting that no member of the Court in dissent in *Furman* or in subsequent capital cases has seen fit to examine and endorse or repudiate any of Brennan's four principles as such.) The worst that can be said about these four principles is that they are only a first approximation to the set of relevant principles pertinent to interpreting the constitutional prohibition against cruel and unusual punishments. Meanwhile, until someone proposes a different set of principles for this purpose, Brennan's deserve the closest scrutiny.

The four principles in question (in the order in which Brennan presented them, perhaps also what he believed to be the order of their descending importance) are these:

1. The "primary principle" is that "a punishment must not be so severe as to be degrading to the dignity of human beings."[18] The sheer painfulness of the punishment, however, is not the only factor determining its severity. "[A severe] punishment may be degrading [to human dignity] simply by reason of its enormity."[19]

2. "The State must not arbitrarily inflict a severe punishment.... [It] does not respect human dignity when, without reason, it inflicts upon some people a severe punishment that it does not inflict upon others."[20]

3. "A severe punishment must not be unacceptable to contemporary society.... Rejection by society ... is a strong indication that a severe punishment does not comport with human dignity."[21]

and Margaret Jane Radin, "Cruel Punishment and Respect for Persons: Super Due Process for Death," *Southern California Law Review* 53 (1980): 1143–85, esp. at pp. 1173–85.
    18. *Furman*, at 271, and cf. 281.
    19. Ibid., at 273.
    20. Ibid., at 274.
    21. Ibid., at 277.

4. "A severe punishment must not be excessive. A punishment is excessive under this principle if it is unnecessary.... The infliction of a severe punishment... cannot comport with human dignity when it is nothing more than the pointless infliction of suffering."[22]

These four principles all concern "severe" punishments; their purpose is to explicate the concept of "cruel and unusual punishments" by laying out the nature of *excessively severe* punishments. It is evidently an implicit tautology in Justice Brennan's reasoning that cruel and unusual punishments are very severe punishments, and that any punishment is unconstitutional when it is excessively severe. (The converse, however, is not a tautology; some punishments very severe by plausible standards—notably, life imprisonment—are not necessarily cruel and unusual, at least not in the relevant constitutional sense of this phrase, because they are not inherently "excessively severe.") It is also assumed that we have an intuitive grasp of what counts as a severe punishment, at least to the extent that everyone will grant that the death penalty is a severe punishment, thereby raising the question whether it is excessively severe.

How do these principles function in Justice Brennan's argument against the constitutionality of the death penalty? And how successfully do they bridge the gap between the value of human dignity and the prohibition against cruel and unusual punishments? To answer the first question, we need to sketch the structure of his reasoning. His conclusion, we know, is this: The death penalty violates the constitutional prohibition against "cruel and unusual punishments."

His argument for this conclusion relies upon two premises. The major one consists of his four principles, which can be treated as a complex conditional proposition and reformulated in this manner:

(P.1) If a severe punishment is degrading, arbitrarily inflicted, publicly unacceptable, and excessive, then it violates the constitutional prohibition against cruel and unusual punishments.

On this interpretation, the four principles do not quite define the concept of an unconstitutionally cruel and unusual punishment; they leave open whether there might be other, so far unstated conditions needed to perform that task. But the four principles do lay down conditions that are sufficient for judging whether a given punishment is unconstitutionally cruel and unusual.

The correct formulation of principle P.1 is somewhat complicated by

22. Ibid., at 279.

the fact that Justice Brennan described the "test" under his four principles as "ordinarily a cumulative one."[23] Assuming that the present instance is not out of the "ordinary," we can give the notion of a "cumulative" role for the four principles two different interpretations. On one interpretation, the four principles form a conjunction in the antecedent of the major premise. This is how they have been treated in the formulation of P.1 above. If so, then *each* of the four principles must be violated for the punishment to be judged cruel and unusual. But there is another interpretation suggested by the term *cumulative*. On this version, it is not necessary that all four principles be violated, because the major premise says in effect: The more of these principles a given punishment violates (or the more extreme the violation of any of these principles by a given punishment), the more cruel and unusual the punishment is.

We need not resolve which is the preferred interpretation, at least not if our only concern is to understand Justice Brennan's argument. It is clear he believes all four of his principles are violated by the death penalty. That is equivalent to asserting as the minor premise of his argument the following:

The death penalty—indubitably a severe punishment—is degrading, arbitrarily inflicted, publicly unacceptable, and excessive.

There is no doubt the argument from these premises is valid; it remains only to see whether it is sound. Before we can turn directly to that question, however, it is important to consider whether the major premise (the four principles) successfully bridges the concept of human dignity with the Eighth Amendment. It may help to answer this question if we reformulate Brennan's four principles in a more uniform manner that emphasizes their connection to human dignity. Taking them in the order in which he mentions them, this is what we get:

First, it is an affront to the dignity of a person to be forced to undergo catastrophic harm at the hands of another when, before the harm is imposed, the former is entirely at the mercy of the latter, as is always the case with legal punishment.

Second, it offends the dignity of a person who is punished according to the will of a punisher free to pick and choose arbitrarily among

23. Ibid., at 282, 286.

offenders so that only a few are punished very severely when all deserve the same severe punishment if any do.

Third, it offends the dignity of a person to be subjected to a severe punishment when society shows by its actual conduct in sentencing that it no longer regards this severe punishment as appropriate.

Finally, it is an affront to human dignity to impose a very severe punishment on an offender when it is known that a less severe punishment will achieve all the purposes it is appropriate to try to achieve by punishing anyone in any manner whatsoever.

These reformulations link the concept of human dignity explicitly with the concept of "cruel and unusual punishments" via the notion of appropriate limits to the permissible severity of punishments. This is easily seen if we recall several of the constitutive elements of human dignity discussed earlier: Respect for the autonomy of rational creatures forbids its needless curtailment in the course of deserved punishment. Respect for the equal worth of persons forbids inequitable punishments of convicted offenders equally guilty. The fundamental equal rights of persons, including convicted offenders (about whom I shall have more to say below), precludes treating some offenders as if they had ceased to be persons.

V

However, these reformulations do not suffice to show us that the principles are the correct ones to elucidate the concept of "cruel and unusual punishments." Nor do they suffice to show that the argument employing them is sound (that is, that both the major and minor premises of Justice Brennan's argument as reconstructed here are true). Both kinds of criticism deserve our scrutiny.

Some critics have argued in effect that Brennan's argument is unsound because one or more of his four principles themselves is incorrect. For example, it can be argued that Brennan's final principle, prohibiting excessive punishment, should not be interpreted as a prohibition against unnecessarily severe punishment, but only as a prohibition against disproportionate punishment—and the death penalty is not disproportionate to the crime of murder.[24] The other form of criticism does not dispute

24. Gregg v. Georgia, 428 U.S. 153 (1976), at 187; also Igor Primoratz, *Justifying Legal Punishment* (Atlantic Highlands, N.J.: Humanities Press International, 1989), pp. 163–64.

the adequacy of Brennan's four principles, but argues that the death penalty as a matter of fact does not violate most, much less all, of them. For example, it can be argued that the death penalty in fact is not "degrading" under the first principle, because there is nothing left for society to degrade in the person who has wilfully committed murder; such a murderer has degraded himself by his own criminal acts. His conduct leaves him with no dignity left to stand on, no moral platform from which to demand, or even plead, that society respect his dignity.[25] Let us consider each of these kinds of criticism further, starting with the second.

Consider Justice Brennan's claim that the death penalty is "unacceptable to contemporary society." Criteria for such unacceptability are multiple and complex, and the evidence under them not uncontroversial. Even so, as Chief Justice Warren E. Burger argued in dissent in *Furman*,[26] anticipating the Court majority four years later in Gregg v. Georgia,[27] there is considerable evidence that contemporary American society *does* "accept" the death penalty in the most plausible sense of that word.[28] Today, nearly two decades after *Furman*, it is difficult to disagree with the Chief Justice: Justice Brennan was almost certainly wrong to argue that American society in the 1970s found the death penalty for murder "unacceptable." If so, then the death penalty at most violates three of Brennan's four principles; and if I have correctly reconstructed the logic of Brennan's argument (and correctly understood his "cumulative" use of his four principles), then he was wrong to think that his argument established that the death penalty really does violate the Eighth Amendment.

It is possible to rescue Brennan's argument against the death penalty from this objection either by abandoning his third principle altogether or by reinterpreting what it means for a punitive practice established in law to be "accepted." Take the second strategy first. This seems to be Brennan's own preferred interpretation, when he wrote that "the objective indicator of society's view of an unusually severe punishment is what society does with it, and today society will inflict death upon only a small

25. See John Cottingham, "Punishment and Respect for Persons," in M. A. Stewart, ed., *Law, Morality and Rights* (Dordrecht: Reidel, 1973), pp. 423–31, at p. 430; also Igor Primoratz, "Murder Is Different," *Criminal Justice Ethics* 8, no. 1 (1989): 46–53, at p. 51.

26. *Furman*, at 385–91 (Burger, C. J., dissenting).

27. *Gregg*, at 179–82, citing "objective indicia that reflect the public attitude" toward the death penalty (173).

28. I have discussed these indicia elsewhere; see my *Death Is Different*, pp. 169–70.

sample of the eligible criminals."[29] He argued in effect that society accepts a severe penalty only if it actually carries out that penalty in all or most of the cases where it is legally relevant. But that presupposes that the relevant convicted offenders are actually sentenced accordingly in the first place—and the actual practice of the nation's criminal justice systems violate both these conditions.

But running against this is evidence of a different sort: the widespread reenactment of death penalty statutes immediately after *Furman*,[30] the willingness of trial juries to use these statutes in two or three hundred cases a year,[31] the willingness of Congress to reenact death penalties (thwarted mainly by a skillful minority in behind-the-scenes maneuvers),[32] and above all by public opinion surveys that show a stable and large majority of the public ready to voice at least nominal support of the death penalty.[33] In light of these facts, it is at best arguable whether Justice Brennan's rebuttal succeeds.[34]

29. *Furman*, at 300.
30. *Gregg*, at 179–80.
31. Ibid., at 181–82.
32. This is a complex story (which I hope to tell in detail elsewhere), some fragments of which can be inferred from U.S. Senate, Committee on the Judiciary, *Establishing Constitutional Procedures for the Imposition of Capital Punishment: Report on S. 239*, 99th Congress, 1st and 2d sess. (Washington, D.C. 1986), and House of Representatives, Committee on the Judiciary, Subcommittee on Criminal Justice, *Hearings on H.R. 2837 and H.R. 343: Capital Punishment*, 99th Congress, 2d sess. (Washington, D.C. 1987).
33. During the 1980s public opinion surveys reported considerably more support for the death penalty than during the 1960s or 1970s. What should be inferred from these polls, however, about public attitudes is more controversial. See Hans Zeisel and A. M. Gallup, "Death Penalty Sentiment in the United States," *Journal of Quantitative Criminology* 5 (1989): 285–96; and P. W. Harris, "Oversimplification and Error in Public Opinion Surveys on Capital Punishment," *Justice Quarterly* 3 (1986): 429–55.
34. Chief Justice Burger insisted that it was "unwarranted hyperbole" to describe "the rate of imposition" of the death penalty in the 1960s as " 'freakishly rare' " (*Furman*, at 387). Instead of trying to decide whether Brennan or Burger had the better of this argument in 1972, when *Furman* was decided, or four years later, when the decision in *Gregg* was announced, let us consider the issue today.
   The *Uniform Crime Reports* tell us that "murders and nonnegligent manslaughters" averaged about 20,000 a year during the 1980s. The National Judicial Reporting Program now informs us that in 1986 nearly 10,000 persons were convicted of "murder." Assuming this to be the annual average for the 1980s, and subtracting the estimated total for all non-first-degree murder convictions as well as all first-degree murder convictions in noncapital jurisdictions, we get a minimum estimated annual total of first-degree murder convictions in capital jurisdictions during the 1980s of 2,500. The Department of Justice's Bureau of Justice Statistics reports an average of 250 persons sentenced to death each year during the 1980s, and an average of 30 executions per year.
   Annually, then, during the 1980s we have this: 20,000 criminal homicides of which perhaps 2,500 result in murder convictions where a death penalty could be handed down, resulting in about 250 death sentences—and 30 actual executions. How much lower the ratio of executions or death sentences to murder convictions or to murders would have to

So let us turn to the other strategy. Here, I believe, we are on much stronger ground. I believe it is a grave error to suppose that there is any significant popular dimension to deciding the *constitutional* status of a punishment as cruel and unusual. Contemporary acceptability of a mode of punishment, measured in the usual ways, as above, is a plausibly relevant consideration only if unusualness of punishments is taken literally, or if arbitrariness and unequal application of the law are at stake (as they are where due process and equal protection of the law in the Fourteenth Amendment are concerned).[35] It seems quite the wrong kind of partial criterion to use as a measure of excessive severity, which is precisely what is at stake in interpreting the prohibition against cruel and unusual punishment.[36] Popular attitudes and practices under law cannot by themselves *make* a severe punishment hitherto acceptable into one that is not, or preserve a widespread punishment from being judged excessively severe.[37] This is not to deny, as the Court has held, that a "cruel and unusual" punishment is one that is at odds with "the evolving standards of decency that mark the progress of a maturing society."[38] One would like to think that popular disapproval of an extremely severe punishment is to be explained at least in part by public belief that the punishment is cruel and unusual. But the converse argument, which Justice Brennan seems to employ, is inappropriate as well as unsound.

Thus, by removing Brennan's third principle altogether from the set of principles that partially define a cruel and unusual punishment, we can circumvent rejection of his argument on the ground that the relevant empirical evidence undermines his claims.

As for the minor premises of Brennan's argument pertinent to his second and fourth principle, I cannot attempt to review here all the relevant evidence marshaled in the research and writing by others that bears on the arbitrary administration of the death penalty and its exces-

---

be before they could fairly be described as "freakishly rare" is, of course, unclear. What is clear is that these ratios have never been lower at any time in this century; see William J. Bowers, *Legal Homicide: Death as Punishment in America, 1864–1982* (Boston: Northeastern University Press, 1984), pp. 25–32, 49–58.

35. Indeed, I am inclined to think that this criterion was introduced (consciously or otherwise) in order to put an equal protection spin on the whole argument.

36. The crude populist abuse to which (what amounts to) this third principle can be put is well illustrated in the opinion for the Court by Justice Antonin Scalia in the recent death penalty case of Stanford v. Kentucky,——U.S.——(1989), at 6–9 (slip opinion).

37. A parallel argument has been made by David Dolinko, "Foreword: How to Criticize the Death Penalty," *Journal of Criminal Law and Criminology* 77 (1986): 546–601, at p. 596 n. 252.

38. Trop v. Dulles, 356 U.S. 86 (1958), at 100–101.

siveness.[39] I can only declare my belief that this evidence amply supports the requirements of the argument.

That leaves only the objection to Brennan's argument to the effect that it fails because the minor premise needed under his first principle is false. That is, Brennan wrongly believes that imposing the death penalty on a convicted murderer is "degrading" to him—although he is right in believing that the Eighth Amendment implicitly prohibits degrading punishments. One must sympathize with this objection; it seems plausible to accept the idea that human dignity affords anyone (who has it) a platform on which he or she may protest certain kinds of treatment to which they are being subjected. Yet, surely, a guilty and convicted murderer is in the worst possible position to lodge a protest of this sort against his impending punishment, whatever it is.

But is it not obvious that if this objection is given full weight, as some defenders of the death penalty apparently want to do, it will prove too much? It will become impossible to see how there can be *any* upper limit to the severity or brutality of punishments, given the gravity of crimes and the brutality of those who commit them. Or, perplexing though it may be, if there is an upper limit to the severity of punishments even for convicted (mass or serial) murderers, we will have to conclude this limit has nothing to do with (is not derived from) the human dignity of the person being punished, because it arises from some completely independent moral consideration. Surely, morality (quite apart from the Bill of Rights) places a principled upper limit to the severity of permissible punishments; the only issue worth disputing is not whether there is such a limit but what it is and why. The prohibition of cruel and unusual punishments in the Eighth Amendment is intelligible only as a prohibition

---

39. See Vivian Berger, "Justice Delayed or Justice Denied?—A Comment on Recent Proposals to Reform Death Penalty Habeas Corpus," *Columbia Law Review* 90 (October 1990): 1665–1714; David C. Baldus, George G. Woodworth, and Charles A. Pulaski, Jr., *Equal Justice and the Death Penalty: A Legal and Empirical Analysis* (Boston: Northeastern University Press, 1990); Ronald J. Tabak and J. Mark Lane, "The Execution of Injustice: A Cost and Lack-of-Benefit Analysis of the Death Penalty," *Loyola of Los Angeles Law Review* 23 (1989): 59–146, esp. at pp. 62–98; and my *Death Is Different*, pp. 164–84, 195–237.

David Dolinko's criticism of arguments against the death penalty that rest on such "procedural" facts suggests that he thinks it is incorrect to interpret the meaning of the prohibition against "cruel and unusual punishments" by reference to principles—such as Justice Brennan's second and third principles—to which facts of this sort are relevant; see Dolinko, "Forward," pp. 571–601. What principles (if any) it would be appropriate to use to interpret this constitutional provision, aside from Justice Brennan's first and fourth principles ("a punishment must not be so severe as to be degrading to the dignity of human beings" and "a severe punishment must not be excessive"), remains unclear.

generated by such a principle. If the principle in question reflects or connects with human dignity, as I believe I have shown that it does, then human dignity *does* provide a platform on which even a convicted murderer may rightfully protest against laws and officials who would punish him in certain ways. Once this is granted, there is no way to prevent arguing that death is among the prohibited punishments.

In order to make this more convincing, a new line of argument needs to be developed that addresses precisely the residue, if we may so speak, of the dignity that even murderers possess, and the cruelty that the death penalty always manifests.

VI

In order to grasp what is at stake in the Eighth Amendment prohibition of cruelty and its tacit recognition and protection of human dignity as a constitutional value, we need to tighten our grip on the idea of cruelty to persons.[40] To do this, we will find it useful to take our cues from reflections not directly or intentionally designed to illuminate cruel punishments under law, and especially not from sources purporting to tell us what the framers and ratifiers of the Eighth Amendment, nor subsequent commentators and interpreters (including the federal courts), have understood by the concept of cruelty as it appears there. Our aim must be in part to test (and not merely repeat or reaffirm) what constitutional authors and interpreters have said and have meant when they condemned cruelty in punishments. To do that without question-begging circularity, we must locate some independent source for the meaning of the term.

In a recent account of the nature of cruelty focused on the eighteenth-century French opponents of the grosser cruelties of their day, we find this definition: *cruelty* is "the willful infliction of physical pain on a weaker being in order to cause anguish and fear."[41] When such a definition is used to judge the death penalty as seen from the vantage point of western Europe two centuries ago, it certainly covers the classic paradigms of cruel executions: crucifixion by the Romans, disembowelment by the Tudors, tearing asunder by the Bourbons. It also applies to one

40. This and the next section are a revised version of an argument that appears in my *Death Is Different*, pp. 123–28, itself a slightly revised version of my essay "Thinking about the Death Penalty as a Cruel and Unusual Punishment," *U.C. Davis Law Review* 18 (1985): 873–923, esp. pp. 917–23.

41. See Judith Shklar, "Putting Cruelty First," in her book *Ordinary Vices* (Cambridge: Harvard University Press, 1984), pp. 7–44.

at least of the forms in which the death penalty is administered under law in our society (the Supreme Court to the contrary not withstanding),[42] namely, the electric chair. Here is a recent description of death by electrocution: "The body burns bright red as its temperature rises. The flesh swells and the skin stretches to the point of breaking. Sometimes it catches on fire. The force of the electrical current is so powerful that the eyeballs sometimes pop out and rest on the cheeks. Witnesses hear a loud, long sound like bacon frying: the nauseating smell of burning flesh fills the room."[43] Death by electrocution mocks the claims made on its behalf when it was introduced a century ago as a humane advance in carrying out the death penalty.[44]

But what about other ways to carry out the death sentence? What about the death penalty as such? Is it cruel, however it is carried out, under this definition of *cruelty*? It would appear not. Where the death inflicted is not "physically" painful, it cannot be cruel. Where the "intention" of the killing is not to cause anyone—the offender, the witnesses, or other criminals—"anguish and fear" but merely to blot out the criminal once and for all, cruelty apparently evaporates. What emerges from this plausible definition of *cruelty* is exactly what the modern friends of the death penalty (including a majority of the Supreme Court since 1976) insist: Capital punishment is not, per se, an excessively severe or cruel punishment, even if (as all honest observers agree) some of its historic modes of infliction were or its use to punish minor crimes would be.[45]

But *cruelty* as defined so far may not be the best, and is certainly not the only, way to understand the term. Mindful of seminal thinking in the eighteenth century about cruelty as well as sensitive to the widespread horrors of this century, we can think about cruelty to persons in a more

42. *In re* Kemmler, 136 U.S. 436 (1890); Malloy v. South Carolina, 237 U.S. 180 (1915).

43. Amnesty International USA, "What's Your Idea of Cruel and Unusual?" (poster, distributed 1989).

44. On the history of electrocution as a "humane" advance in methods of execution, see Berkson, *The Concept of Cruel and Unusual Punishment*, pp. 23–26, and sources cited there.

45. Thus, Walter Berns concedes that carrying out the death penalty by drawing and quartering and disemboweling would be a cruel and unusual punishment; see his *For Capital Punishment: Crime and the Morality of the Death Penalty* (New York: Basic Books, 1979), p. 32. Cf. Raoul Berger on the death penalty by crucifixion or boiling in oil, in his *Death Penalties*, p. 41; and Ernest van den Haag on the death penalty for only "the gravest crimes, in their most aggravated form, e.g., not for rape, but for rape-murder," in his *Punishing Criminals: Concerning a Very Old and Painful Question* (New York: Basic Books, 1975), p. 227. For a list of the "degrading," "shocking," and "horrible" punishments that have been described over the years in Supreme Court dicta as "cruel and unusual punishments," see Berkson, *The Concept of Cruel and Unusual Punishment*, p. 10.

imaginative and thematic fashion. If we do this, we see that "the heart of cruelty" is "total activity smashing total passivity."[46] Cruelty, on this view, consists in "subordination, subjection to a superior power whose will becomes the victim's law." Where cruelty reigns—whether in the hands of a Marquis de Sade or in the galvanic charges used by a modern torturer—there is a "power-relationship between two parties," one of whom is "active, comparatively powerful," and the other of whom, the victim, is "passive, comparatively powerless."[47]

These observations reveal the very essence of capital punishment to be cruelty. Whether carried out by impalement or electrocution, crucifixion or the gas chamber, firing squad or hanging, with or without due process and equal protection of the law, for felonies or misdemeanors, there is *always* present that "total activity" of the executioner and the "total passivity" of the condemned. The state, acting through its local representatives in the execution chamber, *smashes* the convicted criminal into oblivion. The government *annihilates* its prisoner; in the strictest sense of that term it reduces him to inert, lifeless flesh. If this is a fair characterization of cruelty, then the death penalty is a *cruel* punishment.

What is most compelling about the concept of cruelty understood as a "power relationship" in the manner sketched above is that it focuses our attention on the salient common factor in all situations where the death penalty is inflicted, however painlessly, for whatever crime the condemned is guilty, and despite whatever punishment the offender may prefer. For western philosophy, the classic example of capital punishment is provided in the case of Socrates, whose death (if we can believe Plato) was painless, a death he accepted in preference to escape or alternative punishment, a death administered by his own hand from the cup of hemlock he drank in compliance with the order of the Athenian tribunal that had convicted and sentenced him. If such a method of execution were revived today, it could not easily be condemned as "undignified" in the ordinary sense of that term, and to that extent could not be judged to be an assault on human dignity. Today, with the growing popularity of lethal injection—and when medical technology in the future may invent an even less burdensome mode of execution—the same difficulty arises. When death is carried out by the state in a manner that does not disfigure the offender's body, apparently causes little or no conscious pain, brings

46. Phillip P. Hallie, *The Paradox of Cruelty* (Middletown, Conn.: Wesleyan University Press, 1969), p. 90.
47. Ibid., p. 34.

about death within a few minutes, and presents no spectacle of terminal anguish and terror to official witnesses, it is extremely difficult to construct a convincing argument that condemns the practice based on its alleged "cruelty," as that term is often understood. Modern opponents of the death penalty have inadequately acknowledged this difficulty.

But this difficulty is completely outflanked when cruelty is viewed as a power relationship in the manner indicated above. Cruelty seen in this fashion enables us to recognize that the death penalty is and will remain cruel no matter how or on whom or for what reason it is inflicted.

Some will argue that this conception of cruelty is too sweeping, for it condemns *all* punishments—or at least all severe punishments, such as life imprisonment, the usual statutory alternative to death—as cruel. Does not all punishment involve power over the powerless, in precisely the manner essential to the conception proposed and used above to condemn the death penalty?[48] True, punishment requires the punisher to control the punished to whatever extent is necessary to guarantee that the sentence is carried out. But such coercive power usually is not used, and in principle never need be used, to "smash" or "annihilate" the offender, either bodily or spiritually. Its intention is not to destroy life, in body or soul, but only to limit liberty, privacy, and autonomy. Thus the power necessary to carry out severe punishments under law is not "total," even if punitive institutions can be popularly and correctly defined as "total" institutions.[49]

Accordingly, the coercive control needed to incarcerate even dangerous offenders can constitute a morally acceptable alternative mode of punishment not open to attack as excessively severe or inherently brutal or cruel, under the conception of cruelty here being advocated. Imprisonment, including even long-term imprisonment where necessary, also can provide adequate incapacitation, as the long history of its use for dangerous persons convicted of the gravest crimes amply proves.[50] I say this not in complacent dismissal of the miseries of long-term incarceration, but to emphasize the point that incarceration does not *essentially* include

48. See Primoratz, *Justifying Legal Punishment*, p. 50.
49. Erving Goffman, *Asylums: Essays on the Social Situation of Mental Patients and Other Inmates* (New York: Anchor Books, 1961); Samuel E. Wallace, ed., *Total Institutions* (New Brunswick, N.J.: Transaction Books, 1971).
50. This is of course not to deny that observers across two centuries, from Cesare Beccaria (an opponent of the death penalty) to Jacques Barzun (a defender), have claimed that life imprisonment is the more severe punishment or that imprisonment can be and often is turned into a living hell.

annihilative power over any prisoner comparable to what the death penalty manifests over every prisoner.[51] So this alternative to the death penalty cannot be condemned on the ground that it involves merely a subtler form of the very power expressed in, and used here to condemn, the death penalty.

So far, nothing has been said about what makes a punishment "unusual," even though it is only punishments that are "cruel and unusual" that the Eighth Amendment condemns. At face value, cruelty and unusualness are two independent attributes of punishment, each with its own criteria, and capable of various combinations (such as cruel but not unusual punishments, and vice versa). But the Supreme Court has shown little interest in such a construal, however plausible the layperson may find it. Instead, unusualness is more typically taken adjectivally, as a feature of the severity in punishments that is a necessary element in their cruelty. This adjectival role has been given mainly two different interpretations. In one, unusualness means *excessive* severity, or *unequal* severity, or perhaps *arbitrary* severity. In the other, it means *unpopular* severity, or *highly atypical* severity.[52] (Justice Brennan's four principles in effect take both these interpretations into account.)

The two interpretations are hardly of equal plausibility; I have already implicitly rejected the latter as inappropriate because it suffers from the same deficiency that led me to argue earlier against the third of Justice Brennan's four principles. Surely, there is no constitutional objection to a punishment that is merely unusual, in the sense of novel, hitherto unauthorized by statute, or otherwise unpopular—so long as it is not also unusual in the sense of excessively harmful or severe and arbitrary. Unusualness in a punishment is a normative, not a purely descriptive, attribute. Accordingly, the constitutional prohibition of a punishment on

51. Perhaps the most persuasive argument against life imprisonment on the ground that it violates human rights is to be found in Leon Shaskolsky Sheleff, *Ultimate Penalties: Capital Punishment, Life Imprisonment, Physical Torture* (Columbus: Ohio State University Press, 1987), pp. 58–79, 117–50. Elsewhere I have explained why life imprisonment, even without parole, is not essentially as severe or as cruel as death; see my *Death Is Different*, pp. 26–28. Sheleff's critique was not addressed to my argument and left untouched the points I had made. As to why incarceration does not in practice or in theory necessarily take life-destroying forms, see, e.g., Robert Johnson, *Hard Time: Understanding and Reforming the Prison* (Pacific Grove, Calif.: Brooks/Cole Publishing, 1987); Michael Sherman and Gordon Hawkins, *Imprisonment in America: Choosing the Future* (Chicago: University of Chicago Press, 1981); and Norval Morris, *The Future of Imprisonment* (Chicago: University of Chicago Press, 1974).

52. On the interpretation of "unusual" by the Supreme Court, see *Furman* at 277 (Brennan, J., concurring opinion) and 376–79 (Burger, C. J., dissenting). I have discussed the matter further in my *Death Is Different*, pp. 96–98.

the ground that it is "unusual" tacitly alludes to some standard or principle by which to judge degrees and qualities of severity in punishment. On the assumption that the standards or principles that relate to unusualness in punishments insignificantly differ from those that govern unacceptable cruelty in punishment, there is no need to dwell further on what constitutes an unusual punishment per se.

We have yet to explain, however, why cruel punishments offend, frustrate, or violate human dignity and thus are prohibited. What is it that cruelty in punishment destroys? And what does a knowing willingness to impose cruel punishments reveal about punishers?

VII

The argument I propose to use to answer these questions starts from the idea that human dignity is most evidently at stake where violation of the most basic human rights are involved. Thus, if the death penalty violates human dignity, there must be a fundamental human right that it violates. What right could that be? Nothing less than "a nonwaivable, nonforfeitable, nonrelinquishable right—the right to one's status as a moral being, a right that is implied in one's being a possessor of any rights at all."[53] Obviously, such a right seems to be violated by officially sanctioned death in the form of punishment. The possession of such a right is a consequence of one's status as a person, a conceptual product of reflection on our common humanity, our human dignity.

The nature of this right can be best seen by contrast to the "right to life" as it is found in traditional "natural rights" theories of the seventeenth and eighteenth centuries. According to such theories, the right to life is universal (all and only human beings have it), natural (not conferred by society or law), and inalienable (its possessor cannot use it as a bargaining chip). It is also nonwaivable, since that would open the door to such morally reprehensible acts as suicide and euthanasia. But this set of

---

53. Herbert Morris, "A Paternalistic Theory of Punishment," *American Philosophical Quarterly* 18 (1981): 263–72, at p. 270. Morris does not discuss the relevance of this right to the moral or constitutional status of the death penalty.

A rather different argument from mine has been offered by Jeffrie G. Murphy, "Cruel and Unusual Punishments," in M. A. Stewart, ed., *Law, Morality and Rights* (Dordrecht: Reidel, 1979), pp. 373–404, esp. pp. 386, 389, 391–97; a briefer version appears in Murphy, *Retribution, Justice, and Therapy*, pp. 223–49. Murphy's argument rests mainly on "the right not to be dealt with negligently by one's government" and "the right not to have one's basic interests threatened in casual and irresponsible ways."

traits defining the right to life does not entail that someone who possesses this right cannot *forfeit* it. On the contrary, the right to life was traditionally understood to be forfeitable, and it was judged that this right was forfeited by any act of killing another person without justification or excuse.[54] In this way, typical versions of traditional natural rights theories accommodated the lawful (and seemingly necessary) death penalties of their day. The issue before us is whether there is a rational defense of a right connected to human dignity that is invulnerable to demands for its forfeiture.

At the outset, we need to realize how unremarkable such a right is when seen in light of familiar constitutional principles compatible with but having no direct bearing on the Eighth Amendment.

Our Bill of Rights incorporates the principle that even persons accused and convicted of the gravest crimes retain their fundamental rights of due process and equal protection of the law. Whether these rights are absolute in the sense that every countervailing legal consideration must yield before their claims we need not settle here. It is enough to notice that *these rights are not forfeitable* (for present purposes we may ignore whether they can be waived.)[55] If government officers violate these rights in the course of their administration of criminal justice, that is normally sufficient to nullify whatever legal burdens were placed on an accused or convicted person arising from such a violation. What this shows is that our Constitution already has in place, and our society to that extent fully acknowledges, a principle of profound importance: The individual *cannot* do anything that utterly nullifies his or her worth and standing as a person, so far as the processes of the criminal law are concerned.

54. See, e.g., John Locke, *Two Treatises of Government*, ed. Peter Laslett (Cambridge: Cambridge University Press, 1963), "The Second Treatise of Government," secs. 23, 172. It is a curious feature of historical studies of natural rights theories that little or nothing has been said about the role of forfeiture of such rights; see, e.g., Richard Tuck, *Natural Rights Theories* (Cambridge: Cambridge University Press, 1979). For further discussion, see my "Right to Life," *The Monist* 63 (1968): 550–72; and my *Death Is Different*, pp. 55–59.

55. A possible exception to my claim that waiver of this fundamental right is impossible is the case of the death row prisoner who "volunteers" for execution, i.e., who does not permit his attorneys to pursue every possible avenue for relief, or who dismisses his attorneys before such relief has been pursued. Such a "volunteer" could, and I think would more accurately, be described as someone who acquiesced in an infringement of his rights, viz., to due process and equal protection of the laws. In Gilmore v. Utah, 429 U.S. 1012 (1976), Justice White agreed, at least to the extent of arguing that the defendant was " 'unable' as a matter of law to waive the right to state appellate review" (1018). However, the majority of the Court in effect held otherwise, and Gilmore was executed. For discussion and argument on constitutional grounds against the Court's position, see W. S. White, "Defendants Who Elect Execution," *University of Pittsburgh Law Review* 48 (1987): 853–77.

Government *must* treat persons in the criminal justice system as having a worth and dignity that prohibits violation of due process and equal protection of the law.

What is at stake in the present argument over the Eighth Amendment and the death penalty is not, therefore, anything very radical or novel. No concept, value, or principle is being advocated without precedent or analogy to what we find elsewhere firmly embedded in our constitutional law. Rather, what is at stake is the extent to which considerations already familiar in criminal procedure under the constitution can be extended to the evaluation of certain substantive modes of government conduct (viz., lawful punishment) because the same moral factor—human dignity and the equal moral status of all persons—underlies both.

At this point, the overall argument can be advanced by two independent lines of reasoning. The first addresses directly the question of the moral standing of convicted offenders and in particular those guilty of murder and condemned to death, insofar as their standing can be understood as an empirical matter. Convicts on death row typically arrive there with undeniable capacities for action and passion as moral creatures, quite apart from whatever outrageously immoral conduct resulted in their criminal condemnation in the first place. That condemnation and the faulty conduct underlying it does not directly cause these moral capacities to weaken significantly, much less to vanish. The immorality of murder that makes convicted murderers "monsters" in the eyes of the public does not in fact make anyone into a *nonmoral* creature. An act of murder does not cause an offender to lose whatever moral capacities he may have had prior to his crime. Rather, the act of murder is consistent with varying degrees of moral development. (That life, such as it is, on death row sometimes even if not always enhances some of these moral capacities in some offenders, and provides surprising opportunity for their manifestation, also cannot be denied.) However dangerous, pathological, and unreformable such convicts may be (excluding, of course, the severely retarded and the certifiably insane among them), these failings do not overwhelm all capacity in death row convicts for moral action and response—as testimony from friends, relatives, guards, legal counsel, and other visitors overwhelmingly attests.[56] What is true of death row mur-

56. See, e.g., Bruce Danto, John Bruhns, and Austin H. Kutscher, eds., *The Human Side of Homicide* (New York: Columbia University Press, 1982); Doug Magee, *Slow Coming Dark: Interviews on Death Row* (New York: Pilgrim Press, 1980); Robert Johnson, *Condemned to Die: Life under Sentence of Death* (New York: Elsevier, 1981); Bruce Jackson and Diane Christian, *Death Row* (Boston: Beacon Press, 1980); Michael Radelet,

derers is no less true of the enormously larger number of such offenders who are (dare one say only?) imprisoned for their punishment.

Thus, there is no plausible empirical evidence to support the claim that convicted murderers lose their status as moral agents and patients just because they are guilty of horribly immoral crimes. If it is replied that these offenders nevertheless *do* lack such status, what can this mean and how can it be true? It seems to mean that someone, in effect acting in the name of and on behalf of society, *has taken away* the moral status of the individual, stripped the death row murderer of his worth and dignity. But where does anyone get the authority to make such a devastating judgment? Authority to judge an accused and to punish a convicted offender are troubling enough from the moral point of view. Authority in effect to decree that someone no longer has the status of a moral human being is something else altogether. Indeed, the very idea of such a judgment is bewildering, appalling; it is redolent with the odor of magical, superstitious thinking. It is also disingenuous, because it wraps in deceptive legalistic-moralistic language the fact that it is *we* who have decided the murderer shall die, and that *we* are about to kill him.[57] The abstract and anonymous judgment that the murderer forfeits his very status as a person because of his murder all too smoothly paves the way for the sequence of actual lethal decisions made by identifiable persons involved in administering a death penalty system.

If the authority to render such judgment as this is not entirely specious and unjustified, it must be because the best normative *theory* about the sources and limits of human worth and dignity provides for their forfeiture (cancellation, termination, nullification) under certain circum-

Margaret Vandiver, and Felix Berardo, "Families, Prisons, and Men with Death Sentences: The Human Impact of Structured Uncertainty," *Journal of Family Issues* 4 (1983): 593–612; Margaret Vandiver, "Coping with Death: Families of the Terminally Ill, Homicide Victims, and Condemned Prisoners," in M. L. Radelet, ed., *Facing the Death Penalty*, pp. 123–38.

57. Defenders of the death penalty often make the error of supposing that the act of murder destroys the moral dignity of the offender; see, e.g., Walter Berns, "Defending the Death Penalty," *Crime and Delinquency* 26 (1980): 503–11, where he claims that the murderer has "lost his dignity when he freely chose to commit his vile crimes" (p. 507).

Such a view simply ignores the conception of the person as a member of the moral community in the requisite sense. "The moral community is not a club from which members may be dropped for delinquency. Our morality does not provide for moral outcasts or half-castes. It does provide for punishment. But this takes place *within* the moral community and under its rules. It is for this reason that, for example, one has no right to be cruel to a cruel person. His offense against the moral law has not put him outside the law. He is still protected by its prohibition of cruelty—as much so as are kind persons." Gregory Vlastos, "Justice and Equality," in Richard B. Brandt, ed., *Social Justice* (Englewood Cliffs, N.J.: Prentice-Hall, 1962), pp. 31–72, at p. 48.

stances. As was noted above, the judgment that certain persons, who (by virtue of their being persons) are conceded to have had basic human rights prior to their criminal acts, nevertheless forfeit or otherwise relinquish *all* those rights by committing certain crimes—as though they had therewith miraculously ceased to be moral creatures at all—receives no support from experience at all.[58] Everything, then, evidently turns on what the normative theory is that makes this forfeiture the necessary response by society. But there is no adequate theory of the requisite sort at all.

The second line of argument is more abstract and controversial. It starts with the fact that individual human beings are not merely biological specimens of *homo sapiens*. To be sure, the neonate, the hopelessly brain-damaged adult, the senile nonagenarian—as well as the normal and the gifted—are all equally members of the same species. But not all members of the species are equally *persons*; some never will be and others never will be again, even if the criteria of personhood are set generously low.[59] In particular cases, congenital abnormality and abusive or negligent socialization can prevent the development of the relevant traits and thus destroy the possibility that a normal person will ever develop from the human infant that has been given birth. In addition to nature and nurture, what it means to be a person can be understood only as the product of reflective thought about the full range of our characteristic attitudes, abilities, feelings, and deeds. The written documents that trace out this story in all its complexity and variety now span several millennia and dozens of civilizations.

As this record shows, the nature of the person as well as the nature of human society change subtly over time. These changes are partly a result of changes in our self-perceptions, themselves a product of social experience and deeper self-knowledge. History, including the history of morality and moral philosophy, confirms that we are permanently engaged in our own progressive self-understanding, as individuals and as societies. We are thus, in our very natures, at least to some extent, what we take ourselves to be. For several centuries, and in particular since the Age of Enlightenment two centuries ago in Europe, philosophers and

---

58. I have explored this point somewhat further in my *Death Is Different*, pp. 55–59.
59. On these criteria, see D. C. Dennett, "Conditions of Personhood," reprinted in his *Brainstorms*, pp. 267–85. See in general Michael F. Goodman, ed., *What Is a Person?* (Clifton, N.J.: Humana, 1988); Michael Carrithers, ed., *The Category of the Person* (Cambridge: Cambridge University Press, 1985); and A. O. Rorty, ed., *The Identities of Persons* (Berkeley: University of California Press, 1978).

other thinkers have been struggling to enunciate a conception of the person as fundamentally social, rational, autonomous, and relatively immune to change in these respects by the contingencies of actual particular historical circumstances. Such normal personal traits and capacities are, of course, no guarantee against the gravest immorality in individual or collective conduct. Nor does possession of these traits immunize or insulate anyone from mortality.

Short of actual physical destruction, however, these capacities are not and cannot be sensibly thought of as vulnerable to destruction by the agent's own acts, or by the immoral or criminal aspects of those acts. Indeed, there is a paradox at the heart of the idea that a person can forfeit by his own act his status as a person: Action must be deliberate, intentional, and responsible before it can count as a *person's* action. These are also the very qualities in conduct properly deemed necessary before the person whose conduct is in question can be subjected to the criminal law and properly judged, sentenced, and punished. It is conceptually impossible, therefore, for a person in a given act to deserve condemnation by the law for the criminality of that act *and* for the person to have proved by this act that he is no longer a person at all—but only a creature who now lacks any moral standing in the community of persons. Not even the convicted mass or serial murderer is a mere object, a natural force of flesh and bone, a "monster" to be disposed of by the decision of other, as though that were either the only feasible response to his criminal acts or the best response because it is necessary to the preservation of the human community.

With this in mind, one is bound to require that governments accept severe limits on their use of power and coercive force. In particular, a government can have no authority to create and sustain any institution—a lethal institution—whose nature and purpose is to destroy some of its own members, unless these persons are a permanent threat to the innocent and unless there is no nonlethal alternative method of control available. Capital punishment, which of course is designed to annihilate the offender, does constitute just such a lethal institution. Yet for decades it has operated alongside an effective alternative. To defend the death penalty in the face of these facts requires heroic measures.

Standardly, these measures take one of two major forms. One is based, explicitly or implicitly, on the belief that the death penalty is a social defense analogous to individual self-help. The analogy fails, as I have argued elsewhere.[60] The excuse or justification in law and morality that

---

60. I have explained this point elsewhere; see my *Death Is Different*, pp. 51–53.

an individual who kills in self-defense may have provides no rationale for the death penalty. (Contrast this weak analogy with another one: The death penalty in peacetime is like shooting disarmed prisoners of war, a classic violation of international law.) The other line of argument claims that morality itself, insofar as it is based on sound moral theory, permits (some would insist that it requires) society to act against persons who show by their own acts their contempt for the moral nature of others, their victims. Such recourse to vindictive and retributive thinking also fails, either because it begs the question or because it is so flagrantly unrealistic.[61]

The conclusion I reach is that the same moral constraints that have long ago produced constitutional requirements of due process and equal protection of the law argue against any punishment that requires the forfeiture of one's very status as a person. This is what the death penalty requires. A society that understands and respects the dignity of persons will not pretend that it can empower other human beings in their official roles as agents of the criminal justice system to exact such a forfeiture.[62]

61. Ibid., pp. 39–40, 60–62, 171–72. For arguments against the death penalty on retributivist grounds, see Reiman, "Justice, Civilization, and the Death Penalty," and Murphy, *Retribution, Justice, and Therapy*, pp. 223–49.

62. I am grateful to Constance E. Putnam for her helpful comments on an earlier version of this essay.

9

Speaking of Dignity

FREDERICK SCHAUER

A fifteen-year-old girl has been raped and is testifying at the trial of the rapist. On cross-examination the defense attorney elicits from the victim the information that she was not a virgin at the time of the rape. "When I was fifteen," he bellows to the jury, "we had a word for fifteen-year-olds who slept around, and that word was 'slut.' "

At the same time in another part of the world, a black South African has just been arrested for breach of the peace, his crime consisting of walking through a white neighborhood carrying a picture of Nelson Mandela. He protests that he is only trying to honor his hero. "Shut up," one of the arresting officers shouts, "or we'll break your black head!" The victim stands tall and says, with an impassive expression, "Apartheid must end."

Bobbie is ten years old, and one of his legs has been shorter than the other since birth. He is going on an excursion with his schoolmates to a major league baseball game, and in the excitement of the event all the others start to run. Bobbie cannot keep up but silently and gamely tries his hardest to stay with the group. "Gimp!" they taunt back at him, and he starts to cry.

Susan Hernandez is a community organizer in an impoverished urban neighborhood, one in which despair more than hope characterizes the attitude of most residents. It is Sunday, and she is walking through the neighborhood, where many of the residents are outside. "This neighborhood is not poor because we do not work hard," she says to anyone who will listen, "but because the rich and powerful will not give us a chance to succeed."

These vignettes are not designed to tell a single story. Rather, they are designed to rebut the view that there is only a single story to tell. Not uncommonly, the preservation of dignity is marshaled as an argument in favor of freedom of speech, and restrictions on freedom of speech are described as denials of dignity. But as these examples are tailored to suggest, the conflation of dignity and speech, as a general proposition, is mistaken, for although speaking is sometimes a manifestation of the dignity of the speaker, speech is also often the instrument through use of which the dignity of others is deprived.

To drive a wedge between the principles of dignity and free speech is not to suggest that dignity is not a primary human good. Nor is it to suggest that free speech, as a constraint on the ability of some agent in control to limit the communication of some agent under control, is not also a good thing. But noting that dignity and speech are not necessarily conjoined leads to the conclusion that the values of free speech and preservation of dignity will often collide. When that is the case, considering the instances in which an act of speech is an expression of dignity will be of little assistance. Consequently, thinking seriously about dignity may cause us either to recognize its irrelevance to free speech theory or to reevaluate some of that theory itself. But my aim here is not to resolve *that* issue. Instead, it is the more modest one of showing that there is little to be gained by thinking of the right to freedom of speech as but the instantiation of a more general right to dignity.

If the principle of freedom of speech is not the instantiation of a more general principle of dignity, then it should not be surprising that the two will frequently diverge in extension, with freedom of speech often producing deprivations of dignity, and the desire to promote dignity often suggesting restrictions on speech. If this is so, then resolving many hard issues by reference to dignity will be question-begging, and consequently it may be necessary at times to consider directly which of the values of free speech and dignity is more important.

I

I start with the premise that speech is commonly an other-regarding act, capable consequently of causing both good and harm. I recognize that to many this is not self-evident, but I do not wish here to rehearse arguments I have made elsewhere.[1] Instead, I will take as a given that which I recognize is controversial, the capacity of communicative acts to cause the kinds of consequences that would otherwise be sufficient to justify the intervention of government or some other agent in control.[2]

If communicative acts do have the capacity to cause the kinds of injuries or other consequences otherwise sufficient to justify control of those acts, it then appears that any meaningful principle of freedom of speech is an immunization of some communicative acts from control even when those communicative acts produce consequences otherwise sufficient to justify their being controlled.[3] For example, if a product is misused by the consumer in a way that could have been foreseen by the manufacturer, and if the misuse is the "but for" cause of an injury to the user, the manufacturer is likely to be liable.[4] But if a description or instruction published in an article in a periodical is misused by the consumer or reader in a way that could have been foreseen by the publisher, and if that misuse is a "but for" cause of injury or even death, the First Amendment has been held to preclude liability.[5]

Why is this? Why, given the stipulated equivalence of consequences in my formulation of the issue, and the equivalence of consequences in many real instances, would we immunize some but not all acts producing those

1. Especially in *Free Speech: A Philosophical Enquiry* (Cambridge: Cambridge University Press, 1982).

2. I use the infelicitous "agent in control" in order to remain agnostic on the question whether freedom of speech or freedom in general is to be thought of exclusively in terms of freedom from governmental interference, or whether instead it is or can be the freedom of the controlled agent from a certain sort of power otherwise exercised by those individuals or institutions occupying the controlling position. When thought of in this way, it remains possible at least to consider the plausibility of freedom of speech in the context of children vis-à-vis their parents, students vis-à-vis teachers or school administrators, and employees vis-à-vis nongovernmental employers.

3. See my *Free Speech*, pp. 1–15, and also Thomas Scanlon, "A Theory of Freedom of Expression," *Philosophy & Public Affairs* 1 (1972): 204–26; Frederick Schauer, "The Second-Best First Amendment," *William and Mary Law Review* 31 (1989): 1–23.

4. See, e.g., LeBoeuf v. Goodyear Tire & Rubber Co., 451 F. Supp. 253 (W.D. La. 1978), aff'd, 623 F.2d 985 (5th Cir. 1980) (applying Louisiana law).

5. See, e.g., Herceg v. Hustler Magazine, 814 F.2d 1017 (5th Cir. 1987), analyzed at length in Michael Kopech, "Shouting 'INCITEMENT!' in the Courtroom: An Evolving Theory of Civil Liability?" *St. Mary's Law Review* 19 (1987): 173–201. On the contrast between those communicative acts that would commonly generate civil or criminal liability and those that are taken to be protected by a principle of freedom of speech, see Kent Greenawalt, *Speech, Crime, and the Uses of Language* (New York: Oxford University Press, 1989); Frederick Schauer, "Mrs. Palsgraf and the First Amendment," *Washington and Lee Law Review* 47 (1990): 161–69.

consequences? Why would the fact that one act with a given ex ante probability of producing certain consequences, and that does in fact produce those consequences, be subject to official sanction, while another act with the same ex ante probability of producing the same consequences, and which does in fact produce those consequences, is immune from sanction just because the latter act is linguistic or pictorial and the former is not?

The answer to these questions constitutes the full universe of free speech theory (and the failure to address them is fatal for any theory purporting to be a theory of free *speech*), and I can hardly replicate that universe here. Still, it may be useful to divide up the kinds of answers we receive to these questions into three types, for that will enable us to locate more precisely the commonly held conception of the connection between free speech and dignity that I want to challenge here.

The first type of answer given to the questions I raised above is *skeptical*. "Why indeed?" says the skeptic. Once we recognize the consequence-producing and thus the harm-producing capacity of communicative acts, why do we, other than historical coincidence, consider linguistic or pictorial acts, or any discrete subset of the category of linguistic and pictorial acts, different in kind?[6] In asking this question, the skeptic does not imply that the state ought to restrict linguistic and pictorial acts (speech), and accepting the argument of the skeptic does not entail accepting any particular amount of restriction of speech. The absence of a discrete principle of free speech no more entails the conclusion that speech ought to be regulated than the absence of a discrete liberty to drive entails the conclusion that the speed limits on interstate highways ought to be reduced to 35 miles per hour. But accepting the force of the skeptic's question does necessitate not treating the fact that an act (or category of acts) was an act of speech as a reason for treating that act (or category) as different from any other act presenting the same calculus of costs and benefits. Under this view, much of our understanding about freedom of speech is a product of the way in which, at certain times and certain places, speech has been contingently excessively jeopardized by government action. But this, it is said, is not necessarily true

---

6. I say "linguistic and pictorial" rather than "communicative" only because the latter term is slightly indeterminate with respect to whether the actor must have had a communicative intent. Some but not all theories of freedom of speech would require communicative intent on the part of the protected communicator, and I want to avoid these issues here by referring simply to the linguistic and the pictorial.

for all times and places, and no argument for transcendent principle can be given to justify treating deprivations of the freedom to speak as different in kind from other varieties of deprivations of general liberty.[7]

A second variety of response to the "disparate treatment" question of free speech theory is less skeptical and instead sees the class of acts of speech, or some subclass of that class, as serving a range of particularly important social goals. The disparate treatment is thus justified by a desire to grant special protection to this particularly valuable class of acts. Traditional "search for truth" and "marketplace of ideas" theories are of this type, seeing speech as part of a process whose protection justifies the immunization of otherwise sanctionable forms of conduct. Similarly, free speech justifications focusing on protection of (especially political) speech because that speech is a component of democratic processes are also of this social/instrumental variety.[8] And still another variant on this instrumental theme sees free speech as a safety valve, allowing a frustrated citizenry to vent its frustrations in a manner less disruptive than the recourse to violence.[9] Under these and related views, the protection of the speaker (or even the hearer) is not primary, but is rather instrumental to serving the social good in some process that is facilitated by a special immunity for otherwise regulable acts of speech.

As with the skeptical response to the question of why speech is treated differently from otherwise equivalent conduct, my goal here is neither to support nor evaluate these arguments. I describe them primarily in order to show how they differ from a variety of free speech justification that is particularly relevant to the dignity question, and that variety, the one that most interests me here, is the third possible response to the question of special protection of speech. Although I am not in general sympathetic with this class of free speech justifications,[10] I recognize that there is a widely and influentially held view that free speech is an individual right in a strong sense, that it is a deontologically inspired side constraint on otherwise permissible state action, and that the side constraint is justified by the primary good that it protects.[11] Under this view, commonly re-

---

7. For a particularly well-developed argument along these lines, see Lawrence Alexander and Paul Horton, "The Impossibility of a Free Speech Principle," *Northwestern University Law Review* 78 (1984): 1319–57.

8. See esp. Alexander Meiklejohn, *Political Freedom: The Constitutional Powers of the People* (New York: Oxford University Press, 1965).

9. See Thomas Emerson, "Toward a General Theory of the First Amendment," *Yale Law Journal* 72 (1963): 877–955, at pp. 884–86.

10. See Frederick Schauer, "Must Speech Be Special?" *Northwestern University Law Review* 78 (1984): 1284–1306.

11. See, e.g., Martin Redish, *Freedom of Expression: A Critical Analysis* (Charlottesville,

flected not only in the literature but in numerous documents and charters protecting human rights, the right to freedom of speech is of the same species as the right to a fair trial, and the rights to freedom from torture and freedom from discrimination on the basis of race and gender.

Within this last category of free speech justifications, numerous variants appear. To some, what is at stake is self-fulfillment or self-realization,[12] and to others, freedom of speech is a subset of a primary right to self-expression, whether that self-expression be manifested in speaking, length of hair, or manner of dress.[13] One variant, however, one that appears at times in the work of Ronald Dworkin, sees freedom of speech as a manifestation of respect for human dignity.[14] Dworkin and others sometimes use the language of dignity, and sometimes slightly different variants on the same idea, but what emerges is a claim that to deprive a person of the right to speak is to fail to respect her and her choices, and to deprive her of the dignity that is, quite simply, a primary human right.

II

In order to get clear about the argument from dignity as an argument for freedom of speech, we need a more precise notion of just what we mean when we speak of dignity. And here two approaches are particularly important. One approach sees dignity in essentially comparative terms, equating a denial of dignity with a denial of equal status with other human beings. We describe certain conduct as, for example, "dehumanizing" because it treats the victim with *less* respect than is granted to other humans, or because the victim enjoys *less* of something than the otherwise applicable baseline demands. At times references to this kind of dignity tend to sound sufficiently like manifestos that they offer little guidance.[15] At other times, however, the language of dignity is used

---

Va.: Michie, 1984); David A. J. Richards, *Toleration and the Constitution* (New York: Oxford University Press, 1986).

12. See, e.g., Redish, *Freedom of Expression*, and Richards, *Toleration and the Constitution*.

13. See, e.g., C. E. Baker, "Scope of the First Amendment Freedom of Speech," *UCLA Law Review* 25 (1978): 964–1040.

14. Ronald Dworkin, *Taking Rights Seriously* (London: Duckworth, 1977), pp. 197–204. See also Ronald Dworkin, *A Matter of Principle* (Cambridge: Harvard University Press, 1986), pp. 335–97.

15. "The inherent rights of man are based on the ethical denial of respect for human dignity, which is contained in the very idea of law." A. Fernandez del Valle, "Persona y Estado," in Gray Dorsey, ed., *Equality and Freedom: International and Comparative Jurisprudence* (Dobbs Ferry, N.Y.: Oceana Publications, 1977), 1: 109–16, at p. 115.

somewhat more precisely, and here the comparative element tends to drop out in favor of a conception of dignity that refers to certain minimum standards of treatment that are virtually definitional of personhood.[16]

From this second and noncomparative perspective, however, the person whose dignity is deprived is usually passive, performing either a self-regarding act or no act whatsoever. We think, therefore, that persons have been deprived of dignity in this sense when they are tortured, when their privacy is invaded, or when they are the involuntary subjects of medical experimentation. No matter how consequentially desirable such activities may be, so the argument goes, it is simply impermissible to treat people as instruments to be used in any way that others want to use them. To deprive persons of their human status and reduce them to the status of tool, instrument, or weapon is the essence of what a deprivation of dignity is all about.

I do not wish here to evaluate these arguments in their own right. That is, my task is not to determine whether this or that account of dignity is sound. Instead, I want to see what, if anything, various accounts of dignity tell us about freedom of speech. So with that as my goal, I want to turn to the issue of the relationship between freedom of speech and a conception of dignity premised on the right of all not to be the involuntary instrument of the desires of others.

If we conceive of dignity in terms of minimal standards of treatment by others, in terms of a right to be considered as a person and not as a tool for the ambitions or aspirations or goals of another (whether that other be person, institution, or state), and in terms of resistance to the invasions or intrusions or manipulations of others, then arguments from dignity seem much more plausibly to generate arguments for restricting various kinds of speech than for protecting it. Consider the prototypical "hate speech" or "racist speech" situation. In its clearest form, the issue arises when some member of an empowered group directs a racial epithet at some individual member of a disempowered group.[17] Putting aside the

16. See Robert Goodin, "The Political Theories of Choice and Dignity," *American Philosophical Quarterly* 18 (1981): 91–100, at pp. 94–95, arguing that respecting people rather than their choices is the "logical primitive." See also much of A. H. Henkin, ed., *Human Dignity: The Internationalization of Human Rights* (New York: Aspen Institute for Humanistic Studies, 1979).

17. On this increasingly discussed issue, see Richard Delgado, "Words That Wound: A Tort Action for Racial Insults, Epithets, and Name-Calling," *Harvard Civil Rights— Civil Liberties Law Review* 17 (1982): 133–67; Charles Lawrence, "If He Hollers Let Him Go: Regulating Racist Speech on Campus," *Duke Law Journal* (1990): 431–83; Jean Love, "Discriminatory Speech and the Tort of Intentional Infliction of Emotional Distress," *Washington and Lee Law Review* 47 (1990): 123–59; Mari Matsuda, "Public Response

question of likely retaliatory violence,[18] consider whose dignity is at issue when a white yells "Nigger!" at a black, or "Gook!" at an Asian, or "Spic!" at a Latino? In these situations it seems hardly implausible to think of the words, when situated within a preexisting social context involving disparity of social power, as dehumanizing, as invasive, and as using the entirely passive victim as an instrument for the self-indulgence of the user of the epithet. The indignity is suffered by the object of the words, and the words appear to have a plain dignity-depriving intent and effect.

There is little reason to suppose that from the perspective of dignity much changes when we move out of the realm of face-to-face encounters and into that involving more large-scale speech. Suppose that instead of the use of a racial epithet in a face-to-face situation, we imagine a group of white-sheeted Klansmen driving through a black neighborhood shouting racial epithets.[19] Where, as here, the words are directed at involuntary and passive targets, where the intent of the words is to intimidate or to injure or to make the objects in some other way feel worse, and where the preexisting social setting is such that the words have the effect of reinforcing distinctions between oppresser and oppressed, a goal of preservation of dignity in the abstract seems to indicate protection of the targets of the speech in cases such as this.

Many of the same concerns appear applicable when the issue is gender rather than race. Consider a common sexual harassment situation, in which male workers attach degrading and sexually explicit photographs to the lockers of their female coworkers, or display them in other areas where it is expected that women will see the photographs whether they want to or not.[20] As the sexual harassment case law makes plain, these activities, designed to make the woman worker feel less able than the man, or less a fully accepted member of the workforce than the man, are

---

to Racist Speech: Considering the Victim's Story," *Michigan Law Review* 87 (1989): 2320–81; Rodney Smolla, "Rethinking First Amendment Assumptions about Racist and Sexist Speech," *Washington and Lee Law Review* 47 (1990): 171–211.

18. The concern with retaliatory violence pervades the prevailing First Amendment thinking and doctrine about the issue. See, e.g., Gooding v. Wilson, 405 U.S. 518 (1972); Rosenfeld v. New Jersey, 408 U.S. 901 (1972); Lewis v. New Orleans, 408 U.S. 913 (1972); Brown v. Oklahoma, 408 U.S. 914 (1972); Chaplinsky v. New Hampshire, 315 U.S. 568 (1942).

19. The analogy with the "Skokie" issue is intentional. See Collin v. Smith, 578 F.2d 1197 (7th Cir.), cert. denied, 439 U.S. 916 (1978).

20. See generally Catharine MacKinnon, *Sexual Harassment of Working Women: A Case Study of Sex Discrimination* (New Haven: Yale University Press, 1979); Love, "Discriminatory Speech and the Tort of Intentional Infliction of Emotional Distress."

not different in kind from involuntary touching or fondling, in that both deprive the woman of equal status in the workplace, and both impose psychological burdens on the woman that are not placed on the men. Again, when we think of dignity in this context, it is the woman who is just trying to do her job whose dignity is at issue, and if our goal is the protection of dignity, then it seems much less likely that we would protect the speech than that we would protect *against* it.

As with the example of race, little changes when we move the gender situation into somewhat more open settings. When we consider, for example, the woman who is heckled on gender-related grounds by a group of male construction workers, or the effect on women of involuntarily confronting images of women being dismembered or mutilated in a sexualized context, concerns about dignity in the sense now under discussion seem to show us that words and pictures can be and frequently are the vehicles by which women are excluded from equal participation in this society.[21] Where the exclusion is intentional and targeted at women, and where the targeted women are the involuntary recipients of the excluding messages, concerns about dignity appear to suggest dealing with the excluding words rather than protecting them.

The examples of race and gender, although the most obvious and most egregious cases, are not the only ones. Similar accounts could be given with respect to various other divisions—such as religion, ethnicity, sexual orientation, and physical handicap—through which ins are separated from outs, and through which some are made to feel full members of the society while others are kept outside. And when this is the case, speech is often the vehicle of the distinction and thus of the exclusion. If the fact of exclusion is itself a loss of dignity, as it is virtually by definition under this conception of dignity, then a concern with dignity will incline toward minimizing the use of those weapons, including but not limited to speech, by which some people are involuntarily dehumanized.

III

The conception of dignity we have just been working with, however, is neither the only nor even the oldest that is available. Under still another conception of dignity, and a somewhat more common one, dignity is

---

21. See Catharine MacKinnon, *Feminism Unmodified: Discourses on Life and Law* (Cambridge: Harvard University Press, 1987); Rae Langton, "Whose Right? Ronald Dworkin, Women, and Pornographers," *Philosophy & Public Affairs* 19 (1990): 311–59.

about choice. Going back to Kant, and reflected in much of modern liberalism, a common way of thinking about dignity focuses on the ability of the independent moral agent to make choices about her life, the result of which is that deprivations of dignity occur when those choices are neither respected nor permitted. As Alan Gewirth puts it, "Hence, the [human] agent is an entity that, unlike other natural entities, is not, so far as he acts, subject only to external forces of nature; he can and does make his own decisions on the basis of his own reflective understanding. By virtue of these characteristics of his action, an agent has worth or dignity."[22]

If dignity is about choice, and respecting dignity is about respecting the choices of others, then it appears as if the choices made in speaking are among the choices whose respect is required by this conception of dignity. Consider, for example, the following from Ronald Dworkin: "But no society that purports to recognize a variety of rights, on the ground that a man's dignity or equality may be invaded in a variety of ways, can accept such a principle. If forcing a man to testify against himself, or forbidding him to speak, does the damage that the rights against self-incrimination and the right to free speech assume, then it would be contemptuous for the State to tell a man that he must suffer this damage against the possibility that other men's risk of loss may be marginally reduced."[23]

Here we have what seems to be the more common connection between free speech and dignity. Dignity is about choice, speaking is an aspect of choice, and restrictions on speaking are therefore deprivations of dignity. Thus, it appears, to restrict the person who would want to say "Nigger!" to another, or who would want to refer to a gay man as a "queer," or who would want to go to Skokie with his jackboots and his Nazi flag singing the *Horst Wessel* song, or who would want to attach a photograph of a naked mutilated woman to his female coworker's locker, is to deprive that agent of his dignity because some of his choices are being restricted.

Plainly my examples are tendentious, designed to make a point that would not be made were we thinking of the choice-exercising speaker as someone who wants simply to read aloud from Karl Marx, or publicly to urge the virtues of nudism, or to express his objection to war by use of a word that some might find offensive.[24] But it is precisely the differ-

---

22. Alan Gewirth, *Human Rights* (Chicago: University of Chicago Press, 1983), p. 29.
23. Ronald Dworkin, *Taking Rights Seriously* (London: Duckworth, 1977), p. 203.
24. See Cohen v. California, 403 U.S. 15 (1971). It is tempting and more current to mention flag burning—see United States v. Eichman, 110 S. Ct. 2404 (1990); Texas v.

ences between the examples that demonstrate the question-begging nature
of the account of Dworkin and others. Implicit not only in Dworkin's
argument but that of many others is that the choice-reflecting communicative act is largely self-regarding, or is at least not as harm-producing
as some other acts. But how, for example, are we to think about physical
striking rather than speaking? Suppose an agent desires to kick another
agent in pursuit of the first agent's choices. Is restricting the first agent
an infringement of his dignity? In some sense yes, because the first agent
is being told that one of his choices is unworthy, that his choice to kick
the second agent is less worthy a choice than would be his hypothetical
choice to tell the second agent that he would be well advised to consider
the teachings of Jesus.

But when we are thinking about kicking, we respond immediately by
recourse to the harm-producing and other-regarding nature of kicking.
Only those choices that do not interfere with the choices of others, we
say, are entitled to respect under a choice-centered account of dignity.
When an agent chooses to kick another agent, his choice limits the choice
of the other not to be kicked, and it impinges on the dignity of the second
agent. Only those choices that are consistent with respecting the choices
of others, and that do not limit the choices of others, we say, are the
kinds of choices that are worth protecting in the name of dignity.

Suppose our first agent responds to this argument by spitting on the
second agent rather than kicking him. "Spitting is not physically harmful," the first agent says. "After all, we go through life being involuntarily
hit with water, whether from a rainstorm or a car driving through a
puddle or the person next to us in line spilling his soft drink. If those
are not deprivations of the rights of others, then why should I be charged
with failing to recognize the rights or the dignity of others by spitting
on them?"

But spitting is not spilling, we respond. The act of spitting is an
affront, an insult, a dehumanizing act ("Even a dog knows the difference
between being kicked and being stumbled over," Holmes said), and
thus is in no way the kind of self-regarding act that the choice-centered
conception of dignity is all about. But if that is a plausible way of

---

Johnson, 109 S. Ct. 2533 (1989)—but it may be too easy for those of us who have not
been in combat to distinguish the effect of flag burning on the (perhaps disabled) war
veteran from the effect of a racial or religious epithet on members of the targeted group.
I do not deny that there may be distinctions, and I am inclined to think there are, but I
am also inclined to think that finding them may be just a bit too easy in the typical academic
environment.

thinking about spitting, then what of speaking for the same insulting or dehumanizing purpose? There is indeed a physical difference between spitting and speaking, but I use spitting as an example precisely because it tests the importance of the physical/nonphysical distinction. Is speaking, because it is nonphysical, necessarily less harmful, less intrusive, and less violative of the rights and dignity of others than physical intrusions, no matter how trivial these might be? Implicit in the claims of Dworkin and others is that speaking is different in kind, for Dworkin would hardly use "freedom to kick" or even "freedom to spit" in the sentences quoted above.

It is apparent that no plausible choice-based account of human dignity extends the protection of dignity to those who exercise their choices by physically (or financially, for that matter) intruding on the dignity of others. The use of a dignity-based conception of protecting choice as a way of protecting speech thus hinges on the assumption that the decision to speak is either in general or in particular cases not a choice that will infringe on the rights or the dignity of others. But we have seen that the assumption that speech in general cannot and does not infringe on the dignity or the rights of others is untrue. Consequently, it must only be *some* linguistic and pictorial acts that would be protected under this conception of freedom of speech as instantiating a choice-based protection of dignity. But if this is the case, then the argument from dignity is not an argument for protecting speech *simpliciter*, or even an argument for protecting the kind of speech now commonly protected under the First Amendment, but is rather an argument only for protecting substantially self-regarding speech. Under this argument, however, it is unclear what work is being done by the "speech" component of the equation. Protection of dignity as protection of self-regarding choice would protect all self-regarding choices, whether linguistic or not. It is apparent, therefore, that trying to tailor a speech-protective conception of dignity as choice to the need to avoid protecting harmful choices leads to a dropping of speech qua speech from the analysis.[25]

25. We could say that we protect theoretically nonprotectible speech only in the service of categorial simplicity. That is, it could be and has been argued that speech is *in general* much less likely than physical conduct to be other-regarding even if there are some other-regarding and harm-producing instances of speech. Redish, *Freedom of Expression*, for example, relies heavily on this argument. Consequently, although, say, dignity is directly at issue only when self-regarding speech is concerned, we might have to protect all speech, or at least some speech that is not self-regarding, in order to make sure that all of the self-regarding speech is protected. But this conclusion requires accepting one of three quite

IV

Speaking about dignity thus appears not to take us very far in thinking about the protection of freedom of speech. If we start with a choice-centered conception of dignity, we are at a loss to explain that which is most interesting about any free speech system, the way in which it protects not only harmless speech acts, but some number of harmful speech acts despite the harm they may cause. This is not to say that other arguments cannot get us to this point, and indeed I believe that they very well may. But it is to say that arguments from dignity as choice, common as they may be, and useful as they may be in under-girding the right to make those life choices that do not interfere with the life choices of others, take us nowhere in explaining a system that appears to protect those communicative acts that do interfere with the life choices of others.

If instead we start with a conception of dignity that focuses on freedom from dehumanization, we see not only that it is difficult to generate a right of freedom to engage in dehumanizing communicative conduct, but also that it is quite a bit easier to generate arguments for restriction of speech of this type. This has lessons not only for the theoretical issue of how, if at all, to ground a nontrivial principle of freedom of speech, and not only for numerous current controversies about hate speech of all varieties, but also for those various documents and institutions of international human rights that take freedom of speech as fundamental in the same way that freedom from torture is fundamental. That may be the case, but either the argument for freedom of speech is quite different from the argument for freedom from torture, or if the same, the right to freedom of speech appears to be in that context appropriately far narrower than it is according to American law. As a differential protection for or immunization of various other-regarding and harm-producing acts under circumstances in which the

---

controversial premises. One is that empirically the population of speech acts has proportionally fewer other-regarding members than the population of nonspeech acts. Second is
that a greater degree of strategic (or rule-based) overprotection is necessity for self-regarding
speech acts than for other self-regarding acts. And third is that the advances in protection
of dignity attained by using overprotection to guard against underprotection are greater
than the loss of dignity consequent upon the strategic protection of dignity-denying other-
regarding speech acts. None of these premises seem self-evident, and all seem at least as
likely false than true. Nevertheless, this very kind of categorial generalization, empirically
justified or not, necessarily undergirds the identification of a distinct principle of freedom
of speech and a distinct constitutional doctrine protecting it. Schauer, "The Second-Best
First Amendment."

same harms would justify official intervention, freedom of speech is different in dramatic ways from most other individual rights, and thus the idea of dignity, which is highly relevant to thinking about many other rights, may be much less relevant in thinking about freedom of speech.

IO

The Right to Silence and Human Dignity

R. KENT GREENAWALT

How does the concept of "dignity" bear on the privilege against self-incrimination? Dignity is not the central inquiry in determining just what protection that constitutional standard affords, but it nevertheless matters. Deciding what practices are consonant with human dignity is also a crucial inquiry for legislative and executive choices within the outer boundaries of what is constitutionally permitted.

The subject of human dignity and the right to silence covered by the privilege against self-incrimination[1] has a substantial comparative dimension. We would be fortunate if the government could treat everyone with complete dignity all of the time. But that is not possible now in our society, and probably it is not possible in any complex society. Enforcement of much of the criminal law is very important, and reasonably effective enforcement requires some measures that treat some people with less than full dignity. A choice among measures should focus partly on which of them are more consonant with dignity.

This essay does not offer a general analysis of the concept of "dignity"

This essay draws substantially from R. Kent Greenawalt, "Silence as a Moral and Constitutional Right," *William and Mary Law Review* 23 (1981): 15. That article contains more elaborations, citations, and legal analysis than I present here.

1. When I use the term *right to silence* in this essay, I refer to the kind of silence covered by the privilege against self-incrimination, not to silence that is protected by the First Amendment guarantees of freedom of speech and religious exercise nor to the immunity from ordinary searches protected by the Fourth Amendment.

or of how dignity relates to constitutional values and interpretation, so I sketch a few thoughts on those subjects here. Human dignity may be understood as congruent with the idea that all individual human beings have moral worth, that they are important and should not be treated as mere means to the ends of others. In this broad sense, human dignity may be thought to lie behind all guarantees of individual rights.

Human dignity may be thought to follow from some human characteristic, such as reason or choice, or from the relation of human beings to God. Whether dignity is grounded in some such source or is presented more simply as a fundamental normative concept, recognition of dignity affects how people should act toward each other. Most especially, dignity precludes humiliating treatment. In a liberal democracy the concept of dignity is closely related to ideas of respect, individuality, autonomy, tolerance, and equality. To recognize the dignity of liberal citizens involves acknowledgment of their independence of choice, their power to define for themselves the kinds of persons they will be and the lives they will lead. Dignity is something that is to be accorded to all citizens, not only some; and in some basic respect, equality of status is prerequisite for equal dignity.

Constitutional standards protecting individual rights do not reflect one single and identifiable general value. They are based on a sense of needed limits of government coercion. Any constitutional protection draws support from more than one general value, as the privilege against self-incrimination might be said to concern privacy, autonomy, dignity, and other general values. No court interpreting a particular provision can rest comfortably in a reference to one value. Given the dependence of legal interpretation on particular legal materials, history, and institutional considerations, even reference to multiple general values will not usually be the main part of a court's job. Relevant general values will typically be closely related and overlapping in content.

In its broadest sense, human dignity might be understood to lie behind other general values that support individual rights. But that sense of dignity as moral worth is so broad it will not often be a useful tool for interpretation. If one focuses on a narrower sense involving treatment with dignity, respect, and consideration, the value of dignity is likely to be more helpful for analysis, but it should not then be seen as swallowing up other relevant values. Privacy contributes to dignity, but if only that aspect of privacy is regarded, the importance of privacy will be devalued. How people in a culture understand any one value depends heavily on the other values they accept, but reductionist efforts to discover one overarching value that is a key to interpretation are bound to be distorting. Although "human dignity" is not *the key* to judgment about the right to silence, our society should recognize it is a very helpful guide.

Since my main interest in this essay is the relation between dignity and the dimensions of a privilege against self-incrimination, I do not concentrate on what should be decided as a matter of constitutional interpretation and what should be left to legislative and executive choice. My discussion very much has in mind, however, some of the major things the Supreme Court has decided about the privilege against self-incrimination. Talking about its fundamental place in the constitutional scheme, the Court has held that the privilege precludes negative inferences from someone's refusal to speak,[2] that it precludes dismissal from government employment for refusal to testify about crimes relating to government work,[3] and that it applies to police interrogation as well as formal legal demands to testify.[4]

The privilege against self-incrimination, like the Fourth Amendment ban on unreasonable searches and seizures, stands as a barrier to the government's acquisition of information about criminal activities. The moral analogue in private relations to the Fourth Amendment right is quite straightforward. One person should not rummage about the private spaces of another seeking signs of bad behavior unless he has very powerful reasons. The Fourth Amendment similarly limits the government, generally permitting searches only upon probable cause. The private moral analogue to the Fifth Amendment's right of silence is hard to identify; its analysis is more complex, and the judgments of right and wrong are more dubious. When may one person properly ask another if he has done something wrong? What are the responsibilities of the person asked when such questions are put? And what may the questioner assume if no helpful response is forthcoming? Uncertainty about these matters may help explain the profound disagreements over the right to silence, considered by some a pernicious impediment to the discovery of truth and by others "one of the great landmarks in man's struggle to make himself civilized."[5]

Exploration of the ordinary morality that governs questioning of those who may have done something wrong may aid us to understand what

---

2. See Griffin v. California, 380 U.S. 609 (1965).
3. See Lefkowitz v. Cunningham, 431 U.S. 801 (1977).
4. See Miranda v. Arizona, 384 U.S. 436 (1966).
5. Erwin Griswold, *The Fifth Amendment Today* (Cambridge: Harvard University Press, 1955), p. 7.

relations are appropriate between an inquiring state and suspected individuals in the criminal process. By focusing on the respect and concern that individuals owe to each other and that governments owe to their citizens, I do not mean to deny that the efficient pursuit of truth is important for evaluating rights in the criminal process. But whatever one's views about how truth can best be found, arguments about the kind of right to silence that reflects human dignity also deserve attention. These are arguments whose strength citizens and courts can evaluate without relying upon controversial empirical assumptions. Moreover, the crucial disagreements concerning the practices I discuss are over the moral rights of individuals, not over the effective discovery of truth.

SILENCE AND FALSEHOOD IN PRIVATE RELATIONSHIPS

How one person should act toward another whom he suspects of wronging him depends on the precise character of the particular relationship and the wrong, but an abstract and general account can highlight significant factors. I start with two basic distinctions: one between close relationships of trust and other private relationships; the other between substantial and insubstantial bases for suspicion. By close relationships of trust I refer mainly to relations between family members and friends, but some working relations take on this character.

Slender Suspicion in a Close Relationship

Suppose that someone recognizes a slight possibility that another in a close relationship of trust has wronged him: has breached a confidence, taken personal property, or violated some special undertaking, such as the commitment to sexual fidelity in many marriages. Imagine, for example, that Ann cannot find her unusual bracelet and is aware that one of the many things that might have happened is that her roommate, Betty, may have stolen it. At this point, Ann may ask Betty whether she has seen the bracelet, but she should not ask questions plainly directed to the chance that Betty may have taken it. In close adult relationships, trust is a characteristic and central element. If Ann treats seriously the slender chance that Betty has stolen the bracelet, she shows a lack of trust and grants Betty less respect than the relationship calls for.

What may Betty properly do if Ann asks her to account for her activities? Even if she resents the implications of Ann's questions, she may answer honestly, the course many people would choose. But Betty might say something like "That's none of your business," or "I won't dignify that with an answer." Ann's improper questions do not create a duty upon Betty to answer.

With some hesitation, I reach the same conclusion if Betty happens to have taken the bracelet. Betty certainly has a duty to repair the original wrong to Ann, insofar as she can; but unless disclosure is vital to repair the damage, Betty does not have a duty to tell Ann about the wrong. Ann's improper question, though fortuitously on target, does not create a new duty on Betty to disclose her wrong.

What conclusion can Ann properly reach if Betty refuses to respond? Plainly, she lacks sufficient ground to suppose that Betty is guilty, because Betty's silence may well have been the outraged reaction of an innocent, untrusted friend. The more troubling question is whether she can give that silence some weight if further evidence of Betty's guilt appears. She might reason as follows: "I was wrong to question Betty and she was justified in not responding. Still, more guilty than innocent people would refuse to respond, so Betty's silence makes me think it is more likely that she stole the bracelet. My responsibilities to Betty do not require me to disregard this relevant information, though my own improper question produced it." If Ann were capable of dispassionate evaluation, I believe this response would be defensible. In most real situations, however, a person whose excessive suspicions lead her to put improper questions will not be able to judge rationally the weight of a refusal to respond. Once Ann recognizes her own wrong and the propriety of a silent reaction, perhaps she should try to disregard that reaction as possible evidence of guilt.

Solidly Grounded Suspicion in a Close Relationship

I now want to introduce an important change in the facts. Cathy, a mutual friend who is unaware than Ann's bracelet is missing, has written Ann that she was surprised to find Betty's sister wearing a bracelet identical to Ann's. Ann knows that Betty took a trip to visit her family about the time the bracelet disappeared. Although other possibilities cannot be excluded, Ann now sensibly believes that Betty probably took the bracelet and gave it to her sister.

The close relationship of trust no longer bars an attempt by Ann to find out if Betty has taken the bracelet. She cannot be expected simply to discount the chance of Betty's guilt or to carry on the relationship without attempting to resolve the matter. The most natural, open course for Ann is to tell Betty what Cathy's letter says and ask for an explanation. However tactfully Ann phrases the question, Betty will perceive that Ann's confidence in her integrity is less than complete, but if Betty is fair-minded, she will recognize that Ann's shaken confidence is warranted by the external facts.

How else might Ann seek to learn if Betty has stolen the bracelet? She could make a thorough search of Betty's belongings to see if anything else she has lost turns up. She could ask a friend (or a professional detective) to get close to Betty and try to trick her into admissions. She could ask other members of Betty's family how the sister got her bracelet. Ann could simply keep a very close eye on Betty, or lay potential traps for her, leaving jewelry to which only Betty would have access.

Most of these alternatives would avoid directly exposing Ann's suspicions and thus might spare Betty's feelings, but each has serious drawbacks from a moral point of view. The search involves an invasion of Betty's personal space. Getting someone to elicit admissions by deception may be even worse, resting as it does on an extreme manipulation of Betty's social environment. Even the more innocuous techniques of watching Betty carefully and "laying traps" require deceit by Ann, who must simulate full trust in Betty while acting contrary to such trust. Writing first to Betty's family may avoid this objection, but it is an embarrassing insult to a friend.

One perspective for comparing these alternatives is to imagine Betty's feelings about them. If Betty is innocent, she may well be initially hurt by direct questions, but she can come to accept their appropriateness. If she subsequently learns that she has been subject to a search or the attentions of a pretended friend, she will be outraged. We can imagine her anguished cry upon hearing that Ann has written her family, "Why didn't you come to me first?" Discovering that Ann has been "watching" her or laying traps will also make Betty feel wronged. If Betty is guilty, she may feel she has less complaint if other tactics are employed against her, but she still will probably feel some offense that Ann has tried to determine her guilt without first giving her a chance to explain.

Yet another alternative is open for Ann. She could simply assume Betty's guilt on the basis of Cathy's letter and end the relationship without revealing the true reason. That course shows little respect or concern for Betty, who might be innocent and who, even if guilty, might have been able to respond to Ann in a way that would have preserved the value of their friendship.

This analysis suggests the following generalization: in close relationships, when A has strong grounds to suspect B of wrongdoing, A's laying the grounds of his suspicion before B and asking for an explanation is not only appropriate, it is more respectful of B's dignity and autonomy than most alternative approaches to discovering the truth.

When Ann asks her for an explanation, Betty now has powerful moral reasons to respond. Ann undeniably has a legitimate interest in asking what has happened to her bracelet, and external evidence suggests that Betty's honest response will help. Moreover, Ann's justified suspicions threaten their relationship. Betty has a duty as a friend both to aid Ann's search for the facts and to do what she honestly can to prevent a bitter end of the friendship.

If Betty is inclined to conceal the truth,[6] a refusal to respond hardly will be effective. Only lies will suffice, and they require a heavier justification than mere failure to respond. A different ground Betty might assert for refusing to tell the truth is that she has a moral privilege not to bring harmful consequences upon herself. I shall discuss a possible self-preservation justification more fully below and here will say only that when close friends and family members alone are involved, the consequences of admissions of wrongdoing will usually be uncertain. For this reason, and because one is under a powerful duty to respond to questions that have been justifiably put by a close acquaintance, the claim in this context that one can lie or remain silent to protect himself is not very attractive.

How may Ann justifiably react if Betty does refuse to respond? She will rightly perceive Betty's silence now as strongly suggesting guilt. Since her own questioning was appropriate, she may give that silence the weight it naturally has. Further, Ann has the independent complaint that Betty has failed to fulfill an important duty of friendship. In their personal relations, Ann would be justified in acting as if Betty had taken the bracelet.

At this stage the only sense in which Betty has a moral right to silence against Ann in regard to the lost bracelet is the very weak sense in which she has a moral right to silence on every subject. Ann cannot coerce Betty to respond, and if she tricks or pressures Betty into speaking, she violates

---

6. In some situations, as when the original wrong is sexual cheating or conversational breach of confidence, the wrongdoer may think concealment will actually lessen the harm the victim suffers.

Betty's autonomy and dignity. Betty has no special right to silence concerning her possible guilt.

Slender Suspicion in
Less Personal Relationships

Will our conclusions differ if the relationship is less personal? I shall use an example of employer-employee relations, recognizing, of course, its limited power in light of the immense variety of relations into which suspicions can intrude. Arlene owns and runs a grocery store with fifteen employees, including Bob, who has been working for six months. Initially, Arlene starts to suspect that she is missing some food, but she is not sure any theft has occurred, much less which, if any, of her employees might be involved. She may appropriately ask her employees if they have seen anything suspicious, but she should not question each to test his possible guilt. Though Arlene has not the same personal basis for trusting her employees that Ann has for trusting Betty, she still should assume that each is performing his duties honestly until a solid basis exists for supposing otherwise. Each of us needs to be treated as honest and trustworthy in ordinary relationships; focused inquiries based on remote conjecture do not accord due respect to the persons questioned. When genuinely momentous matters are at stake, treating everyone as potentially untrustworthy may be necessary. But even when employees understand the need for periodic lie detector tests or daily searches, they may feel degraded by them, at least until they are numbed by familiarity. Such treatment is to be avoided unless the stakes are very high indeed. So Arlene would be wrong at this point to question Bob as a potential suspect.

If she does so, Bob would be justified in refusing to answer. Unless protected by union contracts, few employees would engage in a job-risking failure to respond. But whatever self-interest may dictate, Bob has no moral duty to answer Arlene—for the same reason Betty had no duty to answer. This conclusion holds even if he has stolen the food. He should stop stealing and repair the original wrong, but he does not have an initial duty to come forward and admit his wrong unless that is required for reparation. Arlene's unjustified inquiries do not create a new duty to admit his guilt.

Because few innocent employees will fail to answer, Bob's refusal may point toward guilt more than a similar refusal by Betty. But because the refusal is consistent with angered innocence, it plainly is not an adequate basis for Arlene to conclude that Bob is guilty. If further evidence of Bob's guilt comes to light, perhaps she may accord Bob's original silence its natural weight. If she, however, recognizes the impropriety of her original questions, she may also assume that she cannot fairly evaluate the likely significance of a silent response and may properly try to disregard it as any evidence of guilt.

Solidly Grounded Suspicion in Less Personal Relationships

If Arlene has special reason to suspect Bob because, for example, another employee has reported him, questions directed toward his possible guilt become appropriate. Indeed, in less personal relationships the point at which such inquiries are acceptable may come earlier than with close friends and family members, since one person's assumption that another is trustworthy will be less deeply rooted, and treatment as a possible suspect will not wound so much. As with the close relationships, direct questioning shows more respect than searches or deceitful attempts to obtain admissions. Employers, however, have recognized supervisory responsibilities over employees, and special scrutiny of a worker, or traps, or initial attempts to get information from others may be more acceptable here than among friends. Nevertheless, inquiries put to Bob are certainly one proper way for Arlene to proceed when she has substantial grounds to think Bob guilty.

One of Bob's responsibilities as an employee is to aid Arlene in resolving legitimate concerns about the business. Both Bob's implied commitment to performance when he took the job and the general benefits of fulfilling such expectations constitute moral grounds for Bob to act as his employee role requires. If Bob is innocent and is now questioned by Arlene, he has a moral duty to explain his activities, so that she will realize that no thefts have taken place or that someone else has committed them.

If Bob is guilty, what he may permissibly do is more difficult. Let us suppose he knows that the police will not be brought in but that he will be fired and will have difficulty getting a new job if he admits to theft. Only some conflicting duty or privilege could override his employee duty to cooperate. Assuming that Bob has no unusual duties toward others that would warrant his refusing to reveal the truth, does he yet have some moral privilege of self-preservation that permits him to do so? The argument to that effect is that no one can fairly be expected to bring an extremely harmful consequence, such as being fired, upon himself.

The strongest version of the suggested principle would treat an individual's self-harming behavior as being actually immoral. A weaker version would consider the right of self-preservation as somehow offsetting Bob's duty to respond honestly to Arlene, leaving Bob in some sense morally free to decide which course to take. How Bob makes the choice might be thought to be morally indifferent. Or the choice to respond honestly, a choice relatively few people would be willing to make, might be regarded as morally preferable, but not demanded by moral duty.[7]

A kind of natural rights argument might be advanced on behalf of a principle of self-preservation. The claim would be that any individual has a basic right to avoid very destructive consequences to himself even if submission would serve the welfare of others.[8] Applied to innocent people, this claim has much appeal, yielding such conclusions as that someone cannot be blamed for declining to donate a kidney to save a life of a stranger. When the person's original wrongful act creates the risk of the very harmful consequences, the claim is more dubious. Still, regrettable as the original wrong was, and justifiable as the threatening response may be, perhaps the person committing the wrong should not be thought to have a moral duty to cooperate in bringing the consequences of that response upon himself.

The self-preservation claim will take on added force in many situations because the wrongdoer's fate is closely tied to that of others. Children, a spouse, other relatives and friends, will be pulled down by any catastrophe that occurs to him. Even if he could somehow disregard his own interests, he might decide that his duties to aid those nearest to him outweigh his duty to his employer.

Assuming that some right of self-preservation relieves Bob of his duty to respond honestly, does it justify his actually lying to Arlene or only his refusing to respond? By lying, Bob would actively try to thwart Arlene's legitimate efforts to learn what happened and perhaps cast suspicion on some innocent person. He would also violate his general duty to tell the truth. Thus, more powerful supporting grounds are necessary for lying than for silence. Yet, remaining silent may be ineffective to protect any of Bob's vital interests. If the principle of self-preservation is understood as concerning actual protection of Bob's interests, his prac-

---

7. The mere fact that most people who find themselves in a particular situation will not perform an act does not foreclose the possibility that the act is required by duty, especially when, as with thieves who are under suspicion, the class of those in the situation is determined by original wrongful acts by members of the class.

8. Cf. Thomas Hobbes, *Leviathan*, chap. 14.

tical choice may be between telling the truth and lying. If instead the principle is taken to mean only that persons have the right not to contribute actively to their own downfall, silence may be an important option to telling the truth even if silence will not ward off harmful consequences.[9]

How can Arlene appropriately react if Bob does refuse to respond? Few innocent people would decline to explain away evidence of their wrongdoing, so a refusal to respond is strongly indicative of their guilt. Although guilty persons more often lie than remain mute, some are unwilling to lie and others are afraid they cannot tell plausible lies. Because Arlene's concern and questions are appropriate, she need not hesitate to accord a silent response its natural weight. Even if Bob is innocent, his refusal to answer is a serious failure of duty. Thus, Arlene will be justified if she dismisses Bob.

Even if Bob enjoys some privilege of self-preservation that allows him to put himself and his family before his employer's interest in discovering the wrong, Arlene need not give Bob's interest priority. And it would be ludicrous to say that in serving her own interests and giving silence its natural effect, she is somehow interfering with Bob's right not to respond. That right is not a right to be thought innocent or escape harmful consequences, but a right not to *help* bring about those consequences. What would otherwise be appropriate actions by Arlene are not turned into wrongs because they reduce the practical value of Bob's right. We should reach the same conclusion about the possibility that questions directed at suspects often produce lies. We do not hold the people who ask proper questions responsible for those lies, or believe that they should disregard the lies if they discover them.

A Right to Silence and the Criminal Process

The Implications of a Moral Right to Silence against the State

So far, I have made a number of suggestions about the morality of silence when one private person questions another about possible wrongdoing. What, if anything, do my conclusions—some drawn confidently, others more tentatively—have to do with the government's efforts to

9. Whatever the strength of the self-preservation principle, it obviously applies to the earlier stage of slender suspicion as well as when questions are based on substantial grounds. Thus, it reinforces the other arguments I have made for why even a guilty person is not under a moral duty to respond at that earlier point.

enforce the criminal law? At the least, the previous discussion illuminates some possibly important distinctions; for example, between the suspected person's weighing of moral claims and the victim's weighing of moral claims. I believe, however, that the discussion also provides an important starting point for resolving questions about the state's use of its power. Moral principles governing private relations should also govern relations between the state and individuals, unless important differences in those relations call for variant treatment. Inquiry about the significance of private relations for the criminal process requires close attention to special features of individuals' relation to their government.

One crucial aspect of government authority is the power to compel people to tell the truth, by confining those who refuse to answer and by treating lies as criminal. Private persons rarely are morally justified in using actual or threatened physical coercion to compel others to speak; the government's employment of such force is often warranted. Persons disagree about the proper occasions for that force and about the ideal scope of various privileges that excuse persons from answering questions. Few doubt, however, that forcing witnesses is sometimes appropriate even though the truth will embarrass the witnesses, put them in an un-complimentary light, or jeopardize important interests of theirs or of persons about whom they care deeply. If incriminating remarks are to receive special treatment, some special justification must apply to them.

One important question is whether a suspect has less moral obligation to tell the truth to criminal investigators than to victims in private re-lationships. The moral grounds in favor of responding honestly might be weaker or some countervailing privilege of self-protection might be stronger. In favor of weaker grounds to tell the truth, it might be said that a criminal's admission of guilt has little to do with compensatory justice. The establishment of criminal guilt is not directly connected to restitution to victims, and many criminal acts either do irreparable dam-age or do not involve specific victims. Moreover, since the questions are not being put by the victims themselves, any special duty to respond to the one who has been wronged is absent. Finally, the ties between suspect and government are less close than the ties in many private relationships and do not involve the voluntary undertaking of responsibilities that typifies friendship and employment.

None of those points is a very powerful reason for considering the moral grounds in favor of truth telling to be weakened. In private contexts, too, compensating for wrongs is often separable from ad-mitting guilt. When redress can be made for criminal wrongs, its ini-

tiation usually depends upon identification of the criminal. And establishment of guilt and punishment accomplish more subtle forms of
partial rectification, relieving victims and others of insecurity, and sat-
isfying normal desires that those who have caused injury be punished.
Because victims usually want crimes solved, officials who investigate
crimes can fairly be seen as representing them, as well as the larger
public. Therefore, the suspect's responsibility to answer honestly seems
little affected by the fact that someone other than the victim is putting
the questions. Nor does the comparative weakness of a suspects's relation to the government mean that the moral bases for his telling the
truth to criminal investigators are correspondingly weaker. Often when
individuals choose whether to comply with government initiatives,
moral responsibilities concerning interests of great moment are involved,
and this is true of most criminal investigations. Everyone has a strong
moral duty not to inflict undeserved harm on fellow members of the
community and to prevent harms others might commit when he can
do so easily. Appalling examples of urban apartment dwellers who do
not pick up their telephones when a neighbor is being viciously assaulted
are a powerful reminder of what life can be like when people do not
act upon this duty. Since the establishment of guilt usually limits a
crime's harmful effects and helps protect the community against future
crimes, powerful moral grounds exist for contributing to the solution
of serious crimes. These grounds apply to persons deciding whether to
admit they have committed crimes.

If a suspect has, all things considered, less moral duty to tell the truth
to criminal investigators than to victims in many private relationships,
the reason is not that the grounds for honesty are weaker, but that some
countervailing privilege of self-protection is stronger, stronger because
of the fearful consequences of admitting serious crimes. Even if we believe
that open admission of guilt is usually the best course of action, we may
hesitate to say that someone has a moral duty to bring conviction and
imprisonment upon himself.

Closely related to this point about self-defense is an argument based
on the character of the relation between government and suspect. Lies
made to enemies are more easily justified than lies made to others, both
because less generally is owed to antagonists and because most antago-
nistic relationships lack the foundation of trust upon which the duty of
honesty partly depends. From the perspective of the person formally
accused of criminal acts, the government plainly has become an enemy
in an important sense.

The criminal process is not a battle between equally meritorious combatants in which the suspect's desire not to be convicted ranks equally with society's interest in convicting the guilty. From society's broader perspective, the aim of the process is to clear the innocent and convict the guilty. The government's pursuit of accurate determinations, however, must be limited by principles of humane treatment. Whether grounds exist to make a suspect's refusal to respond morally acceptable, government compulsion to force admissions is inhumane when strong condemnation and lengthy imprisonment are likely consequences. Though articulation of the grounds of this intuitive judgment is not easy, the broader principle within which it falls is the cruelty of forcing people to do serious harm to themselves, even when infliction of the same harm by others is warranted.[10] That the right to silence rests on this basic moral perception is suggested by judicial talk of "our unwillingness to subject those suspected of crime to the cruel trilemma of self-accusation, perjury or contempt."[11] When most witnesses feared damnation if they lied under oath and the penalty for felonies was death, the choice was particularly excruciating, but it remains cruel for the government to force people to help convict themselves, lie, or be confined for contempt. This is particularly so when the government is not going to take exculpatory statements on their face, but is committed to seeking evidence against, or convicting, someone, despite whatever account he offers.

If the moral basis for the right to silence in ordinary criminal cases is the inhumanity or indignity of forcing admissions, what should the dimensions of the right be? When substantial evidence exists against someone, allowing ordinary inferences from his silence and dismissing him if he refuses to speak about his performance of public duty hardly seems inhumane. These are, rather, natural consequences of his choice to remain silent. Undoubtedly, those practices may affect a suspect's or a defendant's choice to speak, but the moral right to silence should not be viewed as a right to be released from all the normal influences to respond to

10. A disturbing and careful challenge to this idea is made by David Dolinko, "Is There a Rationale for the Privilege against Self-Incrimination?" UCLA Law Review 33(1986): 1063, 1090–1107. Without attempting a full response, I do want to address one point he makes, that the legal system requires people to do other things as damaging to their interests as admitting their own criminality. Compulsion to testify against close relatives in serious criminal cases and against one's own financial interests in civil cases can be worse than self-incrimination in unserious criminal cases; but, in general, self-incrimination is serious enough to warrant special legal treatment.

11. Murphy v. Waterfront Commission, 378 U.S. 52, 55 (1964).

accusations. Rather, it should be viewed as a right to be free of the especially powerful compulsions that the state can bring to bear on witnesses. Some support for this conclusion may be drawn from the practice of other liberal democracies. As far as I am aware, no nation grants silence as absolute protection as our present principles purport to afford. In England, for example, some adverse comment on pretrial silence and on refusal to take the stand is now permitted. In the early 1970s the prestigious Criminal Law Committee proposed expansion of presently permissible inferences and the adoption of other strategies to encourage responses to questions;[12] these proposals failed after heated debate, but even their opponents did not generally argue that existing practices were unfair.[13]

From the moral point of view, pressures and tricks designed to get suspects to confess are much more questionable than inferences from silence and dismissal. When law enforcement officers browbeat suspects, play on their weaknesses, deceive them as to critically relevant facts, such as whether a suspected confederate has confessed, or keep them in a hostile setting, the officials intentionally manipulate the environment to make rational, responsible choice more difficult. Such tactics hardly accord with respect for autonomy and dignity, and they work unevenly by undermining the inexperienced and ignorant and by having little effect on the hardened criminal. These tactics can be defended only under some extreme version of the battle model of the criminal process or, more persuasively, with the argument that some compromise with ideal procedures is required because getting admissions from suspects is so essential to solving crimes. The *Miranda* rules, as well as their predecessor standards for coerced confessions, were formulated largely to curb the worst tactics of this sort, but the Supreme Court has not adopted constitutional principles that would effectively prevent admissions obtained by pressure and deceptions that would be considered immoral in private contexts.

How powerful is the moral right to silence in relation to criminal investigation before a substantial basis exists for suspicion? I have suggested that for private relationships a stronger moral right ordinarily

12. Criminal Law Revision Committee, *Eleventh Report, Evidence (General)* (London: Her Majesty's Stationery Office: 1972), secs. 29–46, 110–12.
13. See Robert S. Gerstein, "The Self-Incrimination Debate in Great Britain," *American Journal of Comparative Law* 27 (1979):81; R. Kent Greenawalt, "Perspectives on the Right to Silence," in R. Hood, ed., *Crime, Criminology and Public Policy* (New York: Free Press, 1974), pp. 239–40, 243–44.

exists before this threshold is passed. Does that idea have application to the criminal process, and if so, how should it affect the right to silence that a legal system grants?

As to most crimes, public officials should not question persons as suspects unless they have a substantial basis for doing so. Murders and other very serious crimes are exceptional in this respect; their solution is so important that anyone who conceivably may have committed them may properly be asked for an account of his activities that will establish his innocence. But, if citizens were commonly questioned by officials about their possible commission of more garden-variety crimes, such as petty theft and income tax evasion, an unhealthy atmosphere of resentment and distrust would result. Nonetheless, it is difficult to conceive the formulation of any legal principle that could effectively forbid such questioning. People are often questioned about their possible knowledge of crimes committed by others, or about their "innocent" mistakes on tax returns. The line is very thin between such questions and those treating someone as a suspected criminal; and the official's view of the respondent may shift because of answers to earlier questions. We must, therefore, rely mostly on the good judgment of officials, and to their paltry resources, to protect citizens from inappropriate fishing expeditions.

Except, perhaps, for the gravest sorts of crimes, an actor does not have a moral duty to come forward and admit his guilt publicly unless that is necessary to provide restitution, to prevent his commission of future similar acts, or to avoid injustice to others. If he happens to be the subject of inappropriate questions directed toward his possible guilt, the questions do not create a new duty to reveal the incriminating facts. His moral right to silence at that point does not, therefore, depend on some privilege of self-preservation overriding what would otherwise be a duty to respond. The right thus rests on a firmer foundation than any right to silence after substantial evidence has been discovered. The history of the privilege against self-incrimination itself supports this distinction. What the initial advocates of a right to silence proclaimed was that they could not be required to respond to incriminating questions in the absence of due accusation.[14]

The moral right not to supply the initial evidence against oneself is much more basic than any right not to respond to inquiry following

14. See, e.g., Leonard Levy, *Origins of the Fifth Amendment* (New York: Macmillan, 1968), p. 62.

substantial evidence; and the argument is powerful that an individual should not suffer serious adverse consequences because he invokes that more basic right. Though the question is close, I think the argument is strong enough to overcome the contrary claims that silence even at an early stage is somewhat indicative of guilt and should be accorded its natural force. Thus, I conclude that although adverse inferences are proper when a person refuses to respond to questions based on substantial evidence of his wrongdoing, those who bear responsibility for determining guilt should not be allowed to draw such inferences from silence that has occurred before substantial evidence of wrongdoing exists. In support of this conclusion is the desirability of reducing incentives for officials to engage in unwarranted fishing expeditions.

Institutions

What might the criminal process look like if a serious attempt were made to implement my suggestions? Though no formal prohibition would bar questioning persons as possible suspects, superiors would discourage investigatory officers from doing so in ordinary cases absent a significant likelihood of guilt. By a "significant likelihood of guilt," I mean a flexible standard that would depend on the seriousness of the crime but would often be less rigorous than probable cause. For example, if an apartment burglary were apparently committed with a set of keys, each of four outsiders with keys could be asked where they were at the time of the burglary. More probing, systematic questioning of a suspect should take place only after probable cause of guilt exists, the point at which arrest is now possible. A neutral official, a magistrate, should determine the presence of probable cause before this more intense questioning occurs. To avoid possible pressure and deceitful manipulation, the questioning should not be done by the police alone, but by a magistrate or in front of him, and the suspect should be accorded counsel. To avoid any subsequent misinterpretation of what took place, a precise record should be kept. At each of these stages, a person would have the privilege of remaining silent. Fact-finders would not be permitted to draw adverse inferences from refusals to respond prior to questioning before the magistrate; but if a suspect then claimed his right to silence, that fact could be introduced as adverse evidence at his trial. If a defendant did not testify at his trial, the jury could be invited by the judge to draw an adverse inference from his silence.[15] Practices like these would more fairly reflect the natural effects of a right to silence than the practices we now have. They would also be more consonant with human dignity, with the respect a government owes its citizens.

15. When officials refused to respond about appropriate questions directed at the performance of public duty, their dismissal would be permissible.

I I

Human Dignity and
Constitutional Rights

LOUIS HENKIN

Others writing in this volume have defined "human dignity" and have explored affinities between that concept and various values implicit in the U.S. Constitution. In this essay I relate human dignity to the idea of individual rights and to the protection of rights by the Constitution.

A standard dictionary defines *dignity* as "the quality or state of being worthy, honored, or esteemed." If so, human dignity can be said to mean that worthiness, honor, or esteem that is recognized as belonging to all human beings, perhaps by virtue of their being human. But "worthiness," "honor" and "esteem" are not identical conceptions, and each is not without ambiguity; none of these terms, moreover, communicates clearly what it entails or brings a recipe for how it is to be achieved.¹ In general, as presently conceived, human dignity requires that in any society every person count, that he (she) be considered worthy as an individual, not merely as part of the collectivity. Specifically, human dignity requires respect for every individual's physical and psychic integrity, for his (her) "personhood" before the law, for her (his) autonomy and freedom; these

---

1. The concept of human dignity is sometimes associated with the ethical writings of Immanuel Kant. As translated into English, he sometimes writes of individual dignity or worthiness (*würde*), sometimes of intrinsic individual worth (*wert*). In a famous statement he declared that a human being should be treated as an end in himself, not as a means to other persons or other ends. See, e.g., Immanuel Kant, *Foundations of the Metaphysics of Morals*, trans. L. W. Beck (Indianapolis: Bobbs-Merrill, reprinted 1969), second section, pp. 52–53.

are not to be lightly sacrificed, even for the welfare of the majority or for the common good. Sometimes human dignity is seen as requiring more—the full development of the individual's personality, respect by society and by one's neighbors, security for one's "honor" and self-esteem.

HUMAN DIGNITY AND HUMAN RIGHTS:
THE CONTEMPORARY LINKAGE

Links between individual rights and human dignity are now commonly assumed. Such links are declared explicitly in the preamble to the Universal Declaration of Human Rights, and in the preamble to the two international human rights covenants that derive from that declaration.[2] The authors of those instruments, seeking a theoretical foundation for the international human rights movement that would be acceptable to all peoples, cultures, and political ideologies, justified human rights by relating them to human dignity.

The framers of the international instruments did not define human dignity; perhaps they thought it needed no definition, in any language. Nor were they precise about the relationship between human rights and human dignity. It was apparently assumed that it went without saying that respect for a person's human rights is necessary to maintain his (her) human dignity. There was no suggestion that respect for human rights was sufficient to that end: other "goods" may also be necessary for human fulfillment in dignity—friendship, love, community, international peace, a healthful environment, human survival.

Having linked human rights to human dignity, the framers of the Universal Declaration proceeded to declare a catalogue of rights. Whether the concept of human dignity determined the specific content of that catalogue is not clear. There has been no studied attempt to invoke human dignity to justify the inclusion of any particular right (or the exclusion of others), either in the declaration or in the many human rights covenants and conventions that derive from it.[3]

2. "Whereas recognition of the inherent dignity and of the equal and inalienable rights of all members of the human family is the foundation of freedom, justice and peace in the world." Universal Declaration of Human Rights, preamble. Compare the International Covenant on Civil and Political Rights, preamble; the International Covenant on Economic, Social and Cultural Rights, preamble.

3. For a list of conventions prepared under the auspices of the United Nations, and a

Perhaps it is self-evident that the commitment to human dignity, however defined, requires freedom from slavery or torture, and personhood and equality before the law.[4] That human dignity also requires, say, the freedom to choose one's own work and a right to a paid vacation, or a right to advanced education,[5] is not as obvious; at least, including such rights requires a broader definition of human dignity. In fact, the principal catalogues of rights include provisions whose relation to human dignity is not undeniable. For example, the International Covenant on Civil and Political Rights, after requiring that "all persons deprived of their liberty shall be treated with humanity and with respect for the inherent dignity of the human person,"[6] requires also separation of accused adults from juveniles, a provision that seems to have purposes other than maintaining respect for the human dignity of either the juvenile or the adult.[7] The International Covenant on Economic, Social and Cultural Rights recognizes the right of everyone to an education that "shall be directed to the full development of the human personality and the sense of its dignity."[8] But the covenant then declares that "primary education shall be compulsory,"[9] though compulsion of any kind might be deemed to be inconsistent with human dignity, and compulsory education might be thought to derogate from the dignity of the parents if not of the child. These and other rights in the international catalogue can be seen as requisite for human dignity only if that conception is given some extraordinary definition. Additional "generations" of rights that have been proposed—a right to peace, to development, to a healthful environment—also seem to have purposes beyond concern for individual human dignity and may not fit comfortably within the ordinary confines of the term.

RIGHTS AND DIGNITY IN THE U.S. CONSTITUTION

Human dignity is not mentioned in the U.S. Constitution and is not a value commonly associated with it. A suggestion that, for the Framers, promoting and maintaining human dignity was a societal purpose and a

---

chart indicating the states that have adhered to them, see *Human Rights—Status of International Instruments*, U.N. Doc. ST/HR/5 (1 Dec. 1990).
4. See, e.g., Universal Declaration, art. 4, 5.
5. Ibid., art. 23, 24, 26.
6. International Covenant on Civil and Political Rights, art. 10(1).
7. Ibid., art. 10(2)(b).
8. International Covenant on Economic, Social and Cultural Rights, art. 13(1).
9. Ibid., art. 13(2)(a).

constitutional value would doubtless claim support in the idea of rights that we consider to be intrinsic to the Constitution.

The Framers' Conception of Rights

The original Constitution of the United States was not a rights instrument. It did not contain any theory of rights or any general commitment to rights, did not recognize most of the rights we now exalt, and it mentioned few other rights. Yet the Framers' commitment to the idea of rights, I believe, is beyond doubt.[10] They built the new government of the United States on a political theory rooted in rights, the theory encapsulated in Thomas Jefferson's famous articulation in the Declaration of Independence: "We hold these Truths to be self-evident, that all Men are created equal, that they are endowed by their Creator with certain unalienable Rights, that among these are Life, Liberty, and the Pursuit of Happiness—that to secure these Rights, Governments are instituted among Men, deriving their just Powers from the Consent of the Governed." ...

Thus, unlike international human rights, rights as conceived by the Framers' generation do not derive from some antecedent conception and are not instrumental to some higher value or purpose, such as human dignity. Individual rights are the basic, irreducible, political conception and political "good." But if the Framers did not derive rights from dignity, the political theory that made rights the "atomic" good reflected a conception of the human being as worthy, as having essential dignity; the source of the individual's rights give evidence to his (her) dignity; the rights that the individual has speak to his (her) dignity.

For historic reasons, the federal Constitution assumed rather than articulated the idea of government rooted in rights that Jefferson had proclaimed. That the Constitution said remarkably little about rights—now a startling phenomenon—is the result of the genesis of the Constitution and of the Framers' limited conception of the constitution they were framing.[11] The new federal government they projected was not to be the primary government or a complete government; governance was left principally to the states. Rights had to be protected against state gov-

10. See generally Louis Henkin, "Rights: American and Human," *Columbia Law Review* 79 (1979): 405, reprinted in *The Age of Rights* (New York: Columbia University Press, 1990), chap. 9.
11. See Henkin, "Constitutional Fathers, Constitutional Sons," *Minnesota Law Review* 60 (1976): 113; see also the article cited in note 10.

ernments, and were in fact protected against them by state constitutions: bills of rights were at the head or at the heart of the early state constitutions. The states and state constitutions were the authentic descendants of the Declaration of Independence, reflecting its political theory and its foundation in rights. The U.S. Constitution was the direct descendant not of the Declaration of Independence but of the Articles of Confederation. The purpose of the U.S. Constitution was primarily not governance but union, "a more perfect union."[12]

The Framers therefore saw no need for a Bill of Rights in the federal Constitution.[13] Rights needed no protection against the new, limited government of the new Union with its few, enumerated powers. In any event, rights would be protected against the new central government by institutional arrangements—by what came to be called federalism, by separation of powers, by checks and balances. Moreover, it was risky to enumerate rights lest some be overlooked and thus jeopardized. During the campaign for ratification, however, opponents and skeptics seized on the absence of a bill of rights. A bill of rights was promised the voters as the first order of business for the new government. The Bill of Rights was adopted by the new Congress in 1789, was ratified, and came into force in 1791.

Dignity and Rights in the Original Constitution

The original Constitution had no bill of rights, yet it clearly reflected values we associate with human dignity. For the Framers of the Constitution, as for the authors of the declaration, the self-evident truth was that all men and women were created equal in human dignity, the dignity that implies autonomy and self-government and certain unalienable rights. For example, the operative clause of the Preamble, "We the people ...ordain this Constitution" implies "popular sovereignty," a political idea that finds support in axiomatic human dignity: Every individual is worthy of and entitled to govern himself (herself), and to join—freely—with other individuals to form societies and institute self-government. The Preamble also refers to the purposes of the "more perfect Union" in terms suggestive for our purposes. The Constitution was ordained to "establish Justice, insure domestic Tranquility, provide for the common

12. U.S. Const., preamble.
13. See The Federalist No. 84 (Hamilton).

defence, promote the general Welfare, and secure the Blessings of Liberty to ourselves and our Posterity"—all "goods" that might be seen as ingredients of or related to human dignity.

Though it contained no bill of rights, the original Constitution clearly reflects the idea of individual rights, and it expressly ordains respect for a few rights. Article I, section 9, provides that "the Privilege of the Writ of Habeas Corpus shall not be suspended, unless when in Cases of Rebellion or Invasion the public Safety may require it." In that provision the Constitution affirms and incorporates an entire jurisprudence of protection against unlawful, arbitrary detention and the right to resort to an independent judiciary for safeguard and remedy against such detention. The Constitution also forbids bills of attainder and ex post facto laws by either the federal government or the states; some concern for individual dignity, for equal human dignity, may be seen also in the prohibition of titles of nobility (Article I, sections 9, 10). The original Constitution also reflected concern for rights in the guarantee of a trial by a jury of one's peers (Article III, section 2); establishing safeguards against abuse of the law of treason (Article III, section 3); in the provision requiring every state to honor the privileges and immunities of citizens of other states (Article IV, section 2); in the prohibition of religious tests as a qualification for U.S. office (Article VI). One might find concern for human dignity in the provision that every human being shall be proportionally represented in the House of Representatives (Article I, section 2), or even the provision forbidding states to impair the obligations of contracts.

The Bill of Rights

History has given the appellation "the Bill of Rights" to a series of amendments to the U.S. Constitution that came into effect simultaneously in 1791. Because these rights were added by amendment after the Constitution came into effect, they do not appear at the head of the Constitution, as did the bills of rights of early state constitutions, and are not integrated into the structure and fabric of the Constitution. For similar reasons the Bill of Rights does not include any theory of government or of rights; it makes no provision for remedies against violation of rights, or for their implementation by Congress or the president, or by the courts.

Even as amended by the Bill of Rights, the Constitution did not become a complete rights instrument.[14] The Framers of the amendments ordained

14. For this sketch of developments in constitutional jurisprudence I draw generally on

what was principally on their mind—the rights they had had as English-
men, and rights to which they thought they were entitled but which they
had not fully enjoyed under English rule. These included the political
freedoms of the First Amendment, security of the person and the home
against unreasonable searches and seizures, protection against being deprived of life, liberty, and property without due process of law, and
various safeguards in the criminal process and against cruel and unusual
punishment.[15]

Even by the Framers' own lights, the constitutional system of rights
that the amendments established had blatant deficiencies. Freedom from
slavery—the ultimate affront to human dignity—was not assured. The
Bill of Rights did not free any slaves or give Congress power to liberate
slaves already in the United States. The Constitution had expressly denied
the power of Congress to restrict importation of slaves for twenty years
(Article I, section 9); the Bill of Rights did not remove or modify that
limitation.[16]

Equally glaring, in a constitution ordained by a people committed to
the principle that all men are created equal, is the absence of any mention
of equality.[17] The Bill of Rights did not remedy that deficiency. Not only
slaves, but free blacks, women, Jews, Catholics, religious dissenters, persons unequal in wealth or social status, found no protection against the
human indignity of invidious discrimination, either in the original Constitution or in the Bill of Rights.[18]

In addition, despite the ringing proclamation in the Declaration of
Independence of the self-evident truth that governments derive "their just
powers from the consent of the governed," the Bill of Rights did nothing
to remedy the failure of the original Constitution to assure that such
consent be secured. Neither the original Constitution nor the Bill of Rights
guaranteed any one the right to vote. Neither the original Constitution
nor the Bill of Rights gave the governed a voice in the selection of the

---

my article, "Constitutional Rights 200 Years Later," in *The United States Constitution:
The First 200 Years*, ed. R. C. Simmons (New York: Manchester University Press, 1989),
reprinted in *The Age of Rights*, cited in note 10.

15. The right to bear arms required for the state militia and not to have troops quartered
in the home in time of peace (amendments 2 and 3) also responded to recent experience.

16. The Constitution expressly precluded constitutional amendment before 1808 that
"shall in any Manner affect" that clause. U.S. Const., art. V.

17. The only reference to equality is to equal suffrage of states in the Senate. U.S. Const.,
art. V.

18. Some four score years later the Fourteenth Amendment provided for the equal
protection of the laws, but that requirement applied only to the states, not to the federal
government. See text at note 28.

president or of senators. The Bill of Rights also left the election of "Representatives" where the original Constitution had fixed it: they were to be chosen by "the People of the several States," but only by those of the people who had "the qualifications requisite for Electors of the most numerous branch of the State Legislature" (Article I, section 2).

There was no mention in the amendments of other rights we consider essential to human dignity. The Bill of Rights did not include the civil rights now recognized in the Universal Declaration of Human Rights[19] and which we take for granted—the rights of "personhood" and personal status before the law, the right to acquire and own property, to make contracts, to pursue legal remedies, to marry and raise a family, to educate one's children, to choose one's occupation and place of residence, to travel, to leave and return to one's country.

Even rights that the Bill of Rights protected were not fully protected. Jefferson had proclaimed that every person was endowed with inalienable rights to life, liberty, and the pursuit of happiness, and he declared that "to secure these rights governments were instituted among men." The Bill of Rights indeed protected some liberty, notably, the important political freedoms in the First Amendment, but "liberty" generally, and life, and property, received only limited protections at best. A person was not to be deprived of liberty without due process of law, but plausibly the liberty protected was freedom from incarceration, not individual autonomy and liberties generally. A person could not be deprived of life, liberty, or property "without due process of law," but on the face of the amendment there was no protection against being deprived of them by arbitrary or unjust law. The Bill of Rights protected life, liberty, and property against deprivation by government, by "state action"; there was no protection against state inaction, against failure by government to enact and enforce laws that would secure the individual's life, liberty, and property against invasion by one's neighbor.[20] Indeed, the Bill of Rights failed to empower Congress to enact laws to implement the rights protected.

To some extent, these lacunae probably reflected a limited conception of the purposes of the Constitution, indeed, of any constitution. Tacitly, framers of constitutions and bills of rights distinguished between natural rights that preexisted society and civil rights enjoyed in society. The line between them was not clear in all respects, but it generally divided rights

19. Cf. Universal Declaration, art. 6, 8, 13, 16, 17.
20. The jurisprudence of state action developed largely in the application of the Fourteenth Amendment (cf. the civil rights cases, 109 U.S. 3 [1883]), but it applies as well to the Bill of Rights.

requiring constitutional protection and others that were the domain of "sub-constitutional" law. Both state and federal constitutions assumed, and built on, an established legal system; both assumed and built on the common law inherited from England, which gave large protection to "civil rights," including in substantial measure a right to the equal protection of laws. Constitution makers in the United States saw no need to "constitutionalize" those common-law rights so as to safeguard them against legislatures or even against executives and judges.

The Ninth Amendment— The Unused Amendment

The enumeration in the Constitution, of certain rights, shall not be construed to deny or disparage others retained by the people. Amendment IX.

The Ninth Amendment was doubtless added from an abundance of caution and to allay the fear that an attempt to express rights might omit some and thereby deny them protection.[21] Incidentally, the amendment also affirmed the Framers' theory of rights. Rights are not granted by the Constitution; they antecede the Constitution. Rights are not granted by government; the people have their rights before government and retain them under government. More than any particular right or the array of rights set forth in the Bill of Rights, the theory of antecedent, retained rights implies the human dignity of every individual member of the people.

But the Ninth Amendment gives no clue as to what those other, antecedent, retained rights might be. In principle, they might well include all those unalienable rights missing from the enumeration, including freedom from slavery, the right to equality before the law and the equal protection of the laws, the right to vote, perhaps even some civil rights implied in personhood.[22] One reason we do not know what is hidden in that amendment is that the courts have not told us. Perhaps from sensitivity about their role as constitutional arbiter in a democratic society, the courts have confined themselves to monitoring and vindicating only rights that are enumerated or that might be inferred from enumerated rights;[23] they have not given effect to, or even identified, any right as

21. See The Federalist No. 84 (Hamilton).
22. But see text at notes 16–20.
23. Cf. the disagreement between Justices Samuel Chase and James Iredell as to judicial enforcement of natural rights. Calder v. Bull, 3 U.S. (3 Dall.) 386 (1798).

included among those which the Ninth Amendment declared to be retained by the people.[24]

Later Rights Amendments

The Bill of Rights, including the Ninth Amendment, imposed limitations on the federal government; it did not apply to the states.[25] Before
the Civil War, the Bill of Rights did little work. As the Farmers had
anticipated,[26] little of the activity of the federal government affected
individual interests and individual dignity in ways that implicated the
Bill of Rights.[27]

The end of the Civil War brought new rights amendments. The
Thirteenth Amendment abolished slavery, finally overcoming the
major affront to human dignity maintained by the Constitution and
by the Bill of Rights. The Fourteenth Amendment was a major rights
amendment, some have called it our Second Constitution, but it did
not address rights in relation to the federal government, only to the
states.[28] That amendment nationalized individual rights and gave
them federal protection against the states: The amendment established
national citizenship, protected the privileges and immunities of
such citizenship against state violation, forbade the states to deprive
any person of life, liberty, and property without due process of
law, or to deny any person the equal protection of the laws. The
Fifteenth Amendment, though strictly it gave no one the right to vote,
prohibited the insult to human dignity implied in denying the right to
vote on account of race. Later amendments forbade the denial of the
right to vote on account of sex, or of age (for citizens eighteen years
or older).

The Constitution has not been otherwise amended to provide protec-

24. Justice Arthur J. Goldberg invoked the Ninth Amendment in his concurring opinion
in Griswold v. Connecticut, 381 U.S. 479 (1965).
25. Barron v. Baltimore, 32 U.S. (7 Pet.) 242 (1833).
26. See text at note 13.
27. Before the Civil War the Supreme Court applied the due process clause of the Fifth
Amendment once, to protect a slaveholder's property rights in a slave, Dred Scott v.
Sandford, 60 U.S. (19 How.) 393 (1857). Issues under the Alien and Sedition Acts of 1798
never reached the Supreme Court. The acts lapsed in 1800 and 1801, respectively, and
were not renewed.
28. Later the citizenship clause was read as denying the federal government the right
to take away citizenship without the individual's consent. Afroyim v. Rusk, 387 U.S. 253
(1967). And see text at note 44.

tion for additional rights.[29] We have not amended the Constitution to supply remaining deficiencies in the protections afforded by the Bill of Rights against the federal government.[30] We have not elucidated the Ninth Amendment by enumerating additional retained rights so as to enable the courts to provide them constitutional protection. Our evolving sense of human dignity[31] has not impelled us formally to recognize and ordain rights that were not recognized by the Framers. We have not seen fit to reconsider the conception of rights we inherited from the Framers; their conception of rights has remained our conception.

Judicial Enhancement of Rights

Perhaps we have not amended the Constitution to increase its protections for rights because the courts have uncovered hidden protections in provisions already there. They did not find them in the Ninth Amendment, probably because the need for additional protection was perceived to be against the states, and the Ninth Amendment did not address the states.[32] Additional protection for rights (and dignity) therefore had to be found in the constitutional provisions applicable to the states, notably, those of the Fourteenth Amendment. The courts might have found such additional protection most plausibly in the privileges and immunities clause of that amendment, but the Supreme Court early gave that clause a restricted meaning and reduced it to insignificance.[33] Instead, the courts

29. Amendment 24 provides that no one shall be denied the right to vote in a federal election for failure to pay a tax.

One may perceive increased respect for individual dignity in the amendment providing for direct election of senators, Amendment 17. The Sixteenth Amendment permitting a progressive income tax made it possible for the United States later to become a welfare state. See text at notes 46–47.

30. To this day, the U.S. Constitution, on its face, does not require the federal government to accord the equal protection of the laws; on the face of it, the Constitution does not forbid the U.S. government to discriminate against blacks or women, or to draw other invidious distinctions. It took ingenious—and intellectually and historically questionable—constitutional construction (in the second half of the twentieth century) to achieve that result. See note 44.

31. The Court invoked "evolving standards of decency" to interpret the prohibition of cruel and unusual punishment in the Eighth Amendment as incorporated into the Fourteenth Amendment. Thompson v. Oklahoma, 487 U.S. 815, 821, 848 (1988) (Opinions of Justice Stevens and Justice O'Connor). In that case the court precluded the death penalty for an act committed by a fifteen-year-old. But see note 50.

32. See note 25.

33. The *Slaughter House* cases ruled that the clause safeguarded only rights that derived from national citizenship, such as the right to come to the seat of the national government, to seek the protection of that government, to hold federal office. 83 U.S. (16 Wall.) 36, 79 (1873).

soon found additional protection against the states in the due process clause of the Fourteenth Amendment.[34]

By their imaginative readings of the due process clause, the courts erected a major bulwark against invasions of rights and dignity. They read the phrase "due process of law" as requiring the rule of law, not rule by executive or administrative fiat. They read due process as requiring not only conformity to traditional legal process but as permitting only procedures that are consistent with "principles of liberty and justice," with "fundamental fairness," with "ordered liberty," measures that do not "shock the conscience."[35] Then, the courts contributed to constitutional protection for human dignity by giving "liberty" in the due process clause large meaning, and finding in that clause not only procedural safeguards but substantive protection against arbitrary deprivations of such liberty even by law. In 1897 the Court said:

> The liberty mentioned in that amendment means not only the right of the citizen to be free from the mere physical restraint of his person, as by incarceration, but the term is deemed to embrace the right of the citizen to be free in the enjoyment of all his faculties; to be free to use them in all lawful ways; to live and work where he will; to earn his livelihood by any lawful calling; to pursue any livelihood or avocation, and for that purpose to enter into all contracts which may be proper, necessary and essential to his carrying out to a successful conclusion of the purposes above mentioned.[36]

In addition to reading "liberty" as tantamount to autonomy, the Court in effect read "due process of law" to mean rational, reasonable law, not arbitrary law, and law serving the legitimate purposes of government, excluding purposes that were not the law's proper business.

Substantive due process was hardly an unmixed blessing for human dignity and rights. For a while, in the age of *Lochner*,[37] the courts took a narrow view of the purposes of government and of the human dignity

---

34. By the perhaps fortuitous choice of that clause instead of the privileges and immunities clause, the courts were able to find additional protection not only for citizens (the beneficiaries of the privileges and immunities clause) but for all "persons" (the beneficiaries of the due process clause). By enriching the due process clause of the Fourteenth Amendment, the courts enriched also the same clause in the Fifth Amendment, thereby giving similar protections for rights against the federal government.

35. See Palko v. Connecticut, 302 U.S. 319 (1937). Also Hurtado v. California, 110 U.S. 516 (1884); Snyder v. Massachusetts, 291 U.S. 97 (1934); Rochin v. California, 342 U.S. 165 (1952).

36. Allgeyer v. Louisiana, 165 U.S. 578, 589 (1897).

37. Lochner v. New York, 198 U.S. 45 (1905).

that the states were entitled to promote. They were concerned only for the dignity implied in formal liberty and autonomy, as in liberty of contract, not for individual freedom in fact; for the dignity of the employer, not of the working man or woman. The courts recognized the right of government to limit individual freedom by regulation to protect health and safety, but they refused to allow the states to recognize and address the effect on health and safety of "starvation wages" and "sweatshop" hours and working conditions.[38] The courts recognized the contribution to the general welfare of free enterprise and laissez-faire but did not allow the states to promote the general welfare by regulating the effect of market forces on employment.[39] The courts recognized the authority of the state to derogate from laissez-faire to benefit women, not from respect for their dignity but rather for their "frailty."[40]

For too long the courts took a narrow view also of what human dignity required as regards equality. The Fourteenth Amendment forbade states to deny to any person the equal protection of the laws, but the courts tolerated and legitimized official segregation alleged to be "separate but equal."[41] The state did not have to respect the dignity of women by honoring their autonomy and equality, as by respecting their right to practice law.[42]

In time, American society, and the courts, began to respond to the evolving sense of what human dignity required. Courts began to read the Constitution as an open, living instrument and to apply what the Framers wrote, in the spirit they intended, to the issues of a new day for a transformed country. Finally, the courts permitted the New Deal and the welfare state. Later they concluded that separate is not equal today, and that women cannot be denied equal rights because of cultural attitudes and stereotypes of a century ago. Recognizing the changed character of the federal system, they "homogenized" constitutional protection by finding that the Bill of Rights, originally governing only the federal government, was largely incorporated into the Fourteenth Amendment and is binding on the states.[43] On the other hand, though explicitly the Constitution requires only the states to provide the equal protection of the laws, the courts concluded that the due process clause of the Fifth Amend-

---

38. Cf. the dissent of Justice John M. Harlan, ibid. at 65; and see Bunting v. Oregon, 243 U.S. 426 (1917).

39. Cf. Justice Oliver W. Holmes's dissent in *Lochner*, 198 U.S. at 74.

40. Muller v. Oregon, 208 U.S. 412 (1908).

41. Plessy v. Ferguson, 163 U.S. 537 (1896), overruled, Brown v. Board of Education, 347 U.S. 483 (1954).

42. Bradwell v. Illinois, 83 U.S. (16 Wall.) 130 (1873).

43. See, e.g., Duncan v. Louisiana, 391 U.S. 145 (1968).

ment effectively requires the federal government as well to accord equal protection.[44]

In time, the courts enlarged the Framers' conception of individual dignity also in other fundamental ways. The Framers, it has been suggested, were concerned for the rights and dignity of gentlemen; in our century, the courts became concerned for the rights and dignity of all men and women, of the least and the worst of them—of all persons accused of crime, of convicted criminals, of prisoners in relation to their wardens, of soldiers in relation to the armed forces, of students in relation to their teachers and schools, of children in relation to their parents. In a development rooted, I believe, in conceptions of the essential dignity and worth of the individual, the First Amendment was interpreted to protect not only freedom of political expression but also other forms of expression, including freedom to advocate even radical ideas and to utter even what is offensive to others. The freedom of the press has been extended to include the individual's right to know; the freedom of speech includes the right not to speak, or to speak anonymously; the right to associate—itself a judicial construct—includes the right not to associate or to be silent about one's associations. Liberty includes autonomy in intimate matters—to marry or not to marry, to practice contraception, to have an abortion. Racial distinctions are suspect, and gender distinctions, too, will be carefully scrutinized. The Supreme Court interpreted the equal protection of the laws to include the right to vote equally, one man (woman), one vote, finally bringing universal suffrage and the consent of all the governed. The courts read the Constitution as recognizing the human dignity of aliens as well as citizens, even aliens abroad who come within the reach of U.S. authority.

By interpreting the constitutional powers of Congress broadly, the courts have unleashed and encouraged Congress to expand individual rights and promote dignity—by the New Deal and the Great Society; by comprehensive civil rights legislation outlawing private as well as official invasions; by a Freedom of Information Act opening government to the scrutiny of the governed.

Rights and Public Order

Human dignity requires respect for human rights, but human dignity requires also community and public order.[45] In the Declaration of In-

44. Bolling v. Sharpe, 347 U.S. 497 (1954).
45. The Universal Declaration of Human Rights provides that "1. Everyone has duties to the community in which alone the free and full development of his personality is possible.

dependence certain rights are declared "unalienable," but men (women) institute government to secure these rights, and inevitably they give up at least some of their liberty and property to government for the proper purposes of government. Even the most liberal state, therefore, must regulate—may interfere with liberty, and tax—may take property—for health, safety, public order, and security against external danger.

The constitutional conception of rights inevitably reflects similar limitations on rights. The Bill of Rights safeguards the individual against deprivation of life, liberty, or property without due process of law, but life, liberty, and property can be taken pursuant to due process of law; substantive due process protects against arbitrary law but not against law that is not arbitrary. Property can be taken for public use if there is just compensation. The people are entitled to be secure against unreasonable searches and seizures, but not against searches and seizures that are reasonable. The individual may not be subject to cruel and unusual punishment but he (she) may be punished by noncruel, accepted punishments, even by the death penalty in some circumstances. Even the fundamental freedoms enshrined in the First Amendment—speech, press, religion, assembly—though written in apparently absolute terms, are not in fact absolute. For example, government can regulate the time, place, and manner of expression, and even content can be regulated for compelling public purposes.

The courts have developed a constitutional calculus of balancing private right and public need, but it requires a political culture of respect for rights, an alert citizenry, and a supreme independent judiciary to monitor the balance if the result is to be respectful of human dignity. Overall our record has been impressive but not wholly glorious. We did not respect the human dignity of the American Indian. We long tolerated racial segregation, separate and not even equal. We excluded Chinese and maintained other racist immigration laws. In time of war we relocated and interned human beings because of their Japanese ancestry. In time of cold war we hunted communists. Expanding notions of human dignity brought "balancing," but we have sometimes given too much respect to

---

2. In the exercise of his rights and freedoms, everyone shall be subject only to such limitations as are determined by law solely for the purpose of securing due recognition and respect for the rights and freedoms of others and of meeting the just requirements of morality, public order and the general welfare in a democratic society. 3. These rights and freedoms may in no case be exercised contrary to the purposes and principles of the United Nations" (art. 29). The International Covenant on Civil and Political Rights recognizes some limitations on rights, and article 4 permits derogations from many rights if strictly required by the exigencies of a public emergency that threatens the life of the nation.

exaggerated claims of national security and other societal claims, too little to the claims of the individual, for instance, the homosexual. We have cut back some women's right to choose to have an abortion.

A BROADER CONCEPTION OF HUMAN DIGNITY

In all, we have done well in enhancing the respect for human dignity implicit in the Framers' conception of rights. But the Framers were content with such respect for human dignity as is implied in the liberal state, as summarized in the Declaration of Independence and reflected in the Ninth Amendment. By today's lights, the Framers' conception of rights and human dignity is incomplete.

For the Framers, rights were "natural." Men and women had moral rights against each other, rights to life, liberty, autonomy, property. They instituted government to secure these rights, the right to be let alone. In the state of nature, apparently, one did not have a right to be assisted by one's neighbor, even to be provided basic human needs if one was old, or sick, or handicapped, or unfortunate. For such assistance one was dependent on neighborly generosity or the neighbor's religious obligation to extend charity.[46] Not being rights in the state of nature, they were not claims upon the governments that men and women instituted, the government of a liberal state.

We have come a long way. Thanks to broad interpretations of the power of Congress to tax and spend so as "to provide for the general welfare" (Article I, section 8), thanks to a constitutional amendment permitting progressive taxation (Amendment 16), thanks to the lessons of the Great Depression, the United States became a welfare state. We have come to recognize that human dignity requires not only political and physical freedom, and equality in freedom, but also Franklin Roosevelt's fourth freedom, "freedom from want." We know that "a necessitous man is not a free man." We have learned from other countries and from the international human rights movement that a right to work and to leisure, a right to food, housing, health care, and education, to an adequate standard of living, are also essential to human dignity. But that knowledge is not part of our constitutional jurisprudence. Some have indeed argued that the Ninth Amendment should be read as incor-

---

46. The would-be recipient had no claims as of right; he (she) was essentially a third-party beneficiary of that religious obligation.

porating a conception of rights demanded by what human dignity requires today. But the courts have not dared.[47] Our constitutional jurisprudence reflects only the conception of rights bequeathed by our eighteenth-century ancestors. For basic needs today, essential to human dignity, we are reduced to relying on the political process, on legislative grace, on political choices between budgetary needs, on the willingness of the governed to be taxed. Our welfare state does not supply what human dignity requires today. There is no respect for human dignity in tolerating poverty and homelessness, de facto segregation, the growth of an "underclass."

A PAROCHIAL SENSE OF HUMAN DIGNITY

Recently, some justices of the Supreme Court have threatened to widen the gap between rights and dignity, or at least between a parochial and a universal sense of dignity. A hundred years ago the Court began to interpret "due process of law" as requiring conformity to a universal standard of decency and human dignity. The Court spoke variously of "fundamental principles of liberty and justice," "fundamental fairness," of Justice Benjamin N. Cardozo's insightful oxymoron "ordered liberty." Justice Felix Frankfurter said that the due process clause condemns that which "shocks the conscience."[48] Clearly, though justices were reluctant to describe it in terms of natural rights, the Court had found in due process some universal, not a parochial, standard. Frankfurter, I am satisfied, invoked not his own conscience, not only the American conscience, but the conscience of mankind.[49]

In 1989 several justices seemed to proclaim retreat from that universal standard of human dignity. In holding that the death penalty for a young person for a crime committed when he was less than eighteen years old was not cruel and unusual punishment, those justices insisted that what

47. E.g., Dandridge v. Williams, 397 U.S. 471 (1970).
48. See note 35.
49. Cf. Rochin v. California, cited in note 35; also Frankfurter, J., concurring in Adamson v. California, 332 U.S. 46, 59 (1947).
The Court took a small step away from a universal standard in the process of incorporating provisions of the Bill of Rights "selectively" into the Fourteenth Amendment. For example, it decided that due process requires a jury trial because "trial by jury in criminal cases is fundamental to the American scheme of justice." Duncan v. Louisiana, cited in note 43, 391 U.S. at 149. But even after selective incorporation prevailed, the Court apparently continued to apply a universal standard of fairness, for example, when it held that "proof beyond a reasonable doubt is among the 'essentials of due process and fair treatment'." In re Winship, 397 U.S. 358, 359 (1970).

is cruel and unusual punishment is to be determined only by an American sense of decency; the fact that the International Covenant on Civil and Political Rights has adopted a different standard is not relevant unless our society had obviously acted to accept that standard.[50]

The ultimate affinity between individual rights and human dignity may be eroding in another respect as well. A hundred years ago the Supreme Court announced that the Constitution did not apply outside the United States.[51] After World War II, however, a plurality opinion of the Court dismissed that old case as a relic of a bygone era and declared that the U.S. government had to respect constitutional limitations wherever it acted.[52] In that case the Court declared that a civilian citizen could not be tried abroad without a jury trial; later a lower court held that even an alien brought to trial in a U.S. court in Berlin was entitled to a jury trial.[53] Other courts have also applied constitutional restraints to official actions by the United States outside the United States, for example, on the high seas, even in relation to foreign nationals.[54]

Some of us have welcomed the view that the Constitution was not merely an internal social compact applicable only in relations among ourselves but a charter for a community of conscience governing the United States wherever it acts.[55] In 1990, however, the Supreme Court rejected a constitutional claim by a foreign national that the Fourth Amendment protected him against unreasonable search by U.S. officials without warrant in Mexico. And several justices saw fit to support that result by a broad declaration apparently implying that the Constitution does not apply abroad, at least where noncitizens are affected.[56]

Developments in the idea and jurisprudence of rights during two hundred years under the Constitution suggest continuing refinement of our society's sense of human dignity and an evolving appreciation of what human dignity requires. However, many find that the U.S. idea of rights is still underdeveloped and has not kept pace with contemporary

---

50. Stanford v. Kentucky, 492 U.S. 361, 370 n. 1 (1989) ("We emphasize that it is *American* conceptions of decency that are dispositive." Emphasis in original.)

51. *In re* Ross, 140 U.S. 453, 464–65 (1891).

52. Reid v. Covert, 354 U.S. 1 (1947).

53. See U.S. v. Tiede, 86 F.R.D. 227 (U.S. Ct. Berlin 1979).

54. See, e.g., U.S. v. Hensel et al., 699 F.2d 18 (1st cir.), *cert. denied,* 461 U.S. 958, 464 U.S. 823, 824 (1983); U.S. v. Williams, 617 F.2d 1063 (5th Cir. 1980); U.S. v. Cadena 585 F.2d 1252 (5th Cir. 1978).

55. See my article, "The Constitution as Compact and as Conscience," *William and Mary Law Review* 27 (1985):11, reprinted in *The Age of Rights,* cited in note 10.

56. U.S. v. Verdugo-Urquidez, 494 U.S. 259 (1990).

international conceptions of human dignity and of what human dignity requires.

Once the United States set the world a standard, the standard of freedom and equality; now the world is showing us a standard of human dignity that includes also the obligation to satisfy basic human needs. Once we invoked "natural," universal standards to support our freedom.[57] Now we refuse to go beyond where we are, to accept an international standard that reflects greater sensitivity to human dignity than our constitutional standard inherited from the eighteenth century. Perhaps that represents a further divergence between constitutional rights and human dignity; at least it reflects a divergence between what some justices believe to be the American sense of human dignity and that of the world at large.

The idea of rights acquired from Europe in the seventeenth and eighteenth centuries is our hallmark and our pride. We gave it our own content, supported it by our own institutions, and helped realize it, perhaps as well as it has ever been realized. The rights we have recognized, rooted in individual autonomy, liberty, equality, surely have strong affinity to human dignity. Commitment to human dignity is implied in our continuing commitment to the basic idea that the individual counts, apart from the group; that one's rights cannot lightly be sacrificed to the majority will, to the good of the majority, even to the common good; that some rights can be sacrificed only to a compelling public interest. But humanity's conception of human dignity has evolved, and there is more in it today than is contained in the concept of rights as defined in our Constitution, even in the Ninth Amendment. The Constitution reflects a conception of rights of liberty and equality, not of fraternity; rights in a liberal state, not in a welfare state. If we will not formally modernize the Constitution, we must continue to refine our political culture and its commitment to human dignity, by adhering to international covenants, by enacting federal and state laws that will help us become and remain the Great Society.

57. See note 35.

12

The Other Goldberg

OWEN M. FISS

Shortly before his retirement in 1990 Justice William J. Brennan, Jr., described Goldberg v. Kelly as the most important decision of his long career. I find it somewhat difficult to know what to make of this statement because, oddly enough, there are two decisions that go by that name. Both were written by Justice Brennan.

The first, decided in 1970, was indeed remarkable.[1] It required an adversarial hearing prior to the termination of welfare benefits and, in so doing, developed the law along two different axes. The so-called due process revolution of the 1960s was extended from the criminal to the civil domain, and the procedural protections traditionally afforded to the property of the privileged classes were now to be provided to the property of the less fortunate.

Although in outcome Goldberg v. Kelly was singular and in that sense a breakthrough, its underlying method of jurisprudence was not. Justice Brennan wrote for the majority and, in so doing, employed a method that characterized the Court's work for the prior twenty-year period and that produced a body of decisions—Brown v. Board of Education,[2] Reynolds v. Sims,[3] Gideon v. Wainwright,[4] New York Times v.

1. 397 U.S. 254 (1970).
2. 347 U.S. 483 (1954).
3. 377 U.S. 533 (1964).
4. 372 U.S. 335 (1963).

Sullivan,[5] and Engel v. Vitale[6] are a few examples—that have come to define judicial review as we know it and that for some time now have been an inspiration for all the world.

The method of all these decisions was, I believe, entirely rationalistic: the justices reflected upon the values and ideals of the Constitution and sought to understand what those ideals would require in the practical world they confronted. In Brown v. Board of Education the justices had to give content to the ideal of racial equality embodied in the Fourteenth Amendment and to ascertain whether the dual school system was consistent with that ideal, that is, whether segregated schools were inherently unequal. In Goldberg v. Kelly the value was not racial equality but procedural fairness—the nature of the process due to a citizen before the state could deprive that citizen of liberty or even property—yet the method that produced that decision was essentially the same.

In calling this method rationalistic, I mean to underscore its discursive nature: The justices listen to arguments about a broad range of subjects—the facts, the history surrounding the laws in question, earlier cases, and the precise wording of the text. This argument goes on with the lawyers, among the justices and their clerks, and among the justices themselves. The justices also think about all that they heard and try to evaluate the strengths and weakness of the arguments. Thinking itself is an interiorization of the discursive process, a continuation of the argument but now wholly within the individual. Thinking is, as Hannah Arendt put it, "the soundless dialogue between me and myself."[7] The process of deliberation comes to a conclusion at the moment of decision, at which time the decision is publicly announced and the justices set forth their reasons for it.

Given its discursive nature, the judicial decision may be seen as the paragon of all rational decisions, especially of a public character. It differs from other decisions only by virtue of the rules or standards determining what counts as a good as opposed to a bad argument, or what constitutes a good as opposed to a bad reason. A member of the city council trying to decide what should be done with public funds, or the superintendent of a park confronting a similar predicament, might consider facts, reasons, or arguments that a judge might not, because of differences in their offices, but each is obliged to decide questions rationally and thus engage

5. 376 U.S. 254 (1964).
6. 370 U.S. 421 (1962).
7. Hannah Arendt, *The Life of the Mind* (New York: Harcourt Brace Jovanovich, 1971), p. 185.

in the deliberative process that is the essence of judging and, for that matter, of law itself.

Some portion of this process is addressed to the elaboration of ends; some, to the means for achieving those ends. The latter goes by the name of instrumental rationality, by which a particular end is stipulated and the decision maker tries to identify the best means for achieving that end. Judgments of this type are almost technocratic and tend to dominate the remedial phase of a lawsuit, in which the judge formulates a plan for bringing a recalcitrant reality into conformity with the norms of the Constitution. What kind of decree, the judge might ask, would most effectively instill within the welfare bureaucracy a proper regard for procedural fairness? On the other hand, the explication of the ideal of procedural fairness, a judgment as to whether it requires a hearing prior to termination, and of what that hearing might consist of, is not technocratic or instrumental, but deeply substantive or normative. It focuses on ends, not means, and on the relationship of these ends or values to social practices, in this instance, the welfare system.

While instrumental reasoning dominates the remedial phase, substantive or normative reasoning—that is, the refinement and elaboration of ends—is the essence of the right-declaring phase of adjudication. In my view, that aspect of adjudication is foundational, for the authority of the judiciary is linked to substantive rationality.[8] The independence of the judiciary and its commitment to public dialogue are the source of the judiciary's special claim to competence, and thus the source of its authority, yet the competence that is produced by independence and public dialogue has more to do with normative than technocratic judgments. We give power to the judiciary because it is "the forum of principle," to use Ronald Dworkin's phrase,[9] not because it has a corner on the social technologies of the world, not because it is more adept than the legislature or the executive in devising the best means for realizing some stipulated end. In fact, we allow the judiciary the power to make instrumental judgments and to be decisive in that domain—to be supreme in the formulation and administration of remedy—only as a way of protecting or safeguarding its declarations of principle or right. In celebrating the Warren Court, and the body of doctrine that it has created, one has in mind more what that institution said about ends, values, ideals—its explication of equality, free speech, religious liberty, procedural fairness,

8. Owen Fiss, "The Forms of Justice," *Harvard Law Review* 93 (1979): 1.

9. Ronald Dworkin, "The Forum of Principle," *New York University Law Review* 56 (1981): 469.

or the more general value of human dignity—than the technologies it devised to achieve those ends. This is true of Goldberg v. Kelly, which was, in my judgment, largely an exercise in, and a triumph of, substantive rationality.

Triumph it was, but the travails of that case and the entire jurisprudence that it exemplified began in the early 1970s, almost at the very moment that decision was rendered. Goldberg v. Kelly marked the end of one era and the beginning of another; it was handed down as American culture turned inward and we began to lose faith in the Constitution as an embodiment of a public morality to be known and elaborated through the exercise of reason. In the academy, those doubts informed and accounted for the rise and extraordinary success of the law and economics movement—a movement that, granted, believed in reason, but only of the instrumental variety.

Law and economics is premised on the idea that there are no public values or ideals about which judges should reason. Ideals exist, but only at a personal or individual level, and as such are not fundamentally different from an individual's interests, desires, or preferences—none of which are especially amenable to reasoned elaboration. Law and economics also assumes that it is arbitrary for any social institution, but especially the judiciary, to choose among these preferences; all are entitled, to use Robert Bork's formula, to equal gratification.[10] In practical terms this means that there can be only one end for social institutions: maximizing the total satisfaction of individual preferences, or as Richard Posner has characterized it, increasing the size of the pie, rather than deciding how it should be divided.[11] The task that remains for the judiciary under this formulation is essentially technocratic: devising or choosing the rules that are the best means for increasing the size of the pie. To say, as law and economics does, that "law is efficiency" implicitly hypothesizes a single, uncontested end and relegates the judge to the formulation of rules—the instruments—that best serve that end.

Law and economics, and its special brand of instrumentalism, has not been confined to the academy. It has had an impact on private law and has even managed to find its way to the High Court. I am referring to Justice Powell's three-pronged test of Matthews v. Eldridge,[12] which bears

10. Robert Bork, "Neutral Principles and Some First Amendment Problems," *Indiana Law Journal* 47 (1971): 1, 10.
11. Richard Posner, "Wealth Maximization and Judicial Decision-Making," *International Review of Law and Economics* 4 (1984): 131, 132.
12. 424 U.S. 319 (1976).

a striking similarity to a formula that Richard Posner had proposed earlier.[13] For Posner, the judge confronted with a claim for new procedure must compare the cost of the proposed procedural innovation against the benefits it was likely to produce, and those benefits are to be calculated by multiplying the costs of an error by the chance of its occurring if the proposed procedure is not instituted. In Matthews v. Eldridge Justice Powell wrote:

> More precisely, our prior decisions indicate that identification of the specific dictates of due process generally requires consideration of three distinct factors: first, the private interest that will be affected by the official action; second, the risk of an erroneous deprivation of such interest through the procedures used, and the probable value, if any, of additional or substitute provided safeguards; and finally, the Government's interest, including the function involved and the fiscal and administrative burdens that the additional or substitute procedural requirement would entail.[14]

As can be seen, Justice Powell's formula confuses the matter slightly by adding to the equation a term that was already there (the value to the individual of the new procedure was already reflected in the error costs), but in spirit and conception, Powell's formula is the same as Posner's. Both understand procedure in wholly instrumental terms, as though it were a machine dedicated to reducing erroneous outcomes. They believe the machine should be acquired if the costs of buying and operating it are less than the benefits likely to be produced, that is, if the machine is efficient.

Such a model for deciding procedural questions can be criticized, and has been, on the ground that it assumes an intellectual capacity that simply does not exist. Operationalizing the cost-benefit methodology requires quantifying factors that cannot be quantified, and any attempt to engage in such an exercise will be worse than useless—it will tend to drive out of the decisional process the "soft variables," those values that are most important to any understanding of procedural fairness.[15] For me, however, the failure of law and economics and the Matthews v. Eldridge approach is of another order: it derives not simply from the

13. Richard Posner, "An Economic Approach to Legal Procedure and Judicial Administration," *Journal of Legal Studies* 2 (1973): 399, 441–42.

14. 424 U.S. at 334–35.

15. Jerry L. Mashaw, "The Supreme Court's Due Process Calculus for Administrative Adjudication in Matthews v. Eldridge: Three Factors in Search of a Theory of Value," *University of Chicago Law Review* 44 (1976): 28, 48.

attempt to quantify that which cannot be quantified, but from the re-
duction of due process and, for that matter, the entire judicial judgment
to instrumental terms.

From my perspective a justice charged with the duty of construing the
due process clause, as Justice Brennan was in Goldberg v. Kelly, should
be seen as engaged in a process of trying to understand what it means
for a society to be committed to procedural fairness, and to elaborate
that understanding in a certain practical context. According to law and
economics and Matthews v. Eldridge, however, the judicial task is transformed into one of choosing an instrument, a means, or a technology
that would serve some specific and relatively uncontested end, such as
reducing the number of erroneous outcomes, or stated more generally,
increasing the size of the pie. Such a view trivializes and distorts the
judicial task entailed in the explication of due process and can be faulted
on that ground; it also might be said that it puts the authority of the
judiciary into question, for the instrumentalization of reason eradicates
that portion of the judicial decision that is the foundation of its authority—the deliberation about ends and values—and thus puts the judiciary on the defensive. There is no good reason for the judiciary to
second guess the legislature or the executive on purely instrumental questions, and as a result, an attitude of deference and passivity on the part
of the judiciary becomes all the more appropriate.

Since the late seventies Matthews v. Eldridge has governed and has
produced a body of decisions that, predictably, deprived Goldberg v.
Kelly of any operative force. *Goldberg* remained on the books, and
though it has not controlled the decisions of the Court, it functioned in
the academy, in the law reviews, and in certain sectors of the profession
as a critical counterpoint—as a reminder of what law once was and might
one day be. It stood as a monument to our own little enlightenment. But
matters became unusually complicated in 1987 when, much to my sur-
prise, a second version of Goldberg v. Kelly appeared, not in the *U.S.
Reports*, to be sure, but in the *Record of the Association of the Bar of
the City New York.*[16] I am referring to Justice Brennan's speech before
the association in September of that year, a speech in which he gave
another account of the jurisprudential method that produced that deci-

---

16. William J. Brennan, Jr., "Reason, Passion, and the Progress of the Law," The Forty-
Second Annual Benjamin N. Cardozo Lecture, *The Record of The Association of the Bar
of The City of New York* 42 (1987): 948. The speech was reprinted in *Cardozo Law
Review* 10 (1988): 3, and all references are to that version of the speech.

sion. He stayed clear of the intrumentalism of law and economics and of Matthews v. Eldridge but nonetheless challenged my understanding of Goldberg v. Kelly as a triumph of substantive rationality. He introduced a new element into the decisional process: passion.

Justice Brennan did not deny any role for reason (either of the instrumental or substantive kind) but insisted that any account of Goldberg v. Kelly that did not include room for the emotional or affective elements would be incomplete and inadequate. He also quoted a passage from one of the briefs describing the plight of some of the welfare recipients involved in the case and characterized that passage in terms of a form of discourse that seems especially tied to the emotive faculty. He saw the brief as telling "human stories."[17] While arguments, whether they be of fact or principle, seem especially addressed to the faculty of reason, storytelling is often seen as being more suited to stirring emotions.

The principal burden of Justice Brennan's discussion of Goldberg v. Kelly before the Bar Association was to criticize the welfare bureaucracy for having become captured by "the empire of reason";[18] but I take him to be making a point about all government officials, including judges. He said as much, and underscored the role of passion in judicial decision—in Goldberg v. Kelly itself—by taking Justice Cardozo as his point of departure: Of Cardozo, Justice Brennan said, "He attacked the myth that judges were oracles of pure reason, and insisted that we consider the role that human experience, emotion, and passion play in the judicial process."[19]

Many factors account for the tremendous stir caused by Justice Brennan's speech, not the least of which is that it coincided with the emergence of a new jurisprudential movement in the academy—spearheaded by critical race theorists[20] and certain feminists[21]—that also places a premium on passion and storytelling. These scholars write from the left, and

17. Ibid., p. 21.
18. Ibid.
19. Ibid., p. 5
20. See, e.g., Richard Delgado, "Storytelling for Oppositionists and Others: A Plea for Narrative," *Michigan Law Review* 87 (1989): 2411; Patricia Williams, "Spirit-Murdering the Messenger: The Discourse of Fingerpointing as the Law's Response to Racism?" *University of Miami Law Review* 42 (1987): 127; Derrick Bell, "The Civil Rights Chronicles," *Harvard Law Review* 99 (1985): 4.
21. See, e.g., Martha Minow and Elizabeth Spelman, "Passion for Justice," *Cardozo Law Review* 10 (1988): 37. Some read Carol Gilligan, *In a Different Voice* (Cambridge: Harvard University Press, 1982), in these terms, but in fact she has been meticulous in presenting the ethic of care as being based on reason, not one of its alternatives.

appear the natural successors to the critical legal studies movement, which emphasized the role of passion.[22] But unlike critical legal studies, the movement I am referring to believes in rights, in the redemptive possibility of law, and in fact draws their inspiration, in one way or another, from a range of theoretical works that is very broad.[23] I am sure Justice Brennan would be surprised to learn that his speech lent comfort and support to a new jurisprudential movement, especially one so hostile to much of the Court's work, but it has turned out that way, and a number of these scholars have in turn returned the favor by endowing his speech with a measure of visibility and energy that is indeed stunning. Judging from my students and some of the commentary published in reaction to Brennan's speech,[24] the second version of Goldberg v. Kelly stands at the verge of supplanting the original.

Mention of Cardozo makes it worth emphasizing at the outset that I do not believe that Justice Brennan was engaged in an exercise in realism and thus merely restating the obvious: judges are people, and as much as they strive to be rational, emotion and passion inevitably creep into the judicial process. If that were all that were involved, I would have no objection. The presence of passion could be safely acknowledged, though on the understanding that it must always be disciplined by reason. My concern arises, however, from the fact that Justice Brennan was not content with repeating the realist's observation but instead quickly moved from the descriptive to the normative. He celebrated passion as a factor that *should* enter the decisional process and criticized Cardozo for not sufficiently encouraging or valuing, as opposed merely acknowledging, the "dialogue between heart and head."[25] For Brennan, passion must be seen as a part of the judicial ideal.

Rational deliberation, whether it be about ends or means, is no easy endeavor. It requires an enormous amount of mental and physical effort, and it always leaves one with an uneasy feeling: Have I done the right thing? I speak from rather mundane personal and professional experi-

22. Roberto Unger, *Passion* (New York: Free Press, 1984). Duncan Kennedy's "fundamental contradiction" had been framed in terms of passion—the love of others and the fear of others. Kennedy, "The Structure of Blackstone's Commentaries," *Buffalo Law Review* 28 (1979): 205.

23. Here I especially have in mind the work of Martha Nussbaum, *The Fragility of Goodness: Luck and Ethics in Greek Tragedy and Philosophy* (Cambridge: Cambridge University Press, 1986), and some of the writing of the law and literature movement. See, e.g., Paul Gewirtz, "Aeschylus' Law," *Harvard Law Review* 101 (1988): 1043.

24. See Stephen Wizner, "Passion in Legal Argument and Judicial Decisionmaking: A Comment on Goldberg v. Kelly," *Cardozo Law Review* 10 (1988): 179.

25. Brennan, "Reason, Passion, and the Progress of the Law," p. 12.

ences, and I am sure the arduousness of the task increases with the magnitude of the responsibility. The sense of uncertainty that a justice must feel, either at the moment of decision or reflecting on past decisions, must be excruciating. It always struck me as a measure of Justice Brennan's greatness that he was not overwhelmed by self-doubt, that for over thirty years, he was able to push on to judgment day in and day out, although he acknowledged, in a paraphrase of Cardozo that dramatically understates the matter, that "judging is fraught with uncertainty."[26]

The temptation to look for ways of curbing that uncertainty is always great. This was, I believe, one of the driving forces behind the rise of law and economics and by implication the Matthews v. Eldridge formula. Evoking the scientism that surrounds economics and the formal language of mathematics associated with that discipline, law and economics, especially at the hands of Posner, promised a method—cost-benefit analysis—that might avoid or relieve the uncertainty of judging. Here was a method that was determinate and certain. There was, of course, nothing to this promise—it presupposed an end that was either vacuous or deeply contested and, in any event, depended on a capacity to quantify values or contingencies that cannot be quantified. But the appeal of the promise could not be denied, and there are passages in Brennan's speech that suggest that his turn to passion might have been impelled by a similar consideration. It may be viewed as an attempt to curb the uncertainty of the law and adjudication or, to use a familiar jurisprudential metaphor, fill the "gaps of the law" that might remain if there were nothing but reason.

A number of aspects of the original Goldberg v. Kelly decision remain shrouded in uncertainty even today. One arises from the risk, and it is only a risk, that the introduction of pretermination adversarial hearings might reduce the funds available for actual or potential welfare benefits. Is that risk a sufficient basis for declining to require pretermination hearings? This strikes me as the central dilemma of Goldberg v. Kelly, and although reason gives no easy answer to it,[27] neither does passion. In his speech Justice Brennan focused on the hardship that would be imposed on the individuals whose benefits might be wrongly terminated and, in

26. Ibid., p. 4.
27. In *Goldberg v. Kelly*, Brennan disposed of the issue in these terms: "Thus, the interest of an eligible recipient in uninterrupted receipt of public assistance, coupled with the state's interest that his payments not be erroneously terminated, clearly outweighs the state's concern to prevent any increase in its fiscal and administrative burdens." 397 U.S. at 266.

the name of passion, specifically invited an empathetic understanding of their situation. Of course, those people deserve our sympathy, but no more or less than those whose welfare checks might be reduced by the institutionalization of the pretermination procedure, assuming the risks that I spoke of were to materialize. Sympathetic figures appear on both sides of the issue, a fact underscored by the division among the justices. Justice Brennan, the author of the majority opinion, is indeed a passionate person, but so was Justice Hugo L. Black, who in dissent spoke out on behalf of those whose welfare checks might be reduced as a result of the new procedural requirement. It may be that one group of recipients is more deserving of our sympathy than the other, but even if that is so, there is no reason to believe that the question of desert—of determining who is more deserving of our sympathy—would itself be resolved on the basis of some feeling.

Often, but not always, our passions seem directed toward or attached to particulars: More often than not, we love particular people or activities, rather than abstract ideas. Building on this insight, one might be tempted to say that passion helps resolve the uncertainty present in Goldberg v. Kelly because it points toward favoring or at least protecting the particular individuals whose welfare benefits are about to be terminated—the plaintiffs in the suit. This might explain why in his Bar Association speech Justice Brennan quoted at length a passage from one of the briefs describing the hardship suffered by four welfare recipients (Angela Velez, Esther Lett, Pearl Frye, and Juan DeJesus) and their families.

While mention was indeed made in the briefs of Angela Velez, Esther Lett, Pearl Frye, and Juan DeJesus, little was known of them by the justices in the actual case other than their names. These persons did not function as particulars, to whom the justices might have become passionately attached; they were used as verbal mannequins, stand-ins for a group of persons consisting of all welfare recipients. Justice Brennan recognized as much when he disposed of the mootness objection that arose from the fact that some or all of the named plaintiffs had already been restored to the rolls. As already noted, Justice Black dissented and in his opinion expressed concern for those who might be in desperate straits because of the newly imposed requirement of adversarial hearings, and though he did not use proper names to make his point, his concerns were no more general or particularized than Justice Brennan's. Both were speaking of aggregates or classes of people. Goldberg v. Kelly was no more about particular named persons, who might suitably be the object of our affections, than Brown v. Board of Education was about Linda

Brown. Both were about social groups and what the Constitution promises them.[28]

In suggesting that passion is no more a determinate guide to judgment than reason, thus far I have focused on the multiplicity of the objects of our affections; I have assumed that the passion was singular (sympathy) but that it may be distributed on both sides of the issue. The indeterminacy of impassioned judgment becomes even more pronounced, however, when we vary that assumption and acknowledge the multiplicity of passions as well: Like all of us, judges are complicated human beings who harbor not only feelings of sympathy but also feelings of fear, contempt, and even hate. A sympathetic attitude to the recipient whose welfare is about to be terminated might point in one direction, say, in favor of the pretermination hearing, as Brennan hypothesized, but imagine the judge (also) feeling that those recipients claiming a right to the hearing might well be the trouble makers who are driving the welfare system into bankruptcy. Once our horizons are thus enlarged, so as to account for both sympathy and its antithesis, the uncertainty of decision will be as acute and as profound as it is under "the empire of reason"; the "gaps of the law" will remain as persistent as ever.

A proper acknowledgment of the multiplicity of passions not only reinforces doubts about the usefulness of introducing passion in the decisional process, but also brings into focus the special danger that would be entailed in using the passions as a basis, even a partial basis, for judicial decisions. The danger I allude to arises from the rather obvious fact that although some passions are good, others are quite bad. In a comment on Justice Brennan's speech, Edward de Grazia draws a distinction between the passions to be allowed and those to be disallowed: he calls one "humanistic" and the other "authoritarian" and then uses "respect for human dignity" as the standard for distinguishing the two categories.[29] Love is to be allowed; hate is not.

As a gloss on Justice Brennan's overarching ambition,[30] Professor de Grazia's scheme seems unobjectionable, but one must wonder at the utility of the entire exercise because de Grazia can rescue passion only by reference to an ideal—"respect for human dignity"—that is itself in

---

28. Owen M. Fiss, "Groups and the Equal Protection Clause," *Philosophy & Public Affairs* 5 (1976): 107.

29. Edward de Grazia, "Humane Law and Humanistic Justice," *Cardozo Law Review* 10 (1989): 45.

30. See also William A. Parent, "Constitutional Values and Human Dignity," this volume.

need of rational elaboration. We need to know, for example, whether fear shows disrespect, or whether it might be a special form of respect. The need to answer questions like this, or otherwise elaborate the ideal of "respect for human dignity," adds a new element of uncertainty into the decisional process. Even more importantly, it renders the entire turn to passion redundant. Once we come to understand what it means to respect the dignity of another, it is unlikely that we need to have recourse to passion in the first place.

Even assuming that somehow we could sort the passions in the way that Justice Brennan or Professor de Grazia wishes, and thus be certain that we are permitted only love, and not hate and its many cognates, there is still reason to be critical of passion as an appropriate basis for public action. By its very nature, love, or at least earthly love, not only invites a certain partisanship (nepotism in all its forms), but allows the person possessed by a love to favor one individual or another for purely arbitrary reasons, for no reason at all, or for reasons that are ineffable.[31] An unanalyzed and unanalyzable sentiment—passion in all its glory— may be an appropriate basis for decision if what is at stake is choosing a friend or a lover, or deciding why I might give more of my resources to my child than some charity, or deciding why I might garden rather than write an article. But it seems to be highly questionable basis for decision when what is at stake is the solemn action of a court of law.

Allowing passion to play a role in the decisional process of the Supreme Court—even if the passion be the most beneficient imaginable or even if the role be a modest or partial one—would be inconsistent with the very norms that govern and legitimate the judicial power: impartiality and the obligation of the judiciary to justify their decisions openly and on the basis of reasons accepted by the profession and the public. These features of the judicial process are not infallible, obviously, but they do at least place the judiciary under a discipline that is gone once passion becomes an appropriate basis of decision. Why, we are left to ask, should the passions of those who happen to be justices rule us all?

At several points in his lecture Justice Brennan seems to be making a point not about passion, but about social reality and the perception of reality. He criticized "*formal* reason"[32] or "*pure* reason"[33] and, speaking of Goldberg v. Kelly, he said that the Court "sought to leaven reason

---

31. Minow and Spelman, "Passion for Justice," p. 47, speak of "nonarbitrary passion," but that strikes me as an oxymoron.
32. Brennan, "Reason, Passion, and the Progress of the Law," p. 17 (emphasis added.)
33. Ibid., p. 10 (emphasis added).

with experience."[34] In this regard, he seems to be recommending that decisions should be based on a true appreciation of social reality, and on that interpretation I am in complete agreement with him. It is important, however, to distinguish Brennan's insistence on empiricism from his claim that reason be leavened with passion or that the commitment of the judge to reason be qualified by allowing a role for passion. Passion is not experience or a privileged means of gaining access to experience, even if the experience in question be the suffering of those on welfare. Experiences may trigger passions, but they may also stir thoughts and be the subject of reflection. Granted, reason sometimes operates at a totally abstract level, wholly removed from experience, as it does in mathematics, but it need not, and when it comes to making practical judgments, as in the case of ethics or law or politics, that is hardly the ideal. In these domains, the best judgment is one that is fully sensitive to and cognizant of the underlying social reality.

As I already acknowledged, passion tends toward the particular and, in that sense, does not pose the danger of abstractness or remoteness, as do certain formal systems of reason, like mathematics. But it is important to understand that passion creates the opposite danger: so thorough an involvement in the particular as to confuse the particular with social reality. The description in appellees' brief of the plight of Angela Velez, Esther Lett, Pearl Frye, and Juan DeJesus and their families—in truth no more a story than a letter to Ann Landers is a work of literature—might trigger an emotional response, but it would be a mistake of the first order for the Court to let these "human stories" stand for the social reality over which it governs.

Because it lays down a rule for a nation and invokes the authority of the Constitution, the Supreme Court necessarily must concern itself with fate of millions of people, all of whom touch the welfare system in a myriad of ways—some on welfare, some wanting welfare, some being denied welfare, some dispensing welfare, some creating and administering welfare, some paying for it. Accordingly, the Court's perspective must be systematic, not anecdotal: it must not focus on the plight of four or five or even twenty families, but consider the welfare system as a whole, which can be understood only as a complex interaction between millions of people and a host of bureaucratic and political institutions. The methods by which a court comes to know and understand a system as far-ranging and as complex as welfare are complicated and, as in the case

34. Ibid., p. 21.

of Goldberg v. Kelly itself, always in need of further refinement and improvement, but to describe these informational methods as "storytelling," as has become fashionable these days on the left, trivializes what is at stake, unfairly disparages the enormous progress modern society has made in developing sophisticated techniques for assembling, presenting, and evaluating empirical information, and throws into doubt the basic aspirations of all these informational processes, namely, finding the truth.[35] A story is a story, sometimes a very good one, even if completely untrue.

For over twenty years Goldberg v. Kelly and its jurisprudential method has been embattled, as has the entire legacy of the Warren Court. As I noted, for the most part it had to be saved from the instrumentalism of law and economics and Matthews v. Eldridge. Justice Brennan's 1987 Bar Association speech, as is true of the work of critical race theorists and a number of feminists, can be understood as part of this struggle—as a rejection of the theoretical underpinnings of law and economics and Matthews v. Eldridge and an expression of the profound inadequacy of what, for the controlling majority of the Supreme Court these days, passes as reason. On this view, Justice Brennan's speech and the new version of Goldberg v. Kelly should be welcomed and embraced and applauded by all who care about law. I am troubled, however, by the terms of his critique, for by valorizing passion, as opposed to calling for an understanding of reason in all its fullness, Justice Brennan appears to have surrendered reason to the instrumentalists and left the idea of substantive rationality more exposed than ever. His celebration of passion not only seems unresponsive to our present needs, which, as far as I am concerned, requires more reflection, not less, but also endangers so much that is good about the law. Qualifying the judiciary's commitment to reason undermines its authority and weakens the principal means we have for guarding against abuses of the judicial power. It reduces the pressure on the justices to reflect deliberately and systematically on the issues before them and to justify their decision in each and every particular.

Of course, on the issue of what actually moved the justices in Goldberg v. Kelly, Justice Brennan will have the last word (I guess), but only by putting the authority of that decision into question. Goldberg v. Kelly might be a great case and, as Justice Brennan said, the most important decision of his career, but no part of its grandeur derives from the pos-

---

35. The relation between storytelling and debunking the idea of truth is explicit in Delgado, "Storytelling for Oppositionists and Others," n. 20.

sibility that some of the justices were emotionally responding to the "human stories" of Angela Velez, Esther Lett, Pearl Frye, and Juan DeJesus. The issue before the Court was whether the welfare system as a whole was being operated in accordance with the ideal of procedural fairness, and in reaching judgment, the justices were guided by reason and reason alone. On that account, Goldberg v. Kelly—the real Goldberg v. Kelly—stands as a magnificent achievement, resisting attacks from both the right and the left, reminding us all of that extraordinary age of American law when we understood all that reason promised and did what was necessary to realize that promise.

Contributors

Hugo Adam Bedau is Austin Fletcher Professor of Philosophy at Tufts University. He is the editor of *The Death Penalty in America*, 3d ed. (1982) and the author of *Death Is Different: Studies in the Morality, Law, and Politics of Capital Punishment* (1987). He is currently working on a book setting forth the liberal foundations of punishment.

Raoul Berger served as Regents Professor at the University of California, Berkeley, and as Charles Warren Senior Fellow in American History at Harvard Law School. He is the author of many articles as well as *Congress v. the Supreme Court* (1969); *Impeachment* (1973); *Executive Privilege* (1974); *Government by Judiciary* (1977); *Death Penalties* (1982); *Federalism: The Founders' Design* (1987); *The Fourteenth Amendment and the Bill of Rights* (1989).

Bernard R. Boxill is Professor of Philosophy at the University of North Carolina at Chapel Hill. He is author of scholarly articles and *Blacks and Social Justice* (1984). His current interests are mainly in the history of African American political thought, international ethics, and the moral issues in economic development.

Owen M. Fiss served as a law clerk to Justice Brennan during the October 1965 term, after having clerked for Thurgood Marshall on the Second Circuit, and is now the Alexander M. Bickel Professor of Public Law at Yale University. He has written widely on issues of civil rights and civil liberties, and he is the author of *The Supreme Court and the*

Rise of the Modern State: 1888–1910, part of the series on the history of the Supreme Court supported by the devise of Oliver Wendell Holmes and soon to be published by Macmillan.

Alan Gewirth is the E. C. Waller Distinguished Service Professor of Philosophy at the University of Chicago. He is the author of many scholarly articles as well as *Reason and Morality*; *Human Rights: Essays on Justification and Application*; *Marsilius of Padua and Medieval Political Philosophy*; *The Defensor Pacis of Marsilius Translated with Introduction and Appendices*; and *Political Philosophy*. He is currently working on a sequel to *Reason and Morality* entitled *The Community of Rights*.

Kent Greenawalt is University Professor and formerly the Cardozo Professor of Jurisprudence at Columbia University's School of Law. He has written widely on the law as it relates to discrimination, religious convictions, free speech, political obligation, and privacy as well as judicial law and procedure. He is the author of *Speech, Crime and the Uses of Language* (1989); *Religious Convictions and Political Choice* (1988); *Conflicts of Law and Morality* (1987); and *Discrimination and Reverse Discrimination* (1983). His *Law and Objectivity* is to be published soon by Oxford University Press.

Louis Henkin is University Professor Emeritus at Columbia University and Chairman of the Directorate of the University's Center for the Study of Human Rights. He is the author of *How Nations Behave: Law and Foreign Policy*; *Foreign Affairs and the Constitution*; *The Rights of Man Today*; *The Age of Rights*; *Constitutionalism, Democracy and Foreign Affairs*. He is coeditor of *International Law, Cases and Materials* and *Constitutionalism and Rights: The Influence of the United States Constitution Abroad*, has edited several other volumes, and has written numerous scholarly articles

A. I. Melden is Professor Emeritus at the University of California at Irvine. He has published numerous scholarly articles in philosophy, especially ethics, as well as *Rights and Right Conduct*; *Free Action*; *Ethical Theories*; *Essays in Moral Philosophy*; *Rights and Persons*; and *Rights in Moral Lives*.

Michael J. Meyer is Assistant Professor of Philosophy at Santa Clara University. He is the author of scholarly articles in political philosophy and ethics, especially on the topics of rights, human dignity, and autonomy. His current work includes a book on the idea of human dignity in modern political thought.

Martha Minow is a Professor of Law at Harvard Law School. She was a law clerk for Justice Thurgood Marshall and Judge David Bazelon. She has written numerous scholarly and popular essays as well as *Making All the Difference: Inclusion, Exclusion and American Law* (1990). Her current research addresses regulations of families and also concepts of representation in the law.

W. A. Parent is Associate Professor of Philosophy at Santa Clara University. He is the author of scholarly articles in jurisprudence and moral theory. His current work includes a book on dignity.

David A. J. Richards is Professor of Law at the New York University School of Law. His books include *A Theory of Reasons for Action* (1971); *The Moral Criticism of Law* (1977); *Sex, Drugs, Death and the Law: An Essay on Human Rights and Overcriminalization* (1982); *Toleration and the Constitution* (1986); *Foundations of American Constitutionalism* (1989). He is currently completing work on a book on the moral and political theory underlying the Reconstruction amendments entitled *"The Political Religion of the Nation": The Reconstruction Amendments and The Second American Revolution.*

Frederick Schauer is Frank Stanton Professor of the First Amendment at the John F. Kennedy School of Government, Harvard University. He is the author of numerous articles in legal and philosophical journals on freedom of speech, legal theory, constitutional interpretation, the structure of rights, and the analysis of rules. He is also the author of *The Law of Obscenity* (1976); *Free Speech: A Philosophical Enquiry* (1982); *Playing by the Rules: A Philosophical Examination of Rule-Based Decision-making in Law and in Life* (1991). His current work focuses on linguistic and metaphysical questions related to the intersection of legal and social categories.

Index

Library of Congress Cataloging-in-Publication Data

The Constitution of rights : human dignity and American values /
  Michael J. Meyer, William A. Parent, editors.
    p. cm.
    Includes bibliographical references and index.
    ISBN 0-8014-2650-2 (cloth : alk. paper). —ISBN 0-8014-9950-X
  (pbk. : alk. paper)
    1. Civil rights—United States. 2. Dignity. 3. United States—Constitutional history.
  KF4749.A2C62 1992
  342.73'085—dc20
  [347.30285]   91-55535